What People Are Saying About *Getting Into College Made Easy*

"If your child has what it takes to get into a major university, stop worrying about all the homework you have to do as a parent. That's because Sari Trompke has done it for you. *Getting Into College Made Easy* gives you the blueprints, tools, and action plans you need to pick and choose from the best academic options available to your child."

—**Dr. MiRan Kim**, Associate Professor at
The School of Hospitality Business at Michigan State University

"Gaining entry into a major U.S. military academy is not an impossible task. From who to contact to how to prepare during each year of high school, *Getting Into College Made Easy* delivers the frameworks, strategies, and plan of action the aspiring candidate needs to be competitive and achieve victory (win an offer of appointment)."

—**Albert Gomez**, West Point class of 1979, Lieutenant Colonel,
U.S. Army Retired, West Point Field Admissions Officer, 1997-2018

"Sari Trompke has written a guide that stands out for its comprehensiveness, candor, and compassion. There is so much valuable information, written in plain English and taking into account the variety of experiences and the value of storytelling. An enlightening and enjoyable read!"

—**Thomas Dingman**, Former Dean of Freshmen at Harvard College,
Special Adviser to the Danoff Dean of Harvard College

"Frustrated? Confused? If getting into one of the military academies, exclusive colleges, or getting your athlete recruited feels out of reach…it isn't. Sari Trompke reveals how to achieve your goals in *Getting Into College Made Easy*. She has over a decade of experience with dozens of success stories from high school students getting accepted into their desired college along with the unbelievable accomplishments of her four children. Get this book now and follow her blueprints, guidelines, and proven methods, and you will find success."

—**John Goodale**, Brigadier General, USA, Retired, West Point Class 1980

"*Getting Into College Made Easy* is a thorough, step-by-step guide to managing the college recruiting process from the moment you walk into high school as a freshman to the day you sign the National Letter of Intent. All levels of student-athlete from Elite to D-3 will walk away from this book with skills that serve them well not only while being recruited, but also for the remainder of their collegiate and professional careers. A requirement for all future college student-athletes and parents!"

—**Joe Villapiano**, Assistant Football Coach/Offensive Coordinator, Cornell University

"*Getting Into College Made Easy* is a step-by-step process that navigates one of the most important processes for our children's future. As a school board member for the past 18 years, I realize that getting into college can be intimidating and confusing. Experience and knowledge are the keys to success and Sari has translated her experiences and knowledge into an easy-to-read comprehensive book. Her methods worked for her own children and many other students as well. In this book, you will find a pathway to educational success, if not for yourself, then for the children you care most about."

—**Mike Vuittonet**, Trustee of the West Ada School Board, Meridian, Idaho

GETTING INTO COLLEGE

Made Easy

The ESSENTIAL and EASY

College Guide for Students, Scholars, and Athletes

SARI TROMPKE

Getting Into College Made EASY
The Essential and Easy College Guide for Students, Scholars, and Athletes
By Sari Trompke

Published by

4Twigs Publishing
Eagle, Idaho

ISBN: 978-1-7327749-0-2 (Print)
ISBN: 978-1-7327749-1-9 (eBook)

Library of Congress Control Number: 2018913597

Editing: Jen Zelinger, TwinOwlsAuthors.com
Book design: NZ Graphics, NZ Graphics.com

Quantity discounts are available to your company, educational organization, association, or other organization for reselling, educational purposes, gifts or fundraising campaigns.

For more information, please contact the publisher at:
gettingintocollege@cableone.net
www.gettingintocollegemadeeasy.org

First Edition 2019

Printed in the United States of America

This book is dedicated to my husband, Ron, who supports me in everything I do. It is also dedicated to my incredible children Rachel, Jordan, David, and Alex who have achieved all we could only dream of.

CONTENTS

Introduction 9

Chapter 1: The Do's and Don'ts of High School 13

Chapter 2: Résumé Building 37

Chapter 3: What Makes You So Different? 57

Chapter 4: The Recruiting Process: Sports, Sports,
and Sports (or the Big "Ds") 62

Chapter 5: SAT, ACT, SAT Subject, and AP Test Preparation 105

Chapter 6: Applying to Military Academies 121

Chapter 7: Determining Which College to Attend 134

Chapter 8: The Nitty Gritty of Applications
(and How Are You Going to Pay for This?) 144

Chapter 9: It's Go Time!: The Admission Process,
the Waiting Game, Decision Time, and Finishing Strong 163

Chapter 10: Don't forget FAFSA, Financial Aid, Loans,
and your CSS profile 171

Chapter 11: Letting Go: A Chapter for Parents 182

Chapter 12: From the Mouths of Babes: College Student's
Perspectives 186

Chapter 13: Worksheets and Charts 219

Endnotes 229

About the Author 233

INTRODUCTION

There are some people out there who look at books (not only about getting into college, but about many other topics on education) and only look at the credentials of the author. A PhD in this or a doctorate in that. I will be clear with you from the get-go, I am not that person. I am more of what I call a "blue-collared individual" who does not have the background that so-called "experts" have in getting students into college. This fact motivated me to find out how the average Joe does it. How can people who have not gone to college (and want a simple guide to help them navigate the waters of getting it paid for) do this? I know that many parents who are looking to get their children into a great college, or college period, may be like me and not have that background themselves. To them, the whole process becomes out of reach or only for families with so-called "pedigreed" backgrounds, a top education, or money.

What about us regular folk? What about our children? What about opportunities for those who do not have the resources, money, connections, or opportunities that many other people have? What about the students who need help with the process? I believe this book will help with direction. This is for both parents and students who are looking for help in getting the best education possible, at the best price, or even better—paid for—and to be prepared for this time in their life. Planning and preparing for it is crucial for success, not only your high school, but as far ahead as your college career.

A little bit about me; I do not have a degree myself. Every person I work with and help is usually surprised that my background does not include a degree. I don't mean to imply that is because I am "oh, so smart" or I live vicariously through my kids. My parents did not go to college and were from a generation where we kids pretty much figured things out on our own. By the time I did figure things out, I realized college wasn't in the cards.

My husband did go to college, working his way through—all on his own—without help from anyone. We both know that he could have done so much more, and he could have had a better education and opportunities with direction and help. We were determined to break that cycle and work hard to direct our children towards a better future than we had education-wise, hopefully setting them up for a great job at the end of it.

I have learned through life's experiences that not everything is determined by a good education, but in today's day and age, it definitely helps get a leg up. The better the school, the better the network system, the better the job opportunities it can create. So what did I do? I became a bit obsessive—yes, full disclosure. I am one of those people who gets fixated on a topic and learns and digs until I get all the information I can on it. I became a "subject matter expert" on upper-tiered colleges and military academies, as well as the recruiting process for athletes.

What was the outcome of my "obsessive behavior"? My daughter, Rachel, went to College of Idaho on a partial debate scholarship, winning Nationals in debate as a freshman too. Rachel attended college for two years, then received a great offer for employment that was the perfect choice for her. She now has an incredible career at a very large company in Austin, Texas. My eldest son, Jordan, attended the United States Military Academy at West Point, being recruited for football and majored in management. Jordan is now a first lieutenant, serving our country out of Fort Hood in Killeen, Texas. My middle son, David, was recruited for track and football at Harvard, and graduated with a degree in economics. He now works in Boston as an analyst at an investment firm. My youngest son, Alex, graduated Michigan State and was recruited for (and received a very healthy scholarship for) swimming. He majored in hospitality business and has a job in New Orleans in hotel management. All different experiences—and all exactly where they wanted to be.

I saw through my children's individual experiences that there wasn't necessarily a formula, but there was a way to improve the odds of getting students into college, receiving scholarships, recruiting, etc. Along the way, my children's friends started asking for my help. The counselor at my children's high school asked me to come speak at the school about getting into college, and my opportunities to help students grew from there. What I have seen through my observations is a need from parents and students when it comes to the college admission process and the "how to's." There are things you can do to help improve the chances of admissions, scholarships, recruiting, and finding that perfect fit. It can be a seriously overwhelming process, and the material I see out there is really not written for the masses or everyday people to use in a practical way. When I was searching for my own children, I had a hard time finding anything that was useful and, quite frankly, some authors made it so complicated, it became confusing and even more overwhelming. With this book, my hope is that you can learn some things that will help guide you towards the right school and find ways to save money, help with the application process and the "choice" process, and give you direction towards a vocation after college. I have seen many parents send their kids to a good school—but then what? Some ended up with a degree that did not give them the options they wanted, and some students went to the school that simply was just an easy choice.

As parents, college is what we want our children trained and prepared for when they are in high school; that is the goal for those who choose this route. What can you do as a student, and what can we do as parents, to increase the odds of finding the college and ultimate career that will be the best fit? I have had parents and students ask my husband and me along the way, "What is the secret? How did we do it?" I don't know if there is a master plan or a checklist, but I can tell you what we did and what we felt was important to improve the opportunities our children had as well as the dozens of students we have been fortunate enough to help. This book comes from many years and many experiences, some good and some bad. But we know all of our children are where they are supposed to be, doing what they love. I have also seen great success from the students that I have worked with and they have been successful wherever they have ended up at.

Full disclosure, I will be using my children and the students I have worked with as examples throughout this book. Because of them, and for them, I learned all of this! I am very proud of them all, but I also want to be able to help others with what I have learned through trial and error; they are truly my human Guinea pigs. Using them as examples is also the best way for me to explain important areas and where I can give real examples of an outcome. I also provide sample worksheets throughout the book with templates in the last chapter under "Worksheets and Charts" to help you utilize them more effectively. They will be blank, so you don't have to recreate them. Hopefully these will be as beneficial to you as they were to our family and the students I have worked with.

I have to preface this book to say that college isn't for everybody. Look at me; look at my very successful daughter! Some find very fruitful careers without having a degree, and that is great. But for those of you who WANT to go to college and need help getting there, I truly believe I can help you.

I consider what I do a passion of mine, and I consider this book an opportunity to reach more people, helping them find the way to THEIR perfect college and setting them up for THEIR best future.

So, let's dive in and get that done!

1

The Do's and Don'ts
of High School

I WISH I COULD talk to parents and kids right before they head into high school.

The main challenge I find when I talk to juniors and seniors is, quite frankly, poor planning. If I'm talking to you in your third or fourth year of high school, and you haven't been one of those students who already has a solid GPA, a good SAT/ACT score, community and school involvement, sports, and more, then it makes it very challenging to have a lot of options going forward. Some students and parents, at this point, are just happy to have college as an option. I love having *all* the options available when talking to a student. You limit your opportunities with poor or no planning.

So, let's come up with a plan for you!

I will occasionally repeat things you've already read in the book. This is on purpose as: 1) some things are worth repeating and are important to emphasize more than once, and 2) I want to ensure readers who skip some chapters receive the relevant and important information mentioned elsewhere.

One thing that should (and will) be highlighted and repeated often is the need for good planning.

Before Your Freshman Year

Forget what you did in middle or junior high school!

Were you a C student? Maybe lackluster in sports and activities? It doesn't matter.

On the flip side: Were you an A student? Great at sports? President of your class?

Okay—it STILL doesn't matter. But this is all a good thing! High school gives you the chance to reinvent yourself. It gives you the chance to try out for the spirit squad or the basketball team or run for class office. It gives you a chance to shoot for straight As, and it is a clean slate and a new beginning!

What you DON'T want to do is decide to be a straight-A student (cumulative) by your junior year. By then, your chances are zero of achieving this, unless you already have that going for you. Otherwise, you are limited in your decisions. I am not saying everyone CAN get straight As. But most of us would agree, if we try our very hardest and set that as the goal, chances are we can get closer than if we don't have a plan or apply ourselves. We can also get into a semantics conversation about how it isn't fair or right that grades and college scores define a student. I would agree, but it IS the system—and it IS what it is. So, we must do our best to function within that system to make it work.

My son is a great example.

Jordan was a poor student in middle school. He received mostly C's. I would say that he didn't apply himself for the most part. We figured he would be the kind of student who ended up at a local college, and we couldn't expect or plan for more. We accepted that.

I don't think that sat well with Jordan though. He worked a lot harder his freshman year and ended up with a 3.33 average for that year. Every year, he built on that and ended up with a 3.6 cumulative GPA by the time he graduated high school and was on the honor roll.

If you had asked me what I had expected after his middle school years, I wouldn't have predicted that based on his previous grades. But that was when the light bulb came on for him. I realized that sometimes you get behind the eight ball, and it is hard to redefine yourself when you are in it, as it was for him in middle school.

So high school is the perfect time to change and raise those standards for yourself. Jordan set a goal, wanted to achieve it, and put the time and effort into it. I also learned something as a parent: that I shouldn't limit my expectations for my children. That was wrong on my part: to settle into thinking of him in a certain way—and to think it was okay for me to do that. As time went on, and I learned more as a parent, I realized that children can follow a path or they can choose to direct themselves to achieve more. This starts before high school even begins.

Before School Starts

- **The summer before high school, read the books recommended by your high school counselor at your future school.**

  It doesn't hurt to contact the school counselor, just to connect, as this is a great opportunity to introduce yourself and start building a relationship.

  Don't laugh, but bring them a plate of cookies or something that they will remember you by. I have always looked at those times as a way to grease the wheels, so to speak. I remembered them at Christmas, Teacher's Appreciation Day, and any other time I could do something nice for them. If it were you, how would you feel if someone did that for you? You would be pretty happy. When the time comes that you need to ask them for a transcript or intervene for you, the establishment of that relationship really comes in handy. Start off on a good foot and make sure you know who the counselor is. They will be a great source of help, especially in the upper-classman years.

If the counselor doesn't have any books they recommend (after you have brought your plate of cookies), there are great lists on the internet to Google. Usually, the list is around five or so books, which is very doable in a summer. It keeps the mind stimulated, and students will have a leg up going into freshman year.

If you, as a student, do not like the books recommended, find a series to get into or pick them out with your parents help. Even some of the "teen" series books are great: just something to keep your mind engaged, so you are not watching TV all of the time. It is a proven fact that students lose around two months of learning over the summer and score lower on the ACT and SAT scores at the end of the summer than before the summer starts. (This is something to think about down the road when planning for the tests.)

With all this being said, for parents, it is critical to your child's success to encourage your children and be part of the learning process with them. Be part of the solution and encourage them to read and maintain their knowledge.

- **Another great tool to get for the summer is puzzle books:**
  Word searches, trivia puzzles, math challenges, brain games, etc. Keep your mind stimulated, but not so much that it feels like school is in session. Be creative with rewards, if you must.

- **Something very simple: limit watching TV.**
  Set an amount of time you will watch, then try to do something else. It is amazing how much knowledge can be lost over the summer. Do not fill your brain with empty information.

- **Parents: Near the end of the summer, sit down with your child. Make a list of goals and ways to achieve them over the next four years.**

This may seem foreign to you and your child, but it is a great practice to start. If nothing is planned or expected, then nothing can be strived for. It may happen by chance—but why leave it to chance?

We become outcome driven when goals are set for us. As parents, this is also a great way to help our children set goals for the rest of their lives. By doing so from the get-go, and looking at them often, you set up great expectations for their high school career. Periodically check in with your child about how they are doing.

If something happens that is out of their control, alter the goal sheet. For example, if they don't make the track team and that was a goal, see what else they can put in its place. If they lose the election for the office they were running for, tell them to put that on for next year and see if there are any other positions they can fill this year.

Setting Goals

- **Set up a level of academic achievement that is doable.**
  Ask these questions: What have you done before? Are you a C or an A student? Can you achieve this goal AND is it enough of a stretch to challenge you?

- **In high school, take more challenging classes in the subjects you enjoy the most.**
  If you are great at art, work to succeed in that area. If you struggle in English, Honors English is setting you up to fail. But getting help for English, such as a tutor (and shooting for an A) is more realistic.

- **Taking more challenging courses will boost an overall GPA and show colleges you can handle more.**
  Looking for more advanced opportunities freshman year will allow for AP courses in the upperclassman years. It is not necessarily a prerequisite to take honors courses first, but at many schools, it can be.

- **Athletics**
  Find out when tryouts, practices, and games take place. Parents: Work with your son or daughter to help them succeed in their sport. By succeed, I mean having a positive experience and being a positive influence on the team! Not everyone can be the best on the team or in a sport, but everyone should

contribute, be respectful, give 125%, be a great teammate, be on time, be leaders by example, and overall be a person of character.

What are other goals, along with having a positive attitude? Is it to make varsity by junior year? Or to run a specific time by the end of freshman year? Each year, set and define those goals. Two of my sons, Jordan and Alex, had a corkboard hanging in their rooms where they hung up their goals and looked at them every day. It was a great motivator and reminder!

- **Extracurricular Activities**

  I had my children pick a few things each year. Their first year, students can select activities like Art, Chess, Debate, or Speech Club, or Student Council, etc. Sophomore year, we set goals together that required a deeper involvement, such as secretary of Student Council, treasurer of the Chess Club, and volunteering for various and specific school-based events. We worked on feeding their earlier experiences into what they would achieve the next year.

  All of my children were established and known in their schools because they were involved in various sports and activities. When it came time for letters of recommendations from teachers, coaches, and those in the administration, my children were not strangers to them. They earned great recommendation letters because my children had made a direct contribution to the school.

  If students are great at math or science, they should find a club at the school that revolves around that subject. Students will even be able to find other opportunities through these clubs, such as internships or volunteer options at science labs and on research projects. These will definitely pave the way for their future opportunities. If they love art or history, or hold a different passion, there are clubs and activities for everything.

  If they don't have it at the school, bring it there yourself next year! (We will talk about that in the sophomore year section.) Getting plugged into activities in the school, or even outside of school, is important and helps with being invested in something positive right away. Some kids do Boy or Girl Scouts programs, or they get involved in student governments that are in their community. These are awesome things to participate and be involved in.

Volunteerism

This, to me, is one of the critical pieces that many parents and students leave out of the equation. For our family, it was so important for us to see our kids look beyond themselves and develop compassion and concern for those less fortunate than us who needed help. This goes for both high-achieving students and struggling students: all students benefit from helping others.

Each child will see an opportunity for them to utilize their God-given talents towards helping others. For those who struggle with self-esteem, this can do so much! There are many wonderful groups out there to get involved in, and many have programs geared towards high school students. They will train you as a junior volunteer, so you have the opportunity to develop in the position and learn many things.

Here are a few ideas to investigate:

- Special Olympics
    - o They always need volunteers, coaches, mentors, and unified partners (individuals with more involved participation in the events).
- Junior Red Cross
- Domestic Abuse Groups:
    - o There are fund-raising activities and some groups even have programs that focus on a younger audience, which would be a great place to get plugged in.
- Junior Lions Club (Leos)
- Animal Shelters and Humane Societies
- Homeless Shelters
- Community Food Pantries
- Environmental Groups
- Big Brother and Big Sister
- Rake America (or Other Community Cleanup Projects)
- Habitat for Humanity
- Key Club
- Senior Citizens Centers
- Ronald McDonald Houses
- Make-a-Wish Foundation
- Military Organization (Veterans, Wounded Warriors, etc.)
- Refugee Groups

Another thing I always tell kids and parents NOT to do is a "one off" (volunteering wise). If you find something you like, join and be connected for at least two years of your high school career, but preferably participate all four years (if at all possible). It is super easy to volunteer only once at a homeless shelter or at Habitat for Humanity, but to actively be involved in a program demonstrates consistency and commitment. It also looks much better on a résumé when you show longevity. Here is an example of what they would want to see on your résumé. It indicates growth, consistency, and continuity with a group.

- Volunteer Winter/Summer Special Olympics; Helped with the track team and worked directly with the athletes in various functions and activities. 2014

- Assistant Coach of Special Olympics Team/Track Team: Assisted athletes and helped coaches with practices and competitions. 2014-2016

- Unified Partner/Coach for Special Olympics Track Team, won State in 2017. 2014-2017

Look for where you (or your child, as the parent) can make a difference. It should be something you feel connected to and passionate about: colleges will want to see that as well. I recommend getting involved with at least one group and volunteering consistently with a few more. This shows that you are well-rounded and that you stretch yourself.

Parents: It is a good idea to help direct them on volunteering options and opportunities. Once they get plugged in, they can navigate the process, but it can be quite overwhelming for them to break the ice by making the first contact. Assist them with the initial steps.

Family Expectations

It is important for not only your child to make commitments about achieving their goals. As parents, we have the responsibility of assistance when paving the way and directing our children towards success. Keeping them on track is definitely part of the parent's job. I hear so many parents say things like:

- "I don't know what my son/daughters grade are until report cards are out."
- "It is their responsibility to determine their future."
- "I didn't have parents that helped me, and I turned out just fine."

What I say to that is, "Really? It isn't our responsibility?" If not ours, then whose responsibility is it? There are ways to track and stay on top of grades and what kids are doing in school. And it isn't that hard!

Freshman Year

- **Most schools offer ways to see grades online.**
  If not, see if you can get updates from the school. If semester grades have already posted, it is too late. It's important to check periodically along the way. I've seen problems and missing assignments. I've even caught a paper or two, turned in by my children, that the teacher forgot to post. If you see a problem in a class, you can resolve it with your child, and you can see if they need help. You can do this BEFORE the end of the quarter or semester when the grades are already posted. Some kids don't know how or what to ask for, and I think it's our job to help them. If they are struggling, we can get tutoring for them before too much time has gone by and they are really far behind. Maybe they were assigned to a class that is too hard for them? Grades show you where they are and how we can better direct them.

- **While we don't want robots or to force our kids to do something they don't want at all, they do need direction.**
  Sometimes they need help figuring out their interests. They will need help finding a career or job where they can use those concentrations. How many fourteen and fifteen year old students have a clear plan for their future? I think, as adults, we have a better gauge of what they can do to move forward, either by experience, age, or knowing there are places to get what is needed. It increases your child's success tenfold when they have accountability to a parent, as well as direction and mentoring from that parent. Even if your child is planning to go to a trade school or maybe not to college at all (it isn't for everyone), success in high school gives them opportunities to make these decisions. They can avoid being forced into a career that they only picked because they did not have a successful high school career.

- **Be involved with your children and get to know their teachers, counselors, principals, and coaches.**
  I volunteered for everything! I mean everything—and I was in charge of EVERYTHING! I don't know if I would necessarily recommend that for everyone, and I know not everyone is in that position, but I didn't want one of

my children to feel I didn't give the same to each one of them in their activities and sports. (But my guilt issues will be saved for another book.)

Anyway, getting to know the coaches and school officials also kept my kids in check. I never really worried about them, but when one or two things came up (my kids are not perfect), I could be involved in the process. The staff knew our family well. They knew my kids, and they knew who we were and what we were about. Make yourself known in a good way!

I mentioned bringing cookies to the counselors. I am a total "schmoozer" when it comes to things like that, but bringing in donuts to the front office, Christmas candy to the teachers and coaches, or even thank you emails at the end of the season or school year are all great ways to show appreciation.

I want to be clear: this is not the way to get yourself (or your son or daughter) playing time or an A in math. But it is a way for relationships to be built, for appreciation to be felt, and for us to show these people they are valued and respected. It is a lesson through our actions. When we do this, our kids see it and hear it, and it changes not only how they see the professionals, but also how they see us.

My kids called me when they got to college to ask what to give their teachers or coaches. I found that amusing. When I was doing it in high school, they would roll their eyes occasionally, thinking it was overkill. But they would be beaming when they came back, telling me how thankful the person was. They could see something: that a small action can have a positive impact on a person and that a relationship can be built from those actions.

- **Be an active part of the process.**

Two of my sons were both in football, and I only missed one team dinner over the four years they played. I attended all but one of their high school games, and only because I went to Parent's Weekend for one of my sons in college. We waited for them every time they were done playing a game to come out from the locker room. We cheered them up when there was a loss or cheered them on for winning. We had a great tradition of getting them tacos from Jack in the Box and watching our local TV station sports show that highlighted high school football after the game. My husband would always talk to them in detail about the game afterwards and give suggestions for next time. It was a great time in our kid's lives. My other son, Alex, is the swimmer in the family. I was the Team Mom of his high school team. It was a great opportunity to help plan and run his high school swim program—it was so much fun! I also got a front row seat (on the deck) when he swam—definitely a great perk for helping. My daughter was in speech and debate for all four years of high school. I went on every trip as a chaperone and judge—not knowing what I was doing at the beginning. But eventually I was able to give her pointers and tips and got to know every kid on that team, even some from other schools. I was president by her senior year. The long bus rides to colleges across the Pacific Northwest and the meets we experienced together are some of my favorite memories with her. It brought us closer together and allowed me a glimpse into her life that I would not have had if I did not help and missed those experiences.

- **Ask yourself: What can I do to be involved and participate in my children's experiences at school?**
  I tell parents that there is no better time to volunteer and get involved because it is usually the time they start not wanting us to! If we have an excuse to be there, they don't even think about it. They actually expect us to be there, and they actually WANT us there. It all leads to success, and we can be part of that process. It is also a great example of giving to others, which we want to translate to our children.

- **Start talking about where they see themselves going to college, but very casually.**
  What do they want to major in? What do they enjoy doing? This is a great time to start thinking about what to shoot for. If they can start visualizing it, it gives them the very thing to shoot for. You do not want to overwhelm them with this conversation. Each child is different, and they may want to look that far ahead. Other students may be freaked out by what is in front of them at that moment.

- **The last, but certainly not least, seems obvious. But I have to say it. STAY OUT OF TROUBLE!**
  There will be times and opportunities for kids to be kids, get into mischief, and sometimes truly be in the wrong place at the wrong time. My husband always had an expression with the kids, "Was it worth it?" (This was generally after they had made a bad decision when they knew they shouldn't have.) I don't think I have ever heard them say, "Yes, Dad, it was worth it." Talk to your kids BEFORE schools start. Discuss your expectations with curfew, drugs, smoking, alcohol, poor choices in friends, etc. Keep them on the right path. If they make

a mistake, help them see why it was a mistake. Work with them to keep the mistakes few and far between. With our kids, there were certain things we had as "hard no's", and drugs were definitely one of them. We were a bit more flexible with curfew. (They could stay out a little later with permission and for special events on occasion.) Give them a little leeway for those things, so when you do say "no" to something that is a "hard no", they can live with it.

- **Keep the dialogue open.**

  Being involved in their lives offers a great opportunity for this (as I mentioned). It helps to see who your sons or daughters hang with in a normal setting. Building relationships with the families of my kid's friends was fantastic. It gave me a great insight into their world without being invasive. I was able to start conversations with things like, "I heard so-and-so got kicked off the team for taking drugs. It's really unfortunate that he did something so destructive, and also let his team down." This offers GREAT conversation starters and opportunities to derail potential dangerous situations before they happen. Not all were negative. Some were about positive things, but it did allow for teachable lessons with my children. Also, if your children know you are involved, that you talk to teachers and counselors, as well as being on a first-name bases with the principal, it's awesome. It is very difficult for your children to get away (or want to get away with) anything! Everyone has a vested interest in your child. As a parent, directing, educating, keeping the channels open, allowing them to still be kids, and keeping the "hard no's" in place is really important stuff. Participating in their lives is crucial to their success and well-being.

- **Here is a well-known fact I am sure you have heard before: The more involved students in activities and sports are the least likely to get into trouble.**

  They either don't have the time or they don't want to let anyone down. With active kids participating in various activities, clubs, and sports, it increases the amount of people they do not want to let down. It also means more is on the line, and they begin to have a vested interest in what they are doing. So, if basketball season is over, there are other activities to keep them engaged and occupied. Common sense will tell you, a busy (even tired) kid doesn't have time and energy to get into trouble. Some need that extra stimulation and distraction as well.

- **Some families do a contract or have specific rules they abide by (and actually are a contractual obligation).**

  It could be things like going to church, a youth group, or family events, or even eating dinner together three nights a week . Whatever you need to make a plan of action is awesome.

- **Be sure you attend the open house at the beginning of the year.**

  You can help organize the paperwork and options available. They may see a new club to join or one may not fit with a sport's practices they have. Get all the information you can and help them navigate through it all. They will be scared, intimidated, and (probably more often than not) afraid to try anything. But when they do, it opens up a whole new world to them!

- **At the end of their freshman year, buy ACT and SAT prep books to read over the summer.**

  These are great for exposure to the tests and knowing what to expect. They don't have to get too in depth at this time, but it's good to start with a glimpse of the tests. I like the books *SAT for Dummies* and *The Real ACT Book*. Both are great and easy to use and read.

On the following page is a sample goal sheet.

FRESHMAN YEAR GOALS (example)

ACADEMIC	ATHLETIC	EXTRACURRICULAR	VOLUNTEER	FAMILY/PERSONAL	COLLEGE GOALS (Only if this is something they are ready for)
Will get at least 4 A's and no lower than 2 B's	Make the freshman basketball team	Join Student Council	Volunteer at Rake America	Eat with family twice a week	Art history major
Will take 1 honors class in history	Score 6 points per game	Join a club: either Art or Spanish	Become a Big Sister	No TV until all homework is done	Dream school: NYU, U of Chicago, or Virginia
Take art all four years	Rebound average of per game	Continue taking piano lessons and perform at the winter carnival	Get involved with a women's shelter. Become a junior ambassador	Help with chores one hour on Saturday	
	Miss no more than 1 practice		Volunteer at Rescue Mission on Thanksgiving and Christmas	Go to church on Wednesday nights when there is no game	
	Try out for the track team			No more soda!	
				No alcohol in high chool and no drugs or smoking EVER!	
				Never get into a car with someone who has been drinking	

With this goal sheet, your child will have a plan set in place for their freshman year. Keep a copy for yourself as well to reference and see where they are in the process. Recommend that they keep a copy of their goals on their bulletin board. Have one set every year going forward. It is great to keep them as a reference of growth and change and, in addition, it helps with résumé building, which we will discuss later.

Sophomore Year

Phew! They made it through freshman year. You have the foundation from the previous year to build on. How do you build off of it?

First, review the past year. Look at what was accomplished and what *wasn't* accomplished the previous year. Understand that not all goals may be met. Those goals were challenges for whatever reason; these can be put on to this year. Goals are a target for us to hit, but we may not hit them right away.

- **Sophomore year is a good time to continue the conversation about what major to select in college and what college to attend.**

   Do this now with more of a purpose than during freshman year. For some students, it can be extremely overwhelming to think about college when they are just starting high school. For many, freshman year is best for looking at what is right in front of them, especially when it feels like they are over a huge hole with a small rope to walk across. Sophomore year starts looking at a broader scope.

   We will get into specifics in a later chapter on looking at schools and finding out the best options and right fit for colleges, so I won't get into that now. But this is a great time to start utilizing that guide. Again, like freshman year, sitting down at the end of summer and creating a set of goals for the coming year is key to developing and making the dream of a great college possible.

- **To create the sophomore year goals, look at the freshman year goals.**

   Which ones were attained and which ones were EASILY attained? If instead of getting four As and two Bs, you received five As and one B, keep that as the goal. This is an excellent opportunity to take ownership of your school year but also gives you direction and validation in the process. (Again, parents: sit down with your student to help them with this.)

- **As you can see from the goals in the sophomore chart, some college goals change.**

   This is expected and a great thing! It will reflect your evolution and being open to new and advanced opportunities and options. You may have a new college on there or a different one than you originally selected. Don't worry if you do or don't stick to what you started with. But having a start is fantastic, and you will start honing in on what you want. Some kids know what career and college they want from an early age, while others take a while—or it can shift each year. High school is an awesome time to try new things but also test your resolve concerning what you truly want out of life and what matters to you. Your dream schools may change depending on grades, logistics, cost, majors offered, etc. These can be factors that shift your wants to more realistic choices. But don't be afraid to have your dream school as a choice at this point, and certainly do not feel bad when you see it change several times. That is why I recommend looking into at least ten schools. If you just continue with only your top two or three college choices, it limits you. Start out small: with just a few your sophomore or freshman year, but as you start developing in high school, you can more clearly see where you will fit and what you want.

- **Sometimes you will change your mind and/or lose interest in a school for various reasons as well.**

My youngest son's dream school was Virginia Tech. He wanted to go there his whole high school career, but he also was interested in University of Nevada Las Vegas (UNLV) because it had a great hospitality program. We visited UNLV his sophomore year, and he did not like it at all. It wasn't what he thought, and there were several factors that were not on his wish list, so he ruled them out. When he got the opportunity to visit Virginia Tech his senior year on an official visit (for swimming), he loved it. It was everything he hoped for and more! But we encouraged him to look at other schools since he had the opportunity to do so. He went to Michigan State and when he came home, he did not want to talk much about it—which was odd. We came to find out (after the coach made a scholarship offer) that he loved the school, loved the program for his major, and loved the coaches and team.

He had initially felt bad about Virginia Tech, and he was working it out in his mind (about liking somewhere more than what he had thought was his dream school). He ended up at Michigan State. It was the right choice for him, and he had a wonderful experience. This happens more than you would think. So keep your options open and investigate the schools you think might be a good fit. This is a great proactive step in the right direction. It also is a great time for students and parents to see how much schools will cost at the time. We will discuss how to do all this in a later chapter, but if you want to go to a school that you know will end up costing you more than you (or your family) can or want to spend, you can start having that discussion early on with your parents. Scholarships will have to be gained, so find out what you have to do to get them. If you plan and start looking early, it gives you the carrot to shoot for, it allows you to take an active role in your future, and it prepares you to set goals and plan for your own future.

- **As parents, we look for teachable moments with our children.**
  Working towards these things with them are defining moments that will set up how they do things in the future when we are not around. As in every year, check in with your son or daughter to be sure they are on track and that they are not overwhelmed.

- **Help adjust goals if they are too hard or too easily achieved, with the academic goals coming first.**
  If something needs to be adjusted, academics will be the last one to tackle as far as an adjustment goes. Academics are always the top priority. This year, your school may offer the PLAN or PSAT that prepares you to take the SAT and ACT. Start reading the ACT and SAT books you may already have (or buy them this year). It will be very helpful to prep for these tests during the summer before you head into your sophomore year.

- **Look at the varying requirements for colleges outside of your state.**
  For example, if you are thinking of attending a college in California, they require you to take a year of visual and performing arts. Idaho requires a credit earned in speech. Some colleges require three foreign language credits, while others require four. These are things you can address at this time, and look at the states outside your own and see how they differ from your home state.

- **Look into a part-time job between your sophomore and junior year (if time permits).**
  You can even look at jobs that only require working a few hours a week. These look great on a résumé and give you the opportunity to experience being interviewed, as well as the responsibility of working.

SOPHOMORE YEAR GOALS (example)

ACADEMIC	ATHLETIC	EXTRACURRICULAR	VOLUNTEER	FAMILY/PERSONAL	COLLEGE GOALS
5 A's and 1 B	Make the starting five in basketball	Run for office: secretary of Student Council	Continue as Big Sister	Eat with family twice a week	Investigate top schools in art history
Take early morning class in debate and speech	Score eight points in the game	Continue in Art Club	Help with the Big Brother/ Big Sister Auction	No TV until all homework is done	Make a list of my favorite schools: cost and admissions standards (pick at least ten)
Study art all four years	Average three rebounds per game	Continue piano: try out for Music Group	Join the student board for the Rescue Mission	Help with chores one hour on Saturday	Dream school: Northwestern or Virginia, Dartmouth
Take Honors II in history	In track: make a relay team		Continue as junior ambassador for women's shelter	Go to church on Wednesday nights when there is no game	Major: art history or history
	Miss no more than one practice in basketball and no more than 2 in track			No more soda!	Take PSAT and PLAN
	Improve my 100 time in track by .20			*No alcohol in high chool and no drugs or smoking EVER!*	Study ACT and SAT books in the latter part of the school year and over the summer
				Never get into a car with someone who has been drinking	

Junior Year

Now we are rolling along. Can you believe it's junior year? You are halfway through—and getting into bigger decisions and seeing some crucial changes. This is the year when you start truly evaluating where you want to go to college and what you want to pick as a major. I want to be clear: this often changes, even in college. But I have worked with a few kids who tell me that they want to go to "XYZ" School and study business and then, when we go to research that school, we discover it doesn't offer an undergraduate business program.

This can be extremely deflating. It is very hard to go down a road and find out it is a dead end, especially when it was your dream. It is important to look at these things your freshman and sophomore year. By the time you are a junior, you should have around ten schools that are a good fit for your major(s) and other important factors (cost, demographics, size, admission standards, etc.). It also is important to research all these things beforehand, especially since I have had discussions with students on various things such as, "I hate large cities, but my top school is University of Chicago." This means that they have not figured out that University of Chicago is in one of the biggest cities in the country. So, do your homework on the schools.

By now you have done all that you should research wise (based on the later chapter on researching schools) and have narrowed it down to ten options. This is the year to meet with your school counselor and start discussing options and plans for these school. It is also a great time to request information from the school. The information is free, and it gets you on the various schools radar. Start applying for outside scholarships at this time. (You do not need to know the exact school you will be attending for this part.)

As with your freshman and sophomore year goals, start setting them at the end of the summer before your junior year. This year, you should have more college goals and tasks. It may be the year you take on a part-time job (if you haven't already), if time permits and your grades are holding steady. If you are not sure, ask how will it affect your grades, sports, or activities. Summertime is a better time to take on a job, but it will all depend on the job and time requirements.

Parents: be sure to listen to your child and question whether they are taking on too much or too little, or setting their goals too high or too low. Get a pulse on where they are, as well as keeping them on task with their goals. Getting a job may be one of their goals for various reasons. But if they seem stressed during the year or when making decisions, have a discussion with them about it. I have found that when my kids have been a bit strained, it is usually around an upcoming big paper or test. Make suggestions to them about time management and/or not going to an optional meeting or event. See if they can use weekends for relaxation and homework, as there is a happy balance between active and overworked. Keep the dialogue going with your child and check in with them periodically. Also, they will start feeling the added stress junior year, knowing that decisions need to be made. Junior year is a great time to take a weekend trip to a school or two on their list to get them more focused and excited about the prospect of college and what it means.

This will also be the year to start looking at AP classes. Pick subjects that you are interested in and that you can excel in. Take the AP test. (See the SAT, ACT, SAT Subject, and AP Test Preparation Chapter.) If you are not great at English, do not take an AP class in it. It will most likely be too demanding, and you will find yourself spending time on it that may not be as productive as other options. If you are great at math, take that AP class.

Look at the college requirements for math and other subjects. If you are looking at upper-tiered schools, military academies, or schools with higher academic requirements, AP courses will be expected from you. Some require a minimum course level for their schools, and some colleges have different requirements on the years you take courses. For example, your high school or state may only require you to take science for two years. However, the college you are applying to "recommends" you to take science all four years. If that is the case, I would highly recommend taking science all four years. Why limit yourself or pull yourself out from an opportunity just because you did not take a class? You also don't want to be in a position where you have to take summer school or an online course, so research the schools' expectations at this time. Then you can accordingly adjust your school course for this year.

Remember you need to keep in mind that sometimes, as you find out more information about schools and majors, your opinions and thoughts might change. As I mentioned before about Alex: it happened with him when he visited the school. But it also can happen during the research process. You can have your heart set on an Ivy League school, but getting straight As doesn't come easily, so you may reevaluate your plans. This may be reflected in "College Goals" on our example goal sheets. It is also very interesting to see how you have changed and grown, and how your opinions have evolved between freshman and junior year.

Start taking SAT and ACT tests. At this point, you should actively be taking the practice tests online and studying for them. Get involved in a work group, hire a tutor, and see what is offered at your high school to help. We will discuss more of the how to's in the ACT and SAT Preparation chapter. This is the year you will be starting the process.

JUNIOR YEAR GOALS (example)

ACADEMIC	ATHLETIC	EXTRACURRICULAR	VOLUNTEER	FAMILY/PERSONAL	COLLEGE GOALS
A's in 4 classes and B's in 2	Make varsity team in basketball	Student Council vice president	On student board for Rescue Mission	Eat with family twice a week	Make excel list and spreadsheet of top ten schools in my major; start ranking them
AP classes in history and art	Score 4 points a game	Art Club treasurer	Continue as junior ambassador for women's shelter	No TV until all homework is done	Major: art history, history, or liberal arts
Take drama	Play 5 minutes or more per game		Help with fund-raiser for Big Brothers and Big Sisters	Help with chores one hour on Saturday	Visit 3 schools this year and 4 over the summer
Join Honor Society	Make 2 relay teams in track			Go to church on Sunday mornings and as often as possible on Wednesdays	Sign up for all the schools to get material and information from them
	Improve time in 200 by .15			No more soda!	Goal schools: Williams, Bowdoin, Carnegie Mellon, NYU, and Virginia
	Make club team in basketball			*No alcohol in high chool and no drugs or smoking EVER!*	Take SAT and ACT
				Never get into a car with someone who has been drinking	

Senior Year

Yes! You are here!

It seems there is so much to do this year, and my biggest recommendation is to try your best to get it done earlier in the year. Most likely, you will start to tune out a bit come spring with the dreaded "senioritis," and you may not be as focused on getting the things done.

Parents, get their attention while you can. You may have to work a little harder to keep them on track and keep their grades up.

I also need to caution you: You might have a false sense of security once you get accepted into a college. You may believe it is carte blanche to not try so hard anymore.

I encourage you to finish strong and to keep your grades up! I have seen schools turn away a student who has failed or dropped their GPA substantially. It also is not the time for you to "have a little fun" and go a bit out of character with your behavior. During this year , it is especially important for you to stay on course.

Parents: Be like Jiminy Cricket, keeping your kids directed and moving towards the light. The senior student tends to feel they are old enough, wise enough, ready to be on their own, and not in need of our direction. While they are getting there, keep them focused on the prize and avoid needing to have the "was it worth it?" conversation. Let them know there is plenty of time to experience and try things when they get to college, but THIS is not the time to risk their future. On the other hand, I do feel it is a great time for students to be more independent and for us, as parents, to be there to talk them through it. Many a child has gone wild, so to speak, when they get to college. They have been riding the straight and narrow for so long during high school that they go a bit bananas when they get to college. This is not something we want to happen either. As parents, it is helpful to find the right balance of activities that allow them to feel they are spreading their wings, but not all at once, allowing them to make good decisions on their own. Senior year was the first year one of my sons went on a road trip with some friends to a school a few hours away. That was hard for me, but he made it back alive, had a great time, and stretched himself a bit. Simple things like that allow them to develop and set their own boundaries.

This is also the year where you can wrap up the school visits (if financially possible) and/or take virtual tours online. It can give you, as a student, a feel for the schools you want to attend. Senior year is the year you apply for the schools you are truly interested in. We will talk about this in depth later, but the application process is early in the year, and you should be done by Thanksgiving, if possible.

I say that for several reasons. 1) As I mentioned before, you will probably start to lose focus slowly after Winter Break. Applying to schools when you are more excited and focused is best. This is especially important when essays and tasks need to get done. 2) Get them in early so you don't have to deal with anything but enjoying your senior year. Then you can just focus on high school and things associated with high school. 3) Why procrastinate? If you have everything turned in, then you are literally just waiting for responses back! (And not stressing about getting the applications in.) 4) Lastly, even if the deadline says January first, for example, many schools are first come/first served for scholarships. Be at the front of the line. (There are also some earlier deadlines for early admissions scholarships that will be discussed in later chapters.)

This is the year you will be taking your SAT subject test(s), if you have not already and if applicable to the schools you are applying for. Not all schools require the SAT subject test(s). I talk about this in detail in the SAT, ACT, SAT Subject, and AP Test Preparation chapter.

As you can see by the senior student's example goal chart, you could have a lot on your plate. But by this time, you have a routine and have learned to juggle several things. This is life, and I feel that this (in itself) teaches you to have balance and to be sure that you're not putting all of your eggs in one basket. You have already learned that you need to make sacrifices and choices to get what you want. Most importantly, it teaches you that Rome wasn't built in a day; this is your body of work—built over your high school career. When you can look back and see all of your accomplishments, you can truly gain the confidence to go to the next level.

SENIOR YEAR GOALS (example)

ACADEMIC	ATHLETIC	EXTRACURRICULAR	VOLUNTEER	FAMILY/PERSONAL	COLLEGE GOALS
A's in 4 classes and B's in 2	Make starting five in varsity basketball	Student Council class vice president	On student board for Rescue Mission	Eat with family twice a week	Goal Schools: NYU and Bowdoin
AP classes in history and art	Score 8 points a game	Art Club president	Continue as junior ambassador for women's shelter	No TV until all homework is done	Major history or liberal Arts
Honor Society member	Make 3 rebounds per game		Help with fund-raiser for Big Brothers and Big Sisters	Help with chores one hour on Saturday	Apply to all schools on wish list
Take AP Tests			Help with fund-raiser and awareness program for women's shelter	Go to church on Sunday mornings and as often as possible on Wednesdays	Look up and apply for ten scholarships a week
Take two SAT subject tests: math and history				No more soda or candy!	
				Learn how to do laundry and balance a checkbook	
				Open checking account	
				No alcohol in high chool and no drugs or smoking EVER!	
				Never get into a car with someone who has been drinking	

It's hard for kids to realize there are no "do-overs" at the end of high school. However, you CAN always work to do better, and you can strive to be better than the previous day, week, month, and year.

In the next chapter, we will look at the development of your résumé. This takes all the things you have done in high school and puts it on paper. Having a well-built résumé is crucial and one you can have available at any given moment for applications, scholarships, recruiting purposes, employment, etc. It's a wonderful tool to create.

2

Résumé Building

IT IS IMPORTANT TO start building your résumé your freshman year.

If you rely on your memory, as a senior, to look back at all the awards, achievements, and accomplishments you have had, you will definitely forget something. Some things can also seem inconsequential during freshman year, but (as mentioned previously) they are all a body of work—and show that you aren't a one year pony. By putting everything into your résumé, you show the continuity, growth, and development that colleges will be seeking. Résumés offer a layering effect, and they should show personal development, progression, growth, and involvement in your school and community.

I will give you some sample résumés further along in this chapter, but for starters, when writing a résumé, break it up into these categories.

- Academic Accomplishments
- Volunteering
- Athletic Involvement and Accomplishments
- Extracurricular/Employment
- Leadership

These do not have to be in that order, as it will also depend on what you are trying to achieve. If it is for athletic recruiting, I would put your athletic accomplishments first. For scholarship applications, you would put academic first, etc. But just like a résumé you would use for employment, you will highlight the area that you will want them to focus on and see first.

Don't wait until the last minute. Parents, creating this (starting freshman year and building it along the way) is a wonderful method for your son or daughter to learn the skill of résumé creation, and you can assist them. This will be essential after they graduate college and they are looking for employment. My kids created their résumés when they started high school and continued building them when they started college. They had learned that résumés will be needed for the next steps, and it helped them immensely when they began their employment searches. These are skills that are invaluable to learn early on in their lives, and it is something that is crucial to their success.

Another benefit of working on your résumé from the very beginning is that creating it gives you a great opportunity to visually look at the areas that may be weaker and need more focus as you are developing them. For example, if you are building your résumé and see that there are no academic accomplishments, you can work on beefing up that area on your résumé. As a parent, this is a great tool as well, as it is so much easier to have them see it and make the corrections themselves than having to nag them for four years. (Believe me when I say this.) It's a great opportunity for them to see what it takes and what they need to do—in order to get where they want to go.

Academics

This area may be easier for some and more challenging for others.

Academics don't come easily to everyone, so you may have to work very hard to achieve this kind of success. If your grades allow for it, become a member of the National Honors Society (NHS). Each school is different, but you typically need to have a cumulative GPA of 3.5. You need to apply at the end of your sophomore year. There are also requirements to stay in the NHS, which starts with maintaining the GPA set by your school, as well as participating in various activities throughout the time you are a member. The NHS is a great thing to shoot for—push for acceptance. It is also universally recognized by all colleges, and it is recognized at most high schools.

The NHS requires an application, essay, and recommendations (to be handed in by a deadline specific to your school). It is a national organization; however, schools have the ability to have higher standards than is required by the NHS. Check with the advisor or counselor at your school to verify the application deadline, so you do not miss out on joining. This is a must for those looking to be considered for an upper-tiered school and an easy thing to be part of. It is also a really great club with students who are focused on their academics.

Some other activities you can look into for building up the academics portion of your résumé are clubs focused on disciplines such as math, science, and history, but also there are various academic challenges and competitions. Another great club is the speech and debate team at your school. Many schools offer this as not only a club team but also give you school credit. Google search some areas of interest for you, and you will be surprised by what you find. For example, if you are interested in science, here are some options for well-known science competitions:

National High School Science Competitions

- Siemens Competition: Research Paper and Presentation
- Intel STS: Research Paper and Interviews
- Google Science Fair: Online Project Submission and Judging Interviews for the Finalist
- National Science Bowl: Team Competition

These range in grade levels for participation, but most are from ninth to twelfth grade.

If you are interested in math, there are almost too many competitions to list! Here are a few that I found interesting and recommend to students. Just Google search the specific competition, and see if they are offered in your area and what the requirements are.

National High School Mathematics Competitions

- American Mathematics Competitions (AMC).
  - o These are the largest set of national high school competitions in the United States. They include the AMC 10, AMC 12, AIME, USAJMO, and USAMO and lead up to the selection of the US team for the International Mathematical Olympiad.
- American Regions Math League (ARML)
- American High School Internet Mathematics Competition (AHSIMC)
- American Scholastic Mathematics Association (ASMA)
- Archimedean Challenge #1
- AoCMM Math Modeling Competition
- Continental Mathematics League (CML)
- Homeschool Math Contests
  - o They offer a chart of math contests open to individuals (homeschooled and otherwise) and also an up-to-date, state-by-state list of regional meets.
- Mandelbrot Competition

- Math League
  - o They offer contests with different names in different states and regions.
- mathleague.org
  - o They organize the state high school math championships in several states
- Moody's Mega Math Challenge
- Mu Alpha Theta
  - o This fraternity hosts both local and a national competitions.
- National Assessment & Testing
- National Internet Math Olympiad
- National Online Math League (NOML): Formerly the Cody Bowl
- Online Math League (OML)
- Purple Comet! Math Meet
- Rocket City Math League (RCML)
- UAB Math-by-Mail
- United States of America Mathematics Talent Search
  - o An excellent competition for students learning to solve proof-oriented problems. (USAMTS homepage.)
- Perennial Math
- Who Wants to Be a Mathematician?
  - o This competition is sponsored by the American Mathematical Society.

I'm also including this awesome website, where you can find out what math competitions are offered in your state:

http://www.artofproblemsolving.com/wiki/index.php/List_of_United_
States_high_school_mathematics_competitions

If history is your thing, here are some ideas for history competitions or things to get involved in.

National High School History Competitions

- National History Bee and Bowl
- US History Bee
- National Mock Trial Championships
- National History Day Contests

Volunteering

As I have mentioned before, I think volunteering for any high schooler, whether you choose to go to college or not, is an important developmental piece of your growth. It allows you to see the world beyond yourself, to find something of yourself that you can give, and sometimes during the whole process, you find something about yourself. It is a very important part of the high school experience, but it can also be challenging to find things you want to do. When volunteering, try to look for something that you have an interest in to begin with. For example, you probably don't want to volunteer at an animal shelter if you don't like animals. If you hate hospitals, then it is not a good idea to help at the local hospital (unless you truly want to overcome a fear).

What you want to look for with volunteering is not quantity, but quality. Instead of volunteering at twenty different groups or organizations over your four years of high school, find two or three that you love and want to commit to. Colleges love to see continuity and depth, but they also want to see a student find connections and progress within those connections. So, it is best to work exclusively with just a few groups or organizations. If you put on your résumé that you helped at a food shelter, but you only did it once during high school, does that really scream commitment or does it show a checkmark in a box that asked, "Did you volunteer?"? Does it show that you were involved and committed? Probably not. That's not to say you can't do a specific fund-raiser for a charitable group as a one-time event because that is a great thing and should be encouraged. I am talking about the one-offs where you volunteer one or two times, and you have nothing else on your résumé. See what is out there and what you are passionate about by helping at various organizations—but the one offs won't and shouldn't fill your whole résumé.

Here are some ideas and groups that you can look into for volunteering. Be sure to Google what you are interested in and see what is in your area as well.

- Hunger Project/Food Bank
- Homeless Shelters
- Women and Children's Shelters
- Military Groups
- Animal Groups (Animal Shelters, Conservatories, or Animal Protection Agencies)
- Habitat for Humanity

- Ronald McDonald House or Other Organizations that Deal with Specific Illnesses
- Hospitals
- Preventing Domestic Violence
- Nursing Homes or Retirement Centers
- Environmental Groups
- Libraries
- Museums
- Waste Project, Recycling, or Clean-up Drives
- Mentoring (Big Brothers, Big Sisters, or Tutoring)

Two of my sons volunteered for the Special Olympics as assistant coaches for their respective sports. One of my sons did powerlifting and another one helped with coaching swimming. What an honor it was for them to work with this great organization! It also really helped them appreciate how talented the people on the Special Olympics teams were. It was life changing for them, and they have some wonderful stories about their time working with the athletes. Another one of my sons worked for the Coalition Against Domestic and Sexual Violence for over four years. He helped educate and bring awareness to middle schoolers and high schoolers on preventing domestic violence before it occurs. He truly loved his time with this group and will continue to be an advocate no matter where he is. My daughter loves animals and helped volunteer at an animal shelter during her high school career.

I mentioned specific one-offs that are great and help groups by raising awareness and funds. You can create fund-raisers and events to raise money for organizations. These are easy and help develop creativity, organization, and leadership skills, while also making a difference in your own backyard. I always tell the students I work with to first find the group that you would want to help. Then contact your principal to see what steps you can take to organize a fund-raiser at school, though it doesn't have to be limited to only your school. Think outside the box—even if the fund-raiser only raises $100, that is okay! That is $100 the group did not have before and, believe me, charitable organizations are thrilled when young people show compassion and concern for the world around them. You also will have done this on your own, learned a lot, raised awareness, and (going forward) will feel more connected to the group or cause that you helped with. Young adults who care turn into grown adults who care.

Fundraising Opportunities

- **Create bracelets made with the group's name, slogan, or motto.**

  If your mascot is a Bronco, it can be "Bronco's Care for _____." Many groups have colors that go with various causes, such as pink for cancer awareness and purple for domestic violence awareness. For the fund-raiser, you can buy bracelets in specific colors to bring awareness to the cause. Sometimes working with Student Council is wonderful because you have the added manpower to help. Since Student Council is already plugged into the school, they can help spread the word, put up posters, get it in your school newspaper, or add it to the announcements that are made each day over the PA system. If you are not on Student Council or having their help is not an option, ask a sports team to help. It could be any team, and you would just talk with the coach for help with recruiting players. For example, if it were basketball, you could sell the bracelets at games and pass out fliers with the bracelets to create awareness. Players on the team would help with this and distributing posters around the school and/or neighborhood. This is a great way to make a difference in your community (and it does look great on a résumé)!

- **Look at things that are happening in the world, country, or community that you can really get behind.**

  Then, create a card (about ten-by-ten inches) about the cause with room for someone's name. Many groups do this fund-raiser in stores, where people donate one to five dollars for causes. The donor puts their name on it, and employees put it up in the store. It is the same concept here but in an approved, designated area of the school. My boys did this when the tsunami disaster happened a few years ago. They raised money and awareness for this relief program and donated the money to the Red Cross. They created this fund-raiser and received help from the football players at the school, along with Student Council. But they created, implemented, and participated in the fund-raiser them-selves. They sold the "cards," which were donated by a local printer, and sold them outside the lunchroom. They put them up after someone made a donation, and they did this for a designated week at their school. (I want to emphasize that any idea like this requires approval from the school administration.)

- **One that is sure to make everyone happy is done near a particular holiday.** Near the holiday, sell lollipops or candy and have a delivery system set up at school to give these to students designated by the buyer. A great holiday to take advantage of is Valentine's Day. Students purchase cards or candy for other students. It's very easy and cheap, but it can be done for any group. You designate the charity and tie it in with your school. For example, "Grizzlies LOVE (Whatever charity you designate would go here)." Many stores will donate candy, and it is an easy way to raise money for charitable organizations.

- **A more elaborate event, that will take more time and development, is to set up a run or walk for a cause.**
  There is no overhead, unless you decide to offer t-shirts.

- **Another simple fund-raiser is a dinner or banquet at your school or lunchroom.**
  Parents can donate food for the fund-raiser, or you can check with restaurants to see if they are able to donate to help with raising funds.

There are plenty of ideas and options out there for volunteering in every area that you can join or even start! If you want to save the forest in the Amazon and there isn't a group in your area, start it yourself!

Athletic

Not everyone can be an athlete, and not every athlete can make the varsity team. But there are things for everyone, and it doesn't have to be at your school either. Maybe you have taken martial arts for years and achieved a red belt. Or you play tennis on a club team or golf. Maybe your school doesn't offer athletics—don't give up! There are plenty of sports and activities for students to get involved in outside of high school. You can run a yoga class, participate in Crossfit, or compete at powerlifting tournaments. This all can be placed under the athletic section of your résumé.

Even if you have not had accomplishments, per se, showing participation and involvement in athletics in some capacity shows that you are balanced and well-rounded. You could even be the junior bass champion for your age group! Be creative in what you do if you are limited in what your school offers or what your abilities are.

My youngest son, Alex, as I mentioned, was a swimmer. He did not like football at all, even though he played on a kid's league for several years. He was always put on the O line, and he did not like that position. He didn't enjoy playing. So he started swimming year-round for a club team during his fifth grade school year. It took until middle school for him to start developing in that sport and become a great swimmer. It also took a lot of hard work and sacrifice on his part, but he didn't want to pick a more traditional sport, like his brothers did. He would have been very unhappy if we had tried to push him in that direction. But, with swimming, he built an incredible résumé in his sport over the years, even achieving an All American status. So don't think it has to be a typical sport. Work with what you like, what you are talented in, and/or what you WANT to do. I have worked with students in varying activities and sports. But whatever they choose, I encouraged them to work hard and to be the best they can be in it.

Parents, this is your part! Encourage and motivate your kids, and help to get them plugged into what they want to be part of as well.

As an athlete, I also want to stress that you do not need to be #1 at a particular sport. But to be part of a team, working hard and being involved shows great team-work—and that is what it is all about. If you are talented at the given sport, that is a bonus, but it isn't the purpose. Find your place in this area and stay with it, so you can gain different experiences and develop along the way.

I have listed some athletic ideas for those not involved in high school sports or who didn't make the high school team in the sport they enjoyed participating in. It does happen, but don't let it curtail your love of a sport or the pure enjoyment of it. What it does show is involvement, and colleges love to see participation and team-work, and it doesn't have to be exclusively at a high school. Many club sports actually perform, compete, and train at a higher level than high school sports, so it may even be something you find helps advance your abilities more in the sport you are pursuing. If there are no club teams available in your area, try something new! High School is a wonderful time for that. Here are some ideas.

- Martial Arts
  - Including, but not limited to, karate, tae kwan do, judo, or jiu jitsu.
- Dance
  - Some options: ballet, tap, jazz, modern, and cultural dances such as Irish, Hawaiian, or Latin.
- Cheerleading Clubs or Groups
- Club Sports of any Kind
  - Volleyball, hockey, swimming, basketball, baseball, football, skiing,

softball, tennis, wrestling, track, cross country, powerlifting, gymnastics, cheer, bowling, rugby, or lacrosse.

o Don't be afraid to try unique or different sports, such as fencing, triathlons, paintball, cricket, roller derby, water polo, handball, or even a cycling team. Many of these sports are offered through your Local YMCA or PAL.

Extracurricular/Employment

This one is so diverse and far-reaching I encourage you to be creative, but definitely get involved. High school is the time to jump in and start looking at what you want to do and who you want to be. It is a time to experience different things and have lots of options to explore.

Most schools offer many clubs and activities to be involved with. When selecting what you want to do, it is always best to start with your interests. If you enjoy art, join Art Club. Depending on the size of the school, many schools have clubs for science, chess, volunteering (Key Club), languages, drama, astronomy, and debate and speech, just to name a few. If you are good at writing and enjoy that, join the school paper or be involved in the school yearbook. One of my favorites is Student Council, which is a wonderful way to be part of the school and really contribute to the whole school experience for yourself and your classmates. Are you a future broadcaster? You should look into the Media Club. There are so many options available at most schools, and if there aren't many options, I always suggest starting one yourself! Talk with your school principal or faculty to see about getting one going. Starting one from scratch would count for extracurricular AND leadership on your résumé.

Band and orchestra is another great extracurricular group. You can participate in your school or master an instrument through training on your own elsewhere. You may even be in a choir at school, church, or through school. These are all opportunities and extracurricular activities to put on your résumé. These activities can also be something that transfer over to colleges that are looking for these type of students to help them in their own clubs, bands, and choirs. They may even recruit you for college! So, if you are thinking of quitting cello lessons, maybe hold on for a while and reconsider. Mastering an instrument or having singing abilities is an incredible gift, and it can really help on your résumé. Not everyone has these talents—and many wish they did. Even if you are a moderate guitar player or a "good" but not "great" singer, continuing with lessons, performing, and working towards improvement shows commitment and heart. Who doesn't admire that? So, try to become the best you can be with your gift.

Some students I have worked with attend smaller private or charter schools that do not offer any clubs or have limited options. My advice is to then look at other options through your community.

- Boys/Girls Scouts
- Leadership groups through the Mayor's or Governor's office
- Photography
- Drama
- 4H
- Crafts
    o Examples: ceramics, pottery, art, weaving, or quilting.
- National Mock Elections
- Junior ROTC and National Guard Programs
- City or state governmental internships

Employment

I know that throwing in a job can be a challenge, and some students just clearly do not have the time for it. If doesn't affect your grades, your most important focus, get a small part-time job on the weekends or even during summer break. Becoming a camp counselor for the summer or lifeguarding are both great ways to spend your summer, make some money, and gain some great skills. Both of these types of employment will come with CPR/First Aid training, which is also a nice add-on to your résumé and knowledge base.

There are many jobs that you can do, such as tutoring, babysitting, cleaning, landscaping, working at fast food restaurants or movie theatres, working in your family business, and even farming or agricultural jobs. In the summer you will have more flexibility and time, so if you can, do something during that timeframe.

As parents, as with anything, encouraging our kids when it comes to employment is very important. It sets them up with skills and develops a great work ethic, which is critical to their own personal development. It isn't just taking on a job; it is building the skills to work for someone and follow a schedule, as well as gaining good customer service skills. (EVERYONE has a customer, but that is for another book.)

Just remember, when they are working they should look at it as another stepping stone for their future. They may need their boss to write a reference or recommendation. Be sure to encourage them to be proud of the job they are doing, and when they do leave the job, they should leave on good terms with clear expectations upfront with their employer of the commitment they can make around school when it starts. This aspect can be hard for teenagers. Sometimes they have a hard time with the communication part. Don't step in and intercede, if at all possible. It is a great opportunity for them to grow and learn about talking and communication on their own with a manager or boss. But do give good, clear direction on what they are to do as far as communication. You have much more experience and maturity, and they will need your guidance.

Leadership

With leadership, you are looking for opportunities to be in charge or in a position where you can make a difference. This can be:

- Captain of a Sports Team
- Student Government
- Boys and Girls State
  - o *See expanded information.
- Junior ROTC
- City, State, or Mock Government
- Boy or Girl Scouts
- Congressional Medal Recipients
  - o They have bronze, silver, and gold levels. (**See expanded information.)
- Outside Club Sports Teams Leadership Opportunities
  - o (Captains, representatives, and managers, etc.)
- Coach, Assistant Coach, Mentor, or School Club Leadership
  - o Be the president, vice president, secretary, treasurer, editor, etc. of a volunteer group.

These are all great ways to develop your Leadership skills and would be great additions to a résumé. Colleges want students with strong leadership skills.

*Boys and Girls State:[1] Boys and Girls State is an awesome way for high school students to participate in a program that helps teach them how government works. When you become involved in this group, you run for office, learn skills in speaking, create laws, and help to enforce them, as well as participate in all the activities through each phase. This is done over the summer, so it doesn't interfere with school. For those students needing leadership development, this is a perfect way for you to get the skills needed, as well as a great résumé builder. Many times it is paid for by local American Legion Groups through scholarships. To see if your state has this program, be sure to look at their website and the criteria for your specific state.

http://www.boysandgirlsstate.org/index.html

Congressional Medal[2]: This award is for young students, between fourteen and twenty-three years of age. You earn various levels of award certificates: bronze, silver, and gold Congressional award medals. You are not competing against other students; this is purely a personal goal-oriented challenge and award program. Each level has its own goals and specific requirements, such as voluntary public service, personal fitness, physical goals, and expedition and exploration. You can do it at your own pace. There is no minimum GPA, which allows a wider range of activities and challenges for all students, irrespective to where they are grade-wise in school.

http://congressionalaward.org/

Some of you may be looking at this and be thinking that there is no way someone can do all of this! There is not enough time in the day and something has to give. My answer is yes and no because each child is different. Each needs a varying amount of time for their studies, based on their own speed, abilities, and capabilities. In my own home, all of my kids were different and unique and each excelled in different areas, but they succeeded at their own pace and with their own expectations.

I have worked with many kinds of students over many years. One boy I worked with spent countless hours participating in his year-round sport, and he still had time to be involved in various activities in and outside of school. He even held down a part-time job during the school year as a lifeguard and interned in the summer as well. How did he do that, you may wonder? Well, he made the decision that his future education, and even beyond that—his future career—required him to make some sacrifices. He chose a more limited social life on the weekends (no parties and limited late night events). He also was highly organized and a great time manager, which is definitely a must.

My daughter, Rachel, was very gifted in speech and debate and was gone a lot during the weekends, which she spent competing from October through May. She could not commit to full-time or even part-time employment, but she did a small cleaning job that was flexible during the week and managed her time around that.

Another student I worked with held down a research internship during the school year, took cello lessons, was involved in a sport, volunteered, and also was #1 in her class. It can be done. It is just about time management, wise choices, and encouragement and direction from us as parents!

As you can see by the résumés attached (these are actual résumés of students I have worked with), there are many activities and ideas for students. Each person has abilities and talents that can be honed and increased during your high school years. It is all about prioritizing, time management, and looking forward to the future this is all leading you towards. Many kids, even adults, live in the moment and don't think about tomorrow or what their actions today will cause. What will the ripple effect be for the future? That is an important question to ask. It is about balance and prioritization. No one is saying to forgo your high school experiences for your college ones, but I am saying DON'T spend it all in one place. Enjoy it and make the most of it, but I have seen many a kid spend it ALL on sports or ALL on academics or ALL on just having fun. Then, when school is over, they more often than not have nothing to show for it. Life is about balance, and if you can learn this in high school, how to manage your life, and how to make good decisions, it will be the key to a bright and great future.

Résumé Examples: Note-I have changed the high school these students have attended as well as any other information to protect their privacy. These students went on to college, received partial to full scholarships, and two of them competed in college sports.

Student #1

Alice Townslet
5555 W. first Drive
Chicago, Illinois 60645
555-555-5555
National Clearinghouse #12345678

Athletic Achievements:
DISTRICTS:
- Won first Place at Districts in 100 Back and 2nd Place in 100 Fly; 2010, Won first Place at Districts in Both 200 Free and 100 Back: 2011, Won first Place in Districts in 100 Backstroke and 100 Freestyle; 2012
- Broke High School District Records in Both 100 Backstroke and 100 Freestyle, 2012
- Made All Metro Team (All Conference) 2010 3rd Place , first Place 2011 and first Place 2012

HIGH SCHOOL:
- Undefeated in Regular High School Swim Season 2011 and 2012
- New Heights High School MVP Swimmer 2010, 2011 and 2012
- Hold 7 out of 8 High School Records at Mountain View High School
- Captain, 2011 and 2012
- Interscholastic All American 100 Backstroke and 100 Fly 2012/2013 Season
- Assistant Coach Helper Mountain View High School 2013

STATE:
- Won 2nd Place at State in 100 Back Stroke and 3rd Place in 100 Fly: The Only Freshmen in the State, as Well as 2nd Place in Medley Relay and 3rd Place in Free Relay; 2010.
- Won 2nd Place at State in Both 200 Free and 100 Back, 2011
- Won 2nd Place at State in Both 100 Back and 100 Fly 2012

NATIONALS-Y NATIONALS:
- Qualified Y Nationals in 5 Events, 2011, 5 Events 2012 and 8 in 2013
- Made Finals at Y Nationals in Both 100 Backstroke and 100 Butterfly 2012
- Won 14th for Backstroke and 24th for Butterfly at Y Nationals, 2012
- Won 5th Place Backstroke and 20th for Butterfly at Y Nationals 2013
- YMCA All American 2013

CLUB:
- Won High Point Scorer (first Place) at Regionals, 2012 and 2013
- Competed In 2012 Sectional Long Course Championships, Qualified for Finals in 4 of 6 events

- Set YMCA Record for: Long Course in 100 Free (53.83), 2012, Short Course 50 Butterfly (27.41), 2012, Short Course 400 Free Team Relay (3:31.58), 400 Medley Team Relay (3:16.19) and 800 Free Relay (7.18:79) 2011-2012, Long Course 200 Free Team Relay (1:41.94) and 400 Free Team Relay (3:44.85) 2012
- USA All American Swimming, 2013
  Captain, 2013/2014 Season
- Won "Hardest Working Award" 2013

Leadership:
- All Student Body President 2013/2014
- All Student Body Treasurer 2012/2013
- Class Secretary/Student Council 2011/2012
- Captain of Swim Team 2011 and 2012
- Assistant Coach High School 2013
- Captain of YMCA Club Team 2013/2014 Season
- Selected as a HOBY representative for New Heights High School 2012 (Hugh O'Brien Youth Leadership)
- New Heights High School, Wendy's Heisman Winner-Student/Athlete Award 2013

Extracurricular/Volunteer/Employment:
- Lunch Reading Program Volunteer at Decatur Elementary School, 2013
- Assistant Coach Swimming Special Olympics, 2012 and 2013
- Junior Red Cross Volunteer 2011, 2012
- City of Springfield Mayor's Youth Advisory Council Representative (MYAC), 2012
- Coach, Summer League Swim Team YMCA, 2012
- Lifeguard YMCA, Springfield, Illinois: February 2011-February 2012
- Custodian, First Mortgage, Chicago, Illinois: July 2010-Present
- Created Purple emPowered Fund-raiser for New Heights View High School, Helping the Women's and Children's Alliance/Shelter, Raised Funds and Awareness for the WAC Shelter and Heelp
  Woman's and Children's Alliance Ambassador, 2013

Academic:
- Maintained a 3.62 Cumulative GPA
- Illinois State All Academic Swimming 2012

Student #2:

James Harwood
333 N. Hempstead Road
Highland Falls, New York 88888
555-555-5555

Athletic Honors:
- 2008 National Power Lifting Champion/USA Power Lifting-Kalamazoo, Michigan
  - Set National Power Lifting Record in Bench Press at 365 Pounds
- Hudson Valley Lineman Challenge Champion 2008
- 5A New York All Conference Second Team Athletic Honors:
- 2008 National Power Lifting Champion/USA Power Lifting-Kalamazoo, Michigan
  - Set National Power Lifting Record in Bench Press at 365 Pounds
- Hudson Valley Lineman Challenge Champion 2008
- 5A Northern New York All Conference Second Team 2008 Defensive Line, as a Sophomore and 5A Northern New York All Conference Second Team 2009 Linebacker, as a Junior and 5A Northern New York All Conference First Team 2010 Linebacker
- New York All State Football 2010, Linebacker
- Selected for the Shriner's All Star Football Team 2010
- 2009 New York State Record in Bench, Squat at 585 and Total Weight Lifted at 1450
  - Won New York State Championship "Best Lifter" Award 2009
- 2009 National Power Lifting Champion/USA Power Lifting-Killeen Texas
  - Set National Power Lifting Record in Squat at 565
- Qualified for World Power Lifting Championship 2008 and 2009
- Invite/Attended 2009 Schuman's Underclassman National Combine in Seattle, Washington
  - Won Best Defensive Player at Combine
  - Won Strongest Player at Combine
- Captain of Varsity Football Team 2009 and 2010
  - Three Year Starter and Varsity Lettered
- Selected for the US Army Combine, Held in San Antonio Texas January 2010-Top 60 Across the Country in each Position selected for this Combine
- Westminster High School Track and Field Participant 2010
  - Shot Put and discus School Record Holder
  - Varsity Lettered
- 2nd Place, New York State Championship Swimming in Both Medley Relay and 200 Free Relay 2010

<u>Academic Achievements:</u>
- NNYC All Academic 2009 and 2010 Football
- NNYC All Academic 2010 Track and Field
- Member of the National Forensic League for Speech and Debate; High School Team won New York State Championship in Speech and Debate 2008
- New York State Tournament first Place Champion in Drama 2009
- Westminster High School Academic Excellence Winner 2009-2010
- Interscholastic Star Nominee for Westminster High School 2010
- New York Hudson Valley Distinguished Student Award Winner 2010

<u>Clubs, Extracurricular and Volunteering activities/Leadership Positions:</u>
- Senior Class Vice President of Student Council, 2010/2011
- Captain of the Varsity Football Team, 2009 and 2010
- President/Founder of Westminster High School Power Lifting Club 2009-2011
- President of the Westminster High School Chess Club 2009-2011
- Employment-Worked at Statewide Insurance, May 2008-current. 1776 W. Liberty Lane, Westminster, NY. Responsible for Filing and Managing Filing System.
- Art Club Member 2009
- Volunteer Winter/Summer Special Olympics; Power Lifting Team and Working Directly with the Athletes in Various Functions and Activities 2008
- Assistant Coach of Special Olympics Team, Power Lifting 2009-2011
- Unified Partner/Coach for Special Olympics Indoor Hockey Team 2009-2011
- Volunteer New York Food Bank 2008

Student #3:

Victoria Wang
2297 W. Medford Lane
Denver, Colorado 80202
555-555-5555

Academic Awards and Accomplishments
- AP Scholar with Distinction
- Valley Visions Published Author
- Research Student of the Year at Valley Math and Science Center
- Algebra Student of the Year at Valley Math and Science Center
- Teachers Choice Award Recipient
- Denver High Mathematical Association of America High Scorer
- National Honor Society Member

Musical Awards and Accomplishments
- Resident Harpist of Denver High School Symphonic Orchestra
- First Chair Harpist

Leadership
- Two-Year Denver YMCA Swim Team Executive Board Member
- Denver YMCA Swim Team Leadership Award
- Front Range LSC Swimming Athlete Junior Representative
- (~750 swimmers in a region covering Colorado, Nevada, and Idaho)
- USA Disability Swimming Committee Athlete Representative and Chair of Communications
- Founder and President of the Cultural Club at Denver High School
- Denver High Swim Team Captain

Athletic Awards and Accomplishments
- Two-year Denver YMCA Swim Team Captain (~350 swimmers)—in charge of organizing various service projects and team activities
- Seven-Time Hardest Worker Award Winner
- Front Range LSC Board of Review Member
- Three Year Varsity Athlete Denver High School Swim Team, State Champions 2013 and 2014
  - State Finalist in the 100 free, 100 fly, and 200 free 2013 and 2014
- Daniel Dewey Sportsperson Award

Volunteer/Employment
- Two Year Assistant Swimming Coach for Special Olympics Idaho
- Four Year Biochemistry Intern—Charlier Research Lab at Colorado State University
- Women and Children's Alliance Ambassador

- Women and Children's Alliance Kick Starter of Teen Champions Program
  - A program designed to spread domestic abuse and dating awareness for youth around the community.
- Women and Children's Alliance Intern - wrote articles for newsletter
- Two Year Volunteer at the Knudsen Nature Center
- Created, Coordinated, and Implemented Team Service Project for USA Swimming with Hawaiian Wildlife Fund in Hawaii
  - Protected Both Greens and Endangered Hawksbill Turtles
- Volunteered with Hawaiian Wildlife Fund in Hawaii
- St. Luke's Junior Volunteer—Interned at Hospital Reception Area and Gift Shop
- Founder and President of Non-Profit Event Organization "Just Keep Swimming," an open water swimming fundraiser for Teen Cancer America

---

As you can see from these résumés, these are very different individuals, active in their schools and communities. They helped others, were successful at school and involved in athletics, but were definitely well-rounded. It can be done with planning, structure, and goal-setting.

3

What Makes You So Different?

IF YOU THINK ABOUT what schools do when they are looking over applications, it does make you wonder, What is the process? What can you do to make your application stand out, whether it be for an actual admission into a college, a scholarship, or a program with a limited acceptance rate?

We will first talk about upper-tiered schools since the requirements for them are higher and different than middle and lower-tiered schools. I want to stress (hopefully over and over again) that there is a place for every person who wants to go to college. Not all should and will get into upper-tiered schools, but I want to make sure I am talking to everyone who wants to navigate the process of getting into college. Also, some students forgo upper-tiered or even higher-tiered schools and end up going to middle or lower-tiered schools because they do not understand what is required of them. They get confused and scared, or it seems too daunting, so they "settle" for a school with an easier process, even if they meet the qualifications of an upper-tiered school.

I want to be sure you have as much information as possible to help you see where you fit and to set realistic expectations for yourself. One college is not better than the other, as it pertains to you. Each of us have a different road and different goals to strive for. This is just a reminder that, for some, it is best to attend a state school, community college, small liberal arts school, etc. For others, it may be going to an Ivy League school, a military academy, or an upper-tiered school. Find your place—and dive into it! It isn't where you start, it is where you finish and what you make of it when you are done.

Okay, now that I got that off my chest, if you are applying to upper-tiered schools, it is important to know that these institutions are looking for standouts, plain and simple. You also may be asking yourself, *What is an upper-tiered school and which ones are they?* There are always questions as to what defines an upper-tiered school, but these are your generalities: They are generally the top twenty-five schools in the country and those with an admission rate below 10%—but this is open to interpretation. I also am not fond of the "upper-tiered" term, with "upper" being those consistently defined as top twenty-five in the country, but that is the term that is consistently used when referring to them. For these type of schools, you will need to be well-rounded, very strong academically (like top-of-the-heap strong), involved in your community and school, and a leader. Involvement in a sport is a plus. For those who are exceptional in a sport, we will discuss more in the recruiting chapter.

Being involved in a sport, activity, or volunteering experience that isn't common can be interesting to an admissions board, such as being an Olympic hopeful in bobsledding, a national frisbee golf champion, part of the Irish dancing team, or experience building houses in Somalia. Being highly talented in an activity is also something that is attractive to a school, such as: acting, modeling, being musically exceptional, debate, etc. While you are doing these activities, if at all possible, be a leader in those areas where you excel. Look for opportunities to take on additional recognition and responsibility as a leader. This can range from becoming a class president to being cheerleading captain or even serving as an officer for a club you participate in. Take your job as a leader seriously because the lessons you learn in this role may set you apart from the crowd when you write your essay or get interviewed.

For the next step, it is crucial to get as much out of academics as possible in high school by challenging yourself. Seek out the most demanding and rigorous opportunities at your school, especially in the academic arena. It is often preferable to do well in a challenging program than to be exceptional in an average one. If your school offers advanced courses, especially those for which college credit is offered, an Ivy League school will expect you to have taken them. Schools can't factor difficult teachers into their decision, they can only go off of your transcript. Look for classes that will be recognized as difficult, but preferably without overly difficult grading. It's most helpful to take difficult classes and work hard in subjects you expect to continue with in college. It will make those subjects easier in college if you challenge yourself in high school.

Sometimes an added circumstance or situation, which people typically consider a detriment to admissions, can actually work in your favor as well—something that makes you or your history unique. For example, things that can make you unique are ethnicity, your social background, where you live, what you are involved in, the circumstances of your life (i.e.; homelessness, tough environments, welfare, deaths in the family, being the first to go to college or the first generation in America, suffering a handicap, etc.). These are the things that mold you into who you are and can ultimately bring diversity to many schools who look for it. If you meet the other requirements with grades, leadership, and activities, these can bring "life" to an application and set you apart from other applicants.

I have worked with students who initially felt uncomfortable bringing up these topics when discussing applications. Some students don't like to highlight them, and some feel uncomfortable. But, believe it or not, schools see it as an opportunity to bring together an array of students from all walks of like, religions, sexual preferences, economic backgrounds, experiences, and cultures.

Let's put it this way: Picture yourself on the admissions board or panel at a great school. You are sitting in a room, looking over thousands of essays and applications from students from all over the world (*literally* all over the world). You have to assume that most everyone in the pile is at the top of their class for an upper-tiered school: In fact, the top 10% of their class and many are valedictorians of their high schools. Statistics show that upper-tiered schools attract those with GPAs of 4.0 and above and, most commonly, a 30 and above on their ACT—if not higher.

Okay, so now you have your pile of accomplished kids. Then what?

What would YOU look for in prospective students who will ultimately contribute to the school? What makes them different than all the other kids who are applying? Activities and connections in their community would be one. Then you look at the ones who were really involved, not just onetime volunteers, but those who were truly involved. You'd also look at WHAT they were involved in. Were they in Peru building a school? Did they work for four years in a project or group that really made a difference in their community?

The next question would be, "Which of these applicants are leaders?" From there, the pile keeps getting smaller, more particular, and specific. It is, therefore, a logical conclusion to assume that there is a narrowing down of the pile by these standards. How else can they differentiate one 4.0 student from another? It's all about what the applicant can bring to the school, what the "value add" is to the school, and sometimes, it is quotas and how they want to be perceived as a school.

That is the business side of it and a lot of the time, they want people who can come together and make a difference in their backyard, period. They, as a school, want to help contribute to that but also take credit for it. That isn't a bad thing; they are seeing something in you and want you to represent their school in that way.

I remember one time, my husband and son David went to Boston to talk with the coach at MIT for basketball. He said something to them both that I never forgot. He said, "Every student that comes to MIT is smart, but we are looking for more than that—someone who can make a difference, who can bring something to the table, and who isn't going to be locked in a room all day studying and doing nothing else." So, in essence, someone who can balance academics and all the other stuff that kids can be doing in this world. I never forgot that and have always stressed it with the students that I help. There are some students who tell me that they don't have time for that or that they struggle with balancing too much. I tell them that there is a place for every student with great grades who may not want to tackle the extra things. There are many schools for them with honor programs, and they will do great things at those schools. It may not be an upper-tiered school, but it may be a place where they are more comfortable. They will "shine" in that environment.

But for those seeking admission to upper-tiered schools, the so-called "all-around well-rounded, very-involved strong leader who is motivated, driven, AND smart" students are what these schools are looking for. Be proud of where you come from, as it has made you who you are—and may be exactly what these schools are looking for.

Now, for those of you who do not have aspirations to attend one of these so-called "upper-tiered" schools but may be more interested in the middle or lower-tiered schools (again, this is just for definition sake): The requirements are not as stringent or high, but if your grades are borderline or if you are applying for merit or academic scholarships, the academics are still important. This will help with your decision-making process as well. I have worked with students who are good academically, maybe not great, but very well-rounded and leaders in their school and community. This mindset not only helped them with admissions but gave them a few thousand dollars a year extra for merit or other talents and contributions. It allows you to shoot for the very best scenario in that situation or school and to find your niche when you are there. There is never a time when I have heard a student say, "Why did I get involved in all these activities? They didn't help me at all!" These experiences and activities will help create who you are, help mold you, and will help you continue that growth into college and beyond. So, continue doing what you are doing and add a thing or two to your résumé. This will give you a bigger scope for scholarship opportunities, even if you are not applying to a school with those requirements or expectations on the application regarding community service or leadership.

In a nutshell, be yourself, but be the BEST you, striving to be involved and doing your best academically, athletically, in extracurricular activities, in leadership and—

quite frankly—let your freak flag fly! Be YOU! Be DIFFERENT—be UNIQUE—if that is who you are. There is somewhere for everyone, somewhere that will appreciate you and who you are and your unique talents and attributes. Don't limit yourself or put yourself in a mold.

"You do you," and the world will find a way to open up to who you are.

4

The Recruiting Process: Sports, Sports, and Sports (or the "Big Ds")

RECRUITMENT FOR ATHLETICS OR talents brings an additional challenge to your college requirements and application process.

But there is a way to break it down to a science, and it takes the "Big Ds." I will explain everything later in the chapter, as well as give you a timeline to follow, but here are the "Big Ds" you will need to follow throughout your high school career.

Dedication

As a recruited athlete, coaches will want to see your dedication and commitment to your sport. If you are a basketball player, were you on a club team during the off-season? If you play soccer, what do you do off-season? They want to see you commit 125% to that sport. Think of it as a job and—if they are going to be paying you money—which ultimately they are since they will be paying for some or all of your education, they will want to know that they are hiring someone who will dedicate themselves to the team and make a contribution. They will want to know you are hardworking and will give them the same amount of effort that you are giving your team now. The only way they will know that is by what they see. This can be through your high school coaches' eyes, as well as what you do in the off-season.

Determination

There is a fine line between persistence and being a pest. Most of us know it, but college coaches want to see someone who truly wants to be at their school, play for them, and who starts the process early. Starting the recruiting process your senior year will get you to the back of the line, unless you are Michael Phelps or LeBron James, as these guys don't need to do anything, people will come to them. But most of us don't have that kind of talent. However, if a coach sees you are someone who has talent and is coachable, that can be enough. They want to see someone who wants it and is willing to push to get it. If you show determination and it is between you and another athlete, who do you think they will pick? They will pick the athlete that they have been in communication with and have a more established relationship with, which they will view as the one who wants it more.

Discipline

Most athletes are disciplined in their sport, but a college coach wants to see more than that. How are you in the classroom? Do you get into trouble at school? What is your GPA? I remember an athlete who went to a local high school, and he was a great football kicker. If I remember correctly, he was ranked top four in the country. There were schools like USC, UCLA, Ohio State, Michigan, and other top schools looking at him for their football team.

However, this athlete only focused on football throughout his high school career and did not pass all of his required high school courses. He had to take those classes during summer school to graduate. He ended up at a smaller college and never got to pursue his God-given football talent. Obviously he did not focus as much attention on his schoolwork as he did his football abilities, and he thought that his kicking skills were enough. If he had put the time and effort into his schoolwork, who knows where he would have ended up? Discipline in all areas of your life, but especially the classroom and especially right when your high school athletic career starts, is crucial. Day One: hit the ground running.

Devotion

Here is another one we have talked about in earlier chapters: being devoted means devotion to helping others and looking beyond yourself. Some people ask, "Why do I need to do anything outside the sport I am in and the classroom?"

First of all, it is incredibly fulfilling and a great opportunity to be an example in the community and to make a difference in people's lives (this is a repeat I know, but worth repeating!). It is also a wonderful way to start building some long-term principles and beliefs beyond high school. Being a great human being is far more important than being a great athlete and, on top of that, college coaches are looking for kids who will be great teammates. If you are applying for upper-tiered schools, this is especially helpful. It gives coaches and colleges one more way to rate you highly, and it gives you more dimension and depth. Every student I have worked with who was involved in their school or community has continued that practice during and after college. It is definitely a gateway to more opportunities and a way for you to see the big picture in life. Showing devotion translates to being a team player and caring about those around you. Again, the reason behind helping others is not to "look good for the coach," but this is how your actions will be translated by college coaches.

The bigger benefit in helping others is how you affect change and make a difference, especially as an athlete. You are a role model to your friends, school, and community. What example are you setting?

Drive

How bad do you want the school, and how bad do you want to play? These are always things to think about when deciding which college to attend. As an example, there are some students who have a 4.0 who may be above average at their sport. If you can get into a great school academically or an average school for sports, what choice do you make? Is playing that important to you or is your education and future more important? On the other hand, if you are a student who struggles in school and have a 2.5 GPA but is gifted at your sport, you definitely don't want to attend a school that is over your head academically. You want to have success and to thrive at school, both athletically AND academically. You also want to grow where you are planted and not struggle, but be fully challenged. There is a fine balance to this. There will be enough challenges at school, so start it off with being driven to do the best you can, while setting yourself up for success and being in the right place.

Detailed Plan

Last, but not least, you need to have a plan and follow it. Keep lists and make goals for yourself. If you do this late in the game, chances are it will limit your options. Be in a position to show that you are not only a great athlete but also someone who contributes to the community and high school. Be a great leader and role model and top of the list, be and plan to be, a great student. You also plan to stay out of trouble and plan to make good choices. This does not happen overnight, but if you follow the plan, your opportunities for success increase 100 times over.

So, where do you start? Let's look at the steps to a successful recruiting process, from sample letters to sample résumés to guidelines to determining if you are a right fit for the school.

PLAN OF ACTION

Freshman Year

Okay, technically you aren't starting the recruiting process your freshman year, but we don't jump ahead to the stage where things happen.

You have to build towards it, and your freshman year is where you start putting your talent to work. It is an inching process, and Rome wasn't built in a day! You have to make choices and set goals from the very beginning of your high school career. I mentioned my son Jordan in an earlier chapter regarding starting fresh in high school and focusing more on his grades. He had a plan, and even though he did not focus on his grades in middle school, he made the decision, set a plan of action, and followed it. You can reinvent yourself at any time, but if you do it from the beginning of high school, it allows for more opportunities and choices when the time comes. It is much harder if you make this commitment your junior year, as it limits options and opportunities for your cumulative GPA and activity involvement.

When it comes to sports, I can (of course) tell you to shoot for being on the varsity team in high school as soon as you can, but that will most likely not happen right away. You will need to put in time and effort and display your commitment and positive attitude to your high school coaches.

When opportunities do arise, be sure to step up. Help out. Set up. Be the first one there and the last one to leave. Practice, practice, practice. Have a positive attitude: Trust me, your high school coach may not get you recruited (that is not their job, it is yours and your parent's), but they can sure derail it with a bad report to a prospective college coach about a bad attitude or work ethic. Remember there are dozens, if not hundreds of kids, seeking that very spot you are aiming for on a roster or team at a college. There are limited spots available on those teams too. Make yourself stand out in all possible ways—and do it early. It is hard for people to shake that first impression, so be sure you start off with a great one.

Also, if not equally as important: in the classroom give it 100%, and go for the most challenging classes possible. I know there are some of you out there who don't see why that is important. You may be thinking that you don't want to go to an academically challenging college so why should it matter? I will tell you why!

An athlete who went to my son's school was absolutely incredible—I mean super-fast, athletic, and could have gone to a D1 school in two sports. However, he did not do well in school. He thought it didn't matter because he wanted to play football. He thought he could get into any college by just being great. He was injured early in his senior year of high school, and he ended up taking some classes at a local college but never played again.

Because of his bad grades, there were no other options. You never know what might happen over the course of your high school career: injuries, a change of heart—even bad coaching or a high school coach who doesn't support you. There are some things that are out of your control. But if you control the things you can, and focus on the things that truly, in the long run, are most important, then you are ahead of the game.

So, your freshman year will be the foundational year for building your plan. I have seen so many students struggle because of that freshman year, if they did poorly grade-wise. You can never overcome it completely, as fighting a low GPA becomes an uphill battle.

To show you how this works, for example, if you have a 3.0 your freshman year and a 4.0 the rest of the time, you still end up with a 3.75. Even though you have perfect grades for three years, you still have to combine that with your freshman year. However, if you do great and maintain or build from a higher GPA, you are off to a great start and will have more options. Trust me when I say that it goes by fast, and when you are in the recruiting process your junior and senior year, it can be really scary to only have a few options because of your grades. Keep the doors open wide, and decide which one you want to go through later. If you limit it with a low GPA from the get-go, the doors are fewer—and so are your options.

Here are the statistics, which can change each year but are a snapshot, divided by each sport and division. It shows how many high school students go on to play sports in college. I want you to be aware of how hard it is to get into college sports, so you know about the challenges. Also be aware that you can take action your freshman year to increase your chances. This includes academics, community service, leadership, etc.

For those who do not know, the National Collegiate Athletic Association (NCAA) is the governing agency for college sports. The participant statistics can change year to year, so if you are checking these statistics, be sure to look at the most updated one. This was for the "2018 Estimated Probability of Competing in College" [3]. Below is the information from the NCAA website, as they are the best ones to determine the likelihood of student-athletes competing in college.

MENS'S SPORTS

	High School Participants	College Sports Participants (those that went on to play	Overall % HS to College Sports	% HS to NCAA Division I	% HS to NCAA Division II	% HS to NCAA Division III
Baseball	491,790	34,980	7.1%	2.1%	2.2%	2.8%
Basketball	550,305	18,712	3.4%	1.0%	1.0%	1.4%
Cross Country	266,271	14,350	5.4%	1.8%	1.4%	2.2%
Football	1,057,382	73,063	6.9%	2.7%	1.8%	2.4%
Golf	141,466	8,527	6.0%	2.1%	1.7%	2.2%
*Ice Hockey	35,210	4,199	11.9%	4.8%	0.6%	6.5%
Lacrosse	111,842	13,899	12.4%	2.9%	2.3%	7.1%
Soccer	450,234	24,986	5.5%	1.3%	1.5%	2.7%
Swimming	138,364	9,691	7.0%	2.7%	1.1%	3.1%
Tennis	158,171	7,957	5.0%	1.6%	1.1%	2.3%
Track & Field	600,136	28,595	4.8%	1.8%	1.2%	1.7%
Volleyball	57,209	2,007	3.5%	0.7%	0.7%	2.0%
Water Polo	21,286	1,013	4.8%	2.7%	0.7%	1.3%
Wrestling	244,804	7,175	2.9%	1.0%	0.8%	1.1%

WOMEN'S SPORTS

	High School Participants	College Sports Participants (those that went on to play	Overall % HS to College Sports	% HS to NCAA Division I	% HS to NCAA Division II	% HS to NCAA Division III
Basketball	430,368	16,532	3.8%	1.2%	1.1%	1.5%
Cross Country	226,039	15,966	7.1%	2.6 %	1.8%	2.7%
Field Hocky	60,549	6,066	10.0%	3.0%	1.3%	5.7%
Golf	75,605	5,372	7.1%	2.9%	2.1%	2.2%
*Ice Hockey	9,599	2,355	24.5%	8.8%	1.2%	14.5%
Lacrosse	93,473	11,752	12.6%	3.7%	2.7%	6.2%
Soccer	388,339	27,638	7.1%	2.4%	1.9%	2.8%
Softball	367,405	19,999	5.4%	1.7%	1.6%	2.1%
Swimming	170,797	12,684	7.4%	3.3%	1.2%	2.9%
Tennis	187,519	8,736	4.7%	1.5%	1.1%	2.1%
Track & Field	494,477	29,907	6.0%	2.7%	1.5%	1.8%
Volleyball	444,779	17,387	3.9%	1.2%	1.1%	1.6%
Water Polo	20,826	1,159	5.6%	3.4%	0.9%	1.3%

A note about ice hockey and something to be aware of: Hockey coaches recommend prospective college recruits take a gap year or two to play on a club team or junior team after high school before actually playing on a college team. It is not a steadfast rule or requirement, but coaches typically require it (there are many leagues and levels). They want potential athletes to play on these junior teams to watch how they develop. The NCAA eligibility rules in hockey are unlike those in any other sport. The NCAA does not start taking away years of eligibility until after your twenty-first birthday, allowing you plenty of time to play on a junior team without negatively affecting your eligibility and hockey scholarship chances.

Also consider, even if you ARE recruited for a sport, every division offers different dollar amounts and emphases that can be expected (based on the division).

Here is more information the NCAA released regarding statistics and explanations about the divisions.

Division I

Division I schools typically have more students, larger athletics budgets, and more athletics department support than schools in Division II or III.

Division II

Schools in Division II emphasize more balance, so academically and athletically talented students can compete at a high level, while still having a more traditional college experience.

Division III

Academics are the primary focus for Division III student-athletes, who experience shorter sports seasons, reducing time away from their academics and other school activities.

If you go onto the NCAA website, you can see all the requirements that are expected for all these divisions. There are minimum requirements for academics, as well as amounts of credits you must have for each subject. At this time, these are the requirements the NCAA has set.

Academic Standards [4]

Division I Eligibility

- All students entering college must have completed sixteen core courses in high school.

- Students must earn a minimum required GPA in core courses and a combined SAT or ACT sum score that matches this GPA on a sliding scale, which can be found in the NCAA Eligibility Center Quick Reference Guide (see below).

Division II Eligibility

- All students entering college must have completed sixteen core courses in high school
- Standards require a minimum GPA of 2.0 and a combined minimum SAT score of 820 or sum ACT score of 68

NCAA Core Courses Definition [5]

- An academic course in one or a combination of these areas: English, mathematics, natural/physical science, social science, foreign language, comparative religion, or philosophy.
- A four-year college preparatory course and a course at or above the high school's regular academic level, for example, an AP class or outside college course.

To be eligible to practice, compete, and receive athletics scholarships in your first full-time year at a Division I school, you must graduate from high school and meet ALL the following requirements:

Complete a total of sixteen NCAA core courses in the following areas:

- Four years of English
- Three years of math (Algebra I or higher)
- Two years of natural/physical science (including one year of lab science, if offered)
- Two years of social science
- One additional year of English, math, or natural/physical science
- Four additional years of English, math, natural/physical science, social science, foreign language, comparative religion, or philosophy

To be eligible to practice, compete, and receive athletics scholarships in your first full-time year at a Division II school, you must graduate from high school and meet ALL of the following requirements:

Complete a total of sixteen NCAA core courses in the following areas:

- Three years of English
- Two years of math (Algebra I or higher)
- Two years of natural/physical science (including one year of lab science, if offered)
- Two years of social science
- Three additional years of English, math or natural/physical science
- Four additional years of English, math, natural/physical science, social science, foreign language, comparative religion, or philosophy

NCAA Divisions I and II schools offer over $2.7 billion in athletic scholarships a year to over 150,000 student-athletes. However, Division III schools do not provide athletic scholarships. They sometimes offer academic scholarships as a supplement for qualifying student-athletes. But students should not expect to receive an athletic scholarship from them.

Division I schools may provide tuition and fees, room and board, books, and other expenses related to attendance at the school. Division II full scholarships cover tuition and fees, room, board, and course-related books and supplies. Most students who receive athletics scholarships get an amount covering a portion of these costs. Division I schools may provide you with multiyear scholarships, but they are not always guaranteed. If a school plans to reduce or not renew your aid, the school must notify you in writing by July 1 and provide an opportunity for you to appeal. In most cases, the head coach decides who receives a scholarship, the scholarship amount, and whether or not it will be renewed.

Also, Division I schools may pay for you to finish your bachelor's or master's degrees after you finish playing NCAA sports. NCAA rules require you to be registered with the NCAA Eligibility Center (we will talk more about that in the junior year section) in order to be recruited, to go on an official visit, to receive an offer of financial aid, or to sign a National Letter of Intent, but it is not required for you to receive an academic evaluation before any of these.

This should give you a bit of an overview on the divisions, expectations for each one, and some criteria to meet before you can participate in athletics at the college level. Be sure to check out the NCAA website for more in-depth information, as well as the place to apply for your clearinghouse number later in your high school career.

I find it very interesting that only around 2% of all high school athletes receive scholarships (athletic) to compete in sports in college. Of those 2%, only 2% of those athletes go on to play professionally. This is another reason to focus on WHY you are going to college. It is for an education, for your future employment, and lastly, for the wonderful experiences you will have there, which includes playing your sport. But playing the sport is not your main reason for being there. Having a skill or talent that can help you pay for your education is a true blessing.

Now, we will move onto Résumé Building, which you will start building your freshman year (as discussed in the Résumé Building Chapter). It is important to keep this up to date, especially for athletes, as it is a work in progress. Each year and opportunity you have, you will just keep adding to it. It is so much better to start at the beginning and add to it than to reflect back on it your junior or senior year (when you will need it). It will keep your activities fresh in your mind, and you can remember all the details, as well as the emotion and excitement of it being translated onto the résumé. It also is beneficial if a coach, teacher, or even a potential employer asks for it. You can provide it for them on the spot!

Résumé Building for the Recruiting Process

The following résumé is from an actual student who played football and ran track in college. I changed his name and other information to protect his privacy (such as high school, state, address, employment, etc.). Remember, even though this is a D1 Athletes résumé, not all who look to be recruited will be considered D1 athletes. I am including this résumé for ideas on things you can be involved in, as well as for structure and information that will be pertinent to a coach or school looking to recruit you. Don't lose heart if you feel you cannot achieve these things or there are way too many things on the résumés. You may be really great at your sport, but other areas might not be so high. Your goal is to try to attain and translate "balance" to coaches. They are always looking for well-rounded student-athletes.

It is always good to look for ways to improve your résumé, so it is good to study examples. There are times students may feel something they have done athletically, academically, or in other areas does not belong on a résumé. However, after seeing other résumés, they recognize it is pertinent. It can help others by giving them a snapshot of who you are. There are a few more résumés available in the Résumé Building Chapter, but here is one specific to an athlete who played a D1 sport:

Tyson Johnson
555-555-5555
1234 W. Main Street
Miami, Florida 66666

Academic Achievements:

- Southern Florida Conference All Academic Football, Basketball and Track 2009, 2010, and 2011
- National Honor Society Member 2010–2011 and 2011–2012
- Penn High School Academic Excellence Award 2009/2010
- Distinguished Student Award January 2012, Presented by the State Dairymen
- SAMMY National Award Winner 2012–Student-Athlete Milk Mustache of the Year Award by USA News and "Got Milk?"
- National Football Foundation Student and College Hall of Fame, Scholar Athlete Award, Florida Chapter-Nominated for the National Scholar Athlete Award October 2012-Finalist, Winner TBD October 2012
- Penn High School Student/ Athlete of the Year Award and Penn High School "Wall of Fame" Recipient 2012
- Graduated in top 2% of my Class at Penn High School, Miami, Florida, May 2012 with a 4.22 Cumulative GPA

Extracurricular Activities/Volunteer:

- Florida State Food Bank Volunteer 2009–2011
- Westbrook Christmas Cares Volunteer 2009–2010
- Start Strong Student Advisor: A Division of Coalition Against Domestic Violence 2009–2012
- Junior Red Cross Volunteer 2011
- Member of Men Today/Men Tomorrow 2009–2011

Leadership:

- Team Captain Basketball 2011-2012, Co-Captain 2010–2011
- Team Captain Track 2011 and 2012
- Team Captain Football 2012
- Student Ambassador of My Life 24/7 2009–2010

Athletic Achievements:

- Eight Varsity Letters in Track, Football and Basketball
- SFC All Conference Football Defensive Back 2010 Season, SFC All Conference Football Wide Receiver 2011 Season, SFC All Conference Basketball 2nd Team 2011/2012 Season
- State Champion Track 4 x 200 relay 2010

- Team State Track Champion 2011 and 2012
- Award-Track Team "Most Motivational" 2011
- Defensive Player of the Year/Penn High School/Basketball 2010 , 2011, and 2012 Seasons
- Selected for the All Star Team for Basketball and Football 2011 and 2012
- Florida All Star Club Team-Basketball, 2007–2012

Employment/Internships:
- Miami, Inc., Miami, Florida; May 2013–August 2013, Internal Audit Intern
- Westbrook Travel Services: Marketing and Phone Soliciting, Fort Lauderdale, Florida July 2010 - August 2012, Marketer

As you can see from this résumé, this person was involved in a lot of things and activities but still had a great GPA! They also still found time to go to Homecoming dances, prom, and other high school activities. It takes determination and focus, but it can be done.

Sample Letters to Coaches

Letters for coaches will slowly evolve. This is a sample introduction letter I recommend sending at the end of your freshman year. You can tweak it or add whatever statistics you want, as well as any highlights of your accomplishments outside of sports (keep thinking well-rounded). This letter gives the college coach a picture of who you are and, from here, you will continue to build and communicate as you progress in your high school career.

A quick comment on email addresses:

Change it if it is inappropriate. If you are unsure if it is, ask your parents.

Having an email address such as onehotchick@myemail.com or numberones-tud@myemail.com is the wrong first impression you want to relay to a coach. It sets a poor example from the beginning, so change it to something more appropriate.

INTRODUCTION EMAIL

Coach Smith,

I want to introduce myself to you. My name is John Jones, and I am currently a sophomore in Timbuctoo, Wyoming at Centennial High School. I am very interested in attending Merlin State. I have heard of your amazing program, and I would love to be part of it. I have filled out the questionnaire online, so you will have specific times and events that I have participated in.

I have been swimming competitively for the last ten years and have continued to improve each year. I received top All Conference Honors this last high school season and recently returned from the YMCA Nationals, where I made finals in two events, winning fourteenth and eighteenth in both of them. I have a 3.4 GPA and also am very involved with Student Council as the student body treasurer. I have started coaching swimming for the Special Olympics this year, and I am currently captain of my high school swim team. I am extremely competitive and work very hard to improve each meet, giving 100% every time I am in the pool.

I feel I would be a great fit for your team and hope that I get that opportunity. Thank you very much for your time, and I hope to hear from you in the near future.

John Jones

jjones@allemail.com

555-555-5555

For most sports, college coaches can begin reaching out to athletes starting September first or June fifteenth going into the athlete's junior year of high school, but not before then. It is important to continue to reach out and put your name on the coach's radar way before that though. When the recruiting process begins each year, coaching staff assemble a "wish list" of student-athletes they are interested in recruiting. The names on this list represents athletes they have heard from and seen at camps, games, etc. They could also be from high school or club coaches. It includes athletes who put in the work and got themselves on the map by reaching out to coaches. I highly recommend filling out questionnaires for each school that interests you before contacting the coaches. Do both around the same time: It shows you are highly interested, and it keeps you on their mailing list for camps or other events they may offer. You will most likely start receiving information from the schools, as well, after you submit the questionnaire.

There are also some important general guidelines on rules on various aspects of recruiting. Be sure to look on the NCAA website for specific sports, as each one is a bit different.

Official Visits

An official visit is any visit to a college or university campus by you and your parents that is paid for by the college. Each official visit may be up to forty-eight hours long or over a weekend. They will pay for your transportation, meals, some entertainment, and lodging. You are able to take up to five official visits during the recruitment process for Division I and Division II schools and only one visit to that school. For example, if you are being recruited for track and field at a school and make an official visit, you cannot go back to that school for an official visit if you are also being recruited for baseball.

Unofficial Visits

College athletic departments, including college coaches, are not allowed to be involved in unofficial visits. Unofficial visits are paid for entirely by the recruit's family. Before the rule changes, unofficial visits were an easy way for underclassmen to visit a college campus, meet with the coach, and get an early verbal offer. However, if athletes want to take unofficial visits now, they cannot schedule them with the coach; they should treat the unofficial visit just like any other student would. If the recruit happens to bump into the coach on campus, they can't have any recruiting conversations at that time.

There is a lot of information out there and a lot to remember—but also four years to build a relationship with the coach or school. It starts your freshman year! You can contact them as often as YOU want to, but communication from them cannot begin until later in your high school career.

Sophomore Year

By this year, you should be starting a stronger communication with college coaches and continuing to hone your athletic skills. Start researching schools. Just like you should academically, athletically look for schools that recruit people like you. For example, if you are a runner in track, look at the average of times and distance for the schools that interest you. They post the best times for the year on their websites, so you can see what you need to achieve to be competitive and interest them. It is very easy to find on the website. Look on the "Athletics" link for each school and narrow your search to the sport you are interested in. This will be an excellent comparative tool to see if you truly could compete at the level of a particular school.

Each sport has different rules set up by the NCAA, but here is a brief overview of those rules, defined by the NCAA*. The graphs and information on the graphs provided were gathered from the NCAA website:

Sophomore Year

Recruiting form of Communication	Division I Men's Basketball	Division I Women's Basketball	Division I Football	Division I Ice Hockey	Division 1 Other Sports	Division II	Division III
Recruiting Material (pamphlets, camps, etc.)	Brochures for camps and questionnaires, NCAA and nonathletic recruiting publications are allowed			All forms of private correspondence beginning January 1st of sophomore year	Brochures for camps and questionnaires, NCAA and nonathletic publications are allowed for most sports	June 15th before junior year	Permissible
	June 15th after your sophomore year, you can receive recruiting material						
Telephone Calls	You can make as many calls as you want at your expense. A coach is allowed to call you starting June 15th before junior year. If college is on a nontraditional calendar, they can begin after the conclusion of sophomore year	You can make as many calls as you want at your expense. A coach cannot contact you	You can make as many calls as you want at your expense. A coach cannot contact you	You can make as many calls as you want at your expense. A coach is allowed to call you starting January 1st of sophomore year	You can make as many calls as you want at your expense. **Women's Ice Hockey:** A college coach may call international college bound athletes once on, or after July 7th-July thirty-first following her sophomore year	June 15th before junior year. No limit on the calls you can receive after the June 15th date	*Permissible
Off campus contact/Official Visit	None allowed	None allowed	None allowed	None allowed	None allowed	Allowed June 15th immediately before junior year	None allowed
Unofficial Visit	You can make unlimited amount of unofficial visits except during dead periods**	You can make unlimited amount of unofficial visits except during dead periods**	You can make unlimited amount of unofficial visits except during dead periods**	You can make unlimited amount of unofficial visits except during dead periods**	You can make unlimited amount of unofficial visits except during dead periods**	You can make unlimited amount of unofficial visits except during dead periods**	You can make unlimited amount of unofficial visits except during dead periods**

*This chart is from the NCAA website and available in its entirety from there. [6]

**Dead periods are the period where coaches may not have any in-person contact with recruits and/or their parents. In other words, coaches are not allowed to talk to recruits at their college campus, the athlete's school, or anywhere. You can still communicate by phone and email but no "in person" contact.

Schools can start contacting you your junior year. Just because they cannot call you or email you directly during your sophomore year, doesn't mean that you cannot call them! If they answer the phone, you can talk to them, but they cannot reach out to you. Sophomore year is a great time to start calling and setting up a foundational relationship. The coach will remember the athlete who took the time to call them, as most athletes do not take the time or are a bit nervous about doing it.

My son Alex was incredible at this. He would make a list of all the coaches and collect their email and phone numbers. He would spend an afternoon once a month and after some events sharing his wins (improving his time, winning a meet, etc.). He developed some great relationships with these coaches—so much so that he received sixteen official visit offers when it came time for it! I know it was because he put in the time calling these coaches, developing these relationships, and keeping in touch with all of them. Not only did he receive sixteen visit offers, they called him on the first day they were allowed to contact him. It was a great validation of his system and of all the work he put into it. Alex did end up at Michigan State and received a great scholarship to swim there.

Finding the best phone number can take a little investigation on your part, but the first step is to go onto the athletic website of the specific school. From there, you will find your sport and information about the coach. Sometimes, depending on the sport, you will have the coaches contact information on their biography. Other times, you will need to look for it on the staff directory, which will be located under another category on the website. You will have to search around a bit, but once you have it, you can keep it for future calls.

A Note for Football Recruits and Other Sports with Specific Position Coaches

Do not call the head coach when calling a DI program for football or other sports that have position coaches. Call your position coach and/or offensive/defensive coach (for football). The head coach likely won't have the time to talk unless it is a DII or

DIII School or a smaller DI school. There is nothing wrong with trying to call a few coaches at the same school. See who you get a hold of and who you connect with.

When Calling a Coach Follow These Guidelines

- **Start the conversation by asking first if it is a good time to talk.**
  If it is not, ask them when the best time is for you to call them back.

- **If it is the first time calling them, be sure to introduce yourself.**
  Let them know you appreciate them taking the time to talk to you. If you struggle with the thought of doing this, practice in front of a mirror, with a friend, in the car, or with your family/parents. Practice makes perfect!

- **Have questions about the school written down in front of you, so you are prepared.**
  Do this for every school you are calling!

- **Have your résumé in front of you to refer to when giving specifics about yourself.**
  Sometimes you may be nervous when talking to the coaches, and this will help you remember to highlight your achievements.

- **Have some specific information and facts about their school, team, and the coach's biography (available on the athletic websites for the school).**
  This can help with opening icebreakers for the first conversation. Such as, "I read that you attended the University of Oregon. My mom went there too! What made you pick that school?" This is a wonderful way to start a more personal connection with the coach, and it gets them talking about themselves. This is a good tip for future employment interviews as well, not just coaches.

- **The coach will, at some point, ask you if you have any questions for them.**
  Always have something! The best questions you can ask a coach are:
  - o What are you looking for in an athlete?
  - o What can I do to improve my chances of making it on your team/roster? And/or what areas would you like me to work on to help improve my chances of playing for you? (Adjust this verbiage, depending on your sport.)
  - o May I call you in a few weeks to keep you posted on my progress?

- **When closing off the conversation, thank them for their time.**
  Let them know you will continue keeping them posted on your progress and that you look forward to keeping in touch through calls and email.

- **Do not worry if you have not gotten a hold of the coach.**
  You will at some point, so keep up the phone and email contact. Remember, until you are in your junior year (for most sports), a coach cannot call you back. Do not take it as a sign that they are not interested in you at this point, just keep laying the foundation and stay in contact on your end. Even if it is just leaving a message, let them know who you are and that you are interested in their school:

When Leaving a Message

- **When leaving a message for a first call:**
  "Good evening, Coach _____. This is_____. I wanted to touch base with you and introduce myself. I will try you back in a few weeks. I emailed you recently and filled out a questionnaire, and I will keep you posted on my progress this season. Good luck against Minnesota this weekend, and I look forward to connecting soon."

- **When leaving a message after you have already introduced yourself:**
  "Hey, Coach_____. This is _____. I wanted to congratulate you on your win against Clemson this weekend. It was a great game! I watched it (or read about it) and was excited to see your win. I had a great game this week as well—a big win. I will email you the specifics but wanted to congratulate you and touch base. Take care, and I will try you again next month."

- **Follow up with an email after the phone call.**
  Let them know about any positive progress in or change to your athletic career, which can include better times, a big win, an achievement or accomplishment in your sport, receiving an honor in your sport, a change of position or event (as well as something positive that went along with it: why did you make the change?), and anything else that is relevant.

- **Never be negative about your high school or club coach, sport, school, teammates, or yourself.**
  Keep it positive and upbeat. If the college coach ever asks you anything about these things, be positive! Remember, they are seeing if you are a good fit for

their team and if you will be someone who will bring not only talent but also good and positive energy that will inspire others. They also want to make sure you are coachable and not someone who will undermine them.

- **Keep it short and sweet when leaving a message, but give a little bit of information.**
  Include something specific to them or their school, as well as a nice bit of information about you.

- **Make sure to let them know who you are when you are calling:**
  Never assume they know.

- **Do not leave your number because they cannot call you back (unless you are further along in the recruiting process).**

Continue calling college coaches. Use a spreadsheet to keep track of who you talk to, when you call, the school where they coach, the coach's name, etc. Add to the note section, so you can keep track of what you discussed or what they are looking for. This is great for follow up for when you talk to them next time.

School	Coach Name	Phone Number	Date/Left Message (LM) or Spoke to Them	Date/Left Message (LM) or Spoke to Them	Date/Left Message (LM) or Spoke to Them	Notes
University of Chicago	Coach Nicholas Stevens	555-555-1111	09/01/17 LM	10/18/17 spoke to coach	01/08/18 LM	Best time to call is after 7p.m./ Likes my defensive skills; looking for that in a player
Whitman	Coach Mark Adams	555-252-2222	09/06/17 spoke to coach	10/16/17 LM	01/09/18 LM	He said to call him after 1/5/18
Stoneybrook	Coach Samantha Bitters	555-222-2222 office 555-999-666 cell	09/05/17 LM	10/20/17 LM	01/10/18 LM	
University of Michigan	Coach Charles Bennett	555-222-6664	09/07/17 LM	10/14/17 LM	01/12/18 spoke to coach	Rival is Ohio State and wife coaches volleyball at Michigan
University of Hawaii	Coach Shannon Smith	555-241-3333	09/09/17 LM	10/19/17 LM	01/20/18 spoke to coach	Will be at basketball tournament in Nevada
University of Minnesota	Coach Timothy Shannon	555-333-6666	09/01/17 spoke to coach	10/22/17 spoke to coach	01/07/18 LM	Can call on weekend
Pepperdine	Coach Leonard Hawks	555-888-3654	09/05/17 LM	10/25/17 spoke to coach	01/06/18 LM	Told me to work on my outside shot

As you continue emailing coaches, you will slowly add in more personal things, not only about yourself but also about their school or specific games and events. For example, "I saw that you had a great win against Wisconsin this weekend. That is great! It looks like it was a close game, but (insert player name of position you are interested in) had a great game. I had a great game this weekend too, with fifteen tackles and two interceptions. Our team beat our rival Century High School with a score of 21-14." This will make it more personal and will allow for there to be more of a personal connection. The coach will also feel you are truly interested in their school and that you are watching and reading up on their team. People love it when you make those connections with and personal observations about them; coaches are no different. It will take time on your part, but it is well worth it.

Here is a sample email for your sophomore year email. Remember, you should have introduced yourself already, so this is a continuation of the email relationship from freshman year.

Coach Thompson,

Good morning, Coach! I was so excited this weekend to see that your team won not only your meet against Mississippi but some of your runners posted their best times. That is really great! I read that Janine Adams did a personal best in the 100 as well. That is really a great accomplishment; she has had a very impressive year.

I came from a great meet myself this weekend, having a personal best in the 200 at 24.13. I took off .17 from my last meet. I am running really well and am excited for our state championship in two weeks.

I also had some great things happen for me at school, as I was just voted in for class secretary in Student Council. I will send you my updated résumé at the end of the school year so you can see some of the other things that I am involved with and some highlights from the year.

The best of luck against Texas this weekend! I will be watching to see how it turns out, but I am sure your team will do great. I look forward to being in touch and will keep you posted on my progress this season.

Sincerely,

Betty Smith

Betty Smith
bsmith@allemail.com
555-555-5555

As you can see, this is a much more personal letter. It shows you are communicating not only about what you are doing in your own world, but you're also aware of what athletes are doings on their team currently—and it shows your interest. It allows them to see you as part of their program, and they can see you would be a great team player.

Make sure you are doing this monthly or when something impressive happens in your sport. This could include improved times, winning a meet or game, an award, an invite to a larger game or event, etc. If you have an accomplishment off the court, field, or other venue, keep that bit of information to include in your email to them when it involves some other information you want to relay. In other words, you would not want to email them every time something happens at school, even if it is great. They do want to see you are well-rounded, but they still want the athletic portion to be the focus. Always include your résumé at the close of each school year so they can track your progress. It keeps you fresh in their mind, and it reminds them of what you've shared so far.

Junior Year

At this time, get a NCAA Clearinghouse number through the website below. This is the perfect year to take this step. The NCAA Clearinghouse is an organization outside of the NCAA that performs academic record evaluations to determine if a prospective student-athlete is eligible to participate at an NCAA Division I or II college as a freshman student-athlete. This is a requirement for you when, and if, you play college sports. You will need to pay a small fee for this: fifty dollars for US citizens and seventy-five dollars for international students.

Here is the registration link [7]:

www.ncaaclearinghouse.net

Your junior year, you will finally be able to receive contact from the coaches, if they are interested. Coaches are looking for something specific, especially if they have a small roster. You may not have the speed or talent that they feel will fit their team. If you are not hearing from a coach by the time they are able to contact you, you may start focusing on other schools that are showing interest. Begin by narrowing down your search this year to schools that are communicating with you, where you have the skills to be competitive, and that you most want to attend. Each year, when the school year starts, I would check out the best times or skill set of the athletes on the rosters at the schools, as I mentioned in the sophomore year section. However, now is the time to judge if you are progressing enough to compete at the schools and to see who they have recruited for the coming year. For example, if you are a wrestler and compete in the 152 weight bracket and they have just recruited three athletes in that same weight class, it is unlikely they will recruit you, even if you're highly skilled.

Filming

Another recruiting tool for this year is the creation of a highlight video you can send to coaches, showcasing your best moments in your sport. Put the video on YouTube and send coaches the link. I put this together for my sons to send to schools. We started this their sophomore year, but definitely start it this year if you have not. You can get video from your coaches and/or, as a parent, you can video tape the games or competitions for your child. One year, we had a family friend videotape the games, and I did the editing afterwards. I recommend purchasing editing software or asking the coaches at the high school if they will allow you to use theirs. You may also have access through the media department at your high school.

Tips for Video Filming and Editing

- Be sure you are easily seen on the video: Have an arrow pointing to you in the film or the focus clearly on you. Some people freeze the film for a second to use the arrow. Make sure the video shows the game or competition around you as well. It should not be so "on" you that viewers have no idea what you are doing within the game or competition.

- Make sure the video quality is clear enough to easily watch. Use a tripod to avoid shaking.

- Make the film short and sweet. It should not be more than five minutes. The coaches view lots of films.

- The film should show the best plays or skills at the beginning. You can never be sure how much of the film coaches watch, and you want them to see your best stuff!

- You do not need sound, but you can use music, although it is not necessary or required. If so, make sure the music you choose is appropriate (no bad language). We used music because we thought it was fun.

- When emailing coaches, include the link (if using YouTube) or other information for them to access it. If sending a DVD, be sure to include it. I recommend YouTube links over DVDs.

- If you purchase your own software, I recommend Pinnacle Studio. I found it very easy to use and not too expensive. (It was around seventy or eighty dollars.)

Academic Expectations

It is also wise to look at the academic expectations of the schools you hope to attend and ensure you are aligned with their academic requirements as well as their athletic expectations. For example, I remember a few years ago, there was a very good baseball player at our local high school. He was sharing with everyone that he was being recruited by Brown (an Ivy League School). I was chatting with his parents shortly after that, and I told them that was a great accomplishment and that he must be doing really well in the classroom. They shared with me that he was a 3.0 student and received a 22 on his ACT: grades and scores that are not bad, but they are not what an Ivy League School requires for admission. The Ivy League will make some concessions for crazily good athletes, but they can only do this for a very small amount of individuals. It will depend on the sport they are able to compete in as well. I will elaborate on this, as it pertains to Ivy Leagues, later in this chapter. Determine the expectations of these schools while, and especially before, making your decision. After our conversation, and me sharing the expectations of Ivy League schools, now and during college, his parents were more aware of that aspect of admissions and expectations of the school. They then pulled Brown off of the list for potential recruiting options as it was too much of a stretch for their son.

It is also important for me to reinforce that, as an athlete, you will be focusing much of your time on your sport. As I have mentioned before, in a way it is a job where you are getting paid (hopefully) by the school where you are competing. They are hopefully paying for your education with a scholarship (again, hopefully).

You want to be sure you attend a school that challenges you, but you don't want the expectations to be so high that it is challenging to stay above water and do it all. Be mindful of the school and academic program that each school offers while narrowing down your search. It is more important to look for the educational aspect AND the athletic aspect of it. But if it is paying for your education, you will definitely have to commit to it and put much of your time towards athletics. These are all factors you will need to think about when selecting potential colleges.

You will have more contact with the coaches your junior year and should have initiated several conversations and emails. Here are the guidelines for your junior year [6]:

JUNIOR YEAR							
Recruiting Form of Communication	Division I Men's Basketball	Division I Women's Basketball	Division I Football	Division II Ice Hockey	Division I Other Sports	Division II	Division III
Electronic Correspondence	You may begin receiving emails June 15th after your sophomore year.	You may begin receiving emails Sept. 1st of your junior year.	You may begin receiving emails Sept. 1st of your junior year.	All forms of private correspondence beginning Jan. 1st of sophomore year.	You may begin receiving emails Sept. 1st of your junior year.	June 15th before junior year.	Permissible
Recruiting Material (pamphlets, camps, etc.)	Allowed-you receive these on June 15th or after of your sophomore year.	You may begin receiving them Sept. 1st of your junior year.	You may begin receiving them Sept. 1st of your junior year.	You may begin receiving them Jan. 1st of your sophomore year.	You may begin receiving them Sept. 1st of your junior year.		
Telephone Calls	You can make as many calls as you want at your expense. A coach is allowed to call you starting June 15th before junior year and it is unlimited calls.	You can make as many calls as you want at your expense. A coach is allowed to call you starting Sept. 1st of junior year and it is unlimited calls.	You can make as many calls as you want at your expense. One call allowed between April 15th and May 31 of junior year.	You can make as many calls as you want at your expense.	You can make as many calls as you want at your expense. Sports other than cross country, track and field, swimming, diving. A coach is allowed to make calls beginning Sept. 1st of junior year. Cross country, track and field swimming, diving one call per week from coaches allowed beginning July 1st following completion of junior year. Women's Ice Hockey-calls are allowed beginning July 7th after junior year.		

JUNIOR YEAR							
Recruiting Form of Communication	Division I Men's Basketball	Division I Women's Basketball	Division I Football	Division I I Ice Hockey	Division I Other Sports	Division II	Division III
Off campus contact/ Official Visit	Off campus contact- Allowed beginning opening day of classes other than April, may only occur at high school. Contact in April can occur at your school or residence. They cannot occur during the time of day that classes are in session. Official visits allowed Jan. 1st of junior year.	Off Campus contact- Sep. 1st of the junior year only at their residence or high school and no contact on the day of of competition. Official visits no earlier than the Thursday following completion the NCAA Division I Basketball Championship game in the student's junior year. These can begin on April 1st of your junior year after the Women's Final Four.	None Allowed		Allowed starting July 1st after your junior year. Women's Gymnastics- Allowed beginning July 15th after junior year. Women's Ice Hockey- Allowed beginning July 7th after junior year.		Allowed following completion of junior year.
Unofficial Visit	You can make unlimited amount of unofficial visits except during dead periods.	You can make unlimited amount of unofficial visits except during dead periods.	You can make unlimited amount of unofficial visits except during dead periods.		You can make unlimited amount of unofficial visits except during dead periods.		

Senior Year

This can be a tough year—or an extremely exciting year.

If you haven't heard back from anyone or haven't had strong interest from the schools you prefer (or any schools for that matter), chances are it isn't going to happen. By now, you would be hearing back from those schools. That doesn't mean things don't change. You could get a walk-on (or even a preferred walk-on). But, by the beginning of your senior year, you should have a good gauge of where you will attend, depending on the sport.

If you are hearing back from schools, especially the schools you want, this can be an extremely exciting time! National signing is the first Wednesday in February for football, and other sports have varying timeframes and dates (National signing is explained later in this chapter). For basketball, the official signing day is in early November. Soccer and men's polo are at the same time as football, and all other sports are in November.

For most sports, you will have heard from schools by July and hopefully offered an official visit, which you will take in the fall. Of course, every athlete looking to play sports in college dreams that their phone will be ringing off the hook come July first before their senior year. This can happen, and it is important to keep a spreadsheet available for this possibility. It may not happen that way, but you will want to be prepared if it does.

I created a spreadsheet you can maintain. We used a ranking system. You would list all of the schools you are in contact with, as well as where they rank (according to your interest). Since you are only allowed to go on five official visits, you will want to select them wisely and rank the schools according to your top choices. This can help if you have two schools that offer a visit on the same weekend. If one is your top choice and the other is your last, you would obviously choose your top choice. You will want to rank the schools you have been in contact in before July first so you are prepared to make decisions (if needed), when they call.

This is where reality sets in, and you know who is truly interested in you as an athlete. You will also have to let them know where they, as a school, stand as well.

I also recommend taking only four out of the five (if you are offered that many) official visits. You will have so much going on your senior year that five visits can be too much, especially when you are still playing or competing in high school and have to maintain your focus on your schoolwork. This is just a suggestion, as some students may need all five visits to make a decision, but you will be feeling it after four of them, trust me! They are so quick (less than forty-eight hours). If you are falling behind in classes and missing games or events at school, be wise when choosing your visits and know you can cancel them.

I also recommend trying to have your top choice at the beginning of your visit schedule for this reason, as they give a limited amount of offers. If it is your first choice, you will want them to offer to you first! If they are a sport or school with limited funds or scholarships, it could literally be too late by the time it gets to you. (I have seen this happen.)

If your first choice makes an offer right out of the gate, which many will do the weekend you go there or immediately after (if you are a good fit for the team), and it is an offer you are happy with, you can forgo the rest of the visits. If it is a close call though, you can ask them for a date when they will need a decision, allowing you to visit your number two school. But do not keep them waiting too long! They have others they will take if you do not accept (or are slow to accept).

Here is a sample spreadsheet, according to the types of calls you would receive. I also put in an example where the student was expecting a response but did not hear from the school. I would follow up with each coach when they call you, with an email either accepting the visit or explaining why you are not able to visit. Either way, be sure to thank them for the offer. Let them know you are attending as soon as possible or that you are not able to attend (and the reason).

Be honest, but be polite. This is a courtesy to them, as there are other student-athletes who will receive calls if you are not interested. When talking with coaches, if you are unsure what you will decide as well as who else will offer you a visit, remember to ask for the date when you need to make your decision. Whether it is a phone call (preferred) or an email, let them know that you appreciate them offering you the visit, and let them know what you have decided. This is where you truly are narrowing it down, to five schools you are interested. You can possibly add a few in there as back-ups, in case there are date and time conflicts.

I also recommend having a calendar available to reference, so you can easily let them know if you have a conflict. You can also quickly record the dates when they are offering you a visit. My sons would fill them in as soon as they heard back from schools. They ranked them beforehand, so when they heard from them, they could pencil in the dates. Most schools will give you a few weekends to pick from.

School	Coach Name	Date called	Official Visit Offered	Notes	Ranking
University of Indiana	Coach Jones	07/01	Yes		1
University of Texas	Coach Thomas	07/01	Yes		3
University of Minnesota	Coach Simpson	07/02	Yes		5
Columbia	Coach Morgan	07/01	Yes		2
University of Idaho	Coach Paul	07/03	No	They wanted me to come out to visit on my own- no official visit offered	8
Tulane University	Coach Talbot	07/02	Yes		4
Pepperdine University		n/a	No	Follow up with coach- emailed on 07/05	7
Florida State	Coach Jones	07/04	Yes		6

Next is a sample prioritization official visit calendar (you will not need weekdays, as visits will only be offered over the weekend). You will want both this and the official visit spreadsheet, so you can capture all the information. But they serve different purposes.

On the sample calendar, I show one weekend blocked out because of a commitment at school. This may happen, so be prepared and plan before selecting your weekends. Talk with your high school coaches to let them know if you are missing a game or event that they expect you to attend after you have committed to an official visit. I have to tell you though, official visits are crucial to the recruiting process, and they should be your priority at this time in your high school career. I know your high school coach may depend on you, but they should also want what is best for you. If you are struggling with your coach on this, have your parents step in to help.

Looking at this calendar, you will quickly be able to see the dates they are offering you a visit, look at your ranking of that school, and determine if you are able to visit all of the schools you want to. In this example, none of the dates conflict with each other, but if University of Minnesota conflicted with University of Texas's visit, you would select University of Texas because you ranked it higher on your list. You would let University of Minnesota know that you were unable to make the visit. Sometimes, if they are still very interested, they will offer another option or date. You can then determine if you want to attend.

School	Sept 7th	Sept 14th	Sept 21st GAME	Sept 28th	Oct 5th	Oct 12th	Oct 19th	RANK
University of Indiana	x		x		x			1
University of Texas		x	x		x			3
University of Minnesota			x		x		x	5
Columbia	x			x			x	2
University of Idaho			x	x		x		8
Tulane University	x	x			x			4
Pepperdine University		x		x			x	7
Florida State	x		x			x		6

For example, if you accept an offer from a specific school on your second visit, cancel the rest of your visits. **I do not mean that you like this school the best and want to attend.** It means they want you, have made an offer, and you have verbally accepted the offer and are happy with it. Do not cancel anything before this has happened!

Cancelling visits happens often, so you can send an email out to the rest of the coaches (each separately, of course), letting them know you have decided to attend such-and-such university, or you can make it generic if you don't want to disclose it to them. Be sure to thank them for the offer.

Here is a sample email—short and sweet.

Coach Simpson,

I wanted to thank you very much for your offer to visit your school in September. Unfortunately, I will not be able to attend. I have decided to play for another school that has made me an offer. Again, I appreciate your interest in me and wish you and your team the best of luck in the future.

Thank you very much,

Samantha Williams

Again, it may be tempting to go on all five visits, but it looks very bad to the school you have committed to. This is a verbal commitment, and it is basically where both parties promise to remain committed until National Signing Day, where it then is contractual. Verbal commitments are not binding, but my question is, "Why go on a visit to another school if you know you won't be committing to them?" There is no purpose to it at all.

Tips on Official Visits

- **Remember:**
  They are seeing if you are a good fit for the team. Be on your best behavior, engage with the team, and be a positive person with the people that you meet.

- **Stay with the "host" that the coach has put you with.**
  This will be someone from the team assigned to show you around and you will stay with. I have heard of visits gone awry because the visiting person has gone off to do something on their own. Remember why you are there: to meet the team and let them get to know you.

- **Dress appropriately!**

  I have heard of visiting athletes wearing other colleges shirts! Literally competing schools! WHHHHYYYYYYY?! Be smart about what you are wearing, and do not wear torn up or dirty clothes. A polo, sweater or casual button-down shirt for guys and girls and nothing skimpy for girls. Jeans are fine for both girls and guys.

- **Do not drink or party at the school.**

  I cannot stress this enough. You will probably be around drinking the weekend you visit, but drink a soda while you are at a party. If you are uncomfortable and do not want the team that you are hoping to be on think you are not "fun," let them know you are in season and your high school coach has strict rules about it. This takes you off the hook.

- **You will have an opportunity to meet with the head coach or position coach one-on-one.**

  Have some questions ready for them. Make sure you are polite, shake their hand firmly, maintain great eye contact, and engage in the conversation. Here are some good questions to have handy:
  - o What is the travel schedule for the team? How does this affect schoolwork?
  - o Where do they see you fitting in on the team or roster?
  - o Do they practice off-season?
  - o How many athletes are they recruiting for the team and/or your position or place?
  - o What is the practice schedule weekly and daily?
  - o Ask what they would typically offer as a scholarship for recruits. This one is tough, I know. You may already know or they may have told you in some way what they offer. But during your official visit, this needs to be a direct discussion.
  - o When will they be making their final decision about recruits? Ask if they have not made an offer yet. This will give you the timeline concerning when you will hear back from them.

- **Follow up with your college host.**

  Use a text, an email, a Facebook message, Instagram, or other social media you both use. Let them know you appreciated them hosting you. It also goes a long way when the team talks to the coach about you. Make this an easy decision for everyone.

- **Email the coach.**

  Let them know how much you enjoyed the visit and that you hope to hear from them soon. Let them know you are very interested in attending their school and being a part of the team. This does two things: it lets them know you are very interested (even if it is not your first choice, until you have all the data in, do not discount anyone), and you are polite! I would do this as soon as you get home from your visit. This keeps you fresh in their minds, especially since they may have had several other recruits there that weekend.

- **Do not assume that you don't have to be on your best behavior just because you are talented.**

  Be nice to the team, school, coaches, and counselors you meet. Be polite to everyone, and be engaged in the process.

- **Lastly, remember, it will be a whirlwind weekend, and you will take in a lot.**

  Ask yourself if you'd fit in on the team and at the school. As I have mentioned before, things can change when you visit a school, even if it is initially your first choice. Be open and observant based on being there.

Now with all that being said, here is the recruiting timeline for your senior year [6]:

SENIOR YEAR							
Recruiting form of Communication	Division I Men's Basketball	Division I Women's Basketball	Division I Football	Division I Ice Hockey	Division I Other Sports	Division II	Division IIII
Electronic Correspondence	See rules that apply for sophomore and junior year	See rules that apply for sophomore and junior year	See rules that apply for sophomore and junior year	See rules that apply for sophomore and junior year	See rules that apply for sophomore and junior year	See rules that apply for sophomore and junior year	See rules that apply for sophomore and junior year
Recruiting Material pamphlets, camps, etc.)	Allowed	Allowed	Allowed	Allowed	Allowed	Allowed	Allowed
Telephone Calls	You can make as many calls as you want at your expense Unlimited	You can make as many calls as you want at your expense Unlimited	You can make as many calls as you want at your expense One call per week beginning Sept 1st of senior year	You can make as many calls as you want at your expense Unlimited	You can make as many calls as you want at your expense Unlimited	You can make as many calls as you want at your expense Unlimited	You can make as many calls as you want at your expense Unlimited

			SENIOR YEAR				
Recruiting form of Communication	**Division I Men's Basketball**	**Division I Women's Basketball**	**Division I Football**	**Division I Ice Hockey**	**Division I Other Sports**	**Division II**	**Division IIII**
			Unlimited calls after you sign a National Letter of Intent*** or after the college receives a financial deposit from you Unlimited during contact period, which is the time that coaches are allowed to come off campus and meet you. This coincides with the same timing as the Unlimited calls				
Off campus contact/Official Visit	You can make only one official visit per college and up to five college visits total for Division I schools.	You can make only one official visit per college and up to five college visits total for Division I schools.	Off-campus contact Sunday after the last Saturday in November Official visits can begin the opening day of classes of senior year You can make only one official visit per college and up to five college visits total for Division I schools.		Off-campus contact can start July Ist, prior to senior year or the opening day of classes of student-athletes' senior year in highs school, whichever is earlier Women's Hockey, July 7th prior to senior year or the opening day of classes of athletes' senior year in high school, whichever is earlier Women's Gymnastics-July 15th prior to senior year or the opening day of classes of athletes' senior year in high school, whichever is earlier	Official visits can begin opening day of classes and are unlimited for Division II schools	Official visits can begin opening day of classes

SENIOR YEAR							
Recruiting form of Communication	Division I Men's Basketball	Division I Women's Basketball	Division I Football	Division I Ice Hockey	Division I Other Sports	Division II	Division IIII
					Official Visits can begin opening day of classes of the senior year		
Unofficial Visit	You may make an unlimited amount of official visits, except for dead period	You may make an unlimited amount of official visits, except for dead period	You may make an unlimited amount of official visits, except for dead period	You may make an unlimited amount of official visits, except for dead period		You may make an unlimited amount of official visits, except for dead period	You may make an unlimited amount of official visits, except for dead period

***What is the National Letter of Intent (NLI)?* [8] *It is a binding agreement between a prospective student-athlete and an NLI institution. The prospective student-athlete agrees to attend the institution full-time for one academic year (two semesters or three quarters) and play sports for that school. In return, the school agrees to provide athletic financial aid for one academic year (two semesters or three quarters). There is a penalty for not fulfilling the NLI agreement: You must serve one year in residence (full-time two semesters or three quarters) at the next NLI member institution and lose one season of competition in all sports. So, you forfeit time to play sports at the new (or other school) that you decided on. It is a big deal to sign a NLI, and it is just like any other contract. Coaches have released players from their obligation, if requested by an athlete, but it is a decision at the discretion of the coach and school.*

National Signing Day

National Signing Day can be an incredible day for many student-athletes. I do want to stress at this point in the recruiting process, your education is the most important thing to focus on (I know you keep hearing that!). Sports can be an incredible means to an end, a great experience, a way to gain scholarship money, an opportunity to meet new people—and for the very gifted (professional athlete potential), it can provide a gateway for future opportunities. But it is not the MAIN reason you are attending college. If you don't have offers at this time, please remember this and know that there are other doors open to you—it just may not be the one you want right now.

I also want to share with you, this time can even be heartbreaking for great athletes. They may get strung along by coaches at colleges who are not going to offer much in the form of scholarship money, or they will expect you to walk-on to their team. They may sense your strong interest and feel that you, as an athlete, will compete even if you are not receiving a scholarship. It is very important to start having that conversation with the college coaches this year. Ask them what they typically offer and if they are interested in having you be part of their team. This can be done at the official visits when you are talking to the coaches, but the conversation definitely needs to happen at some point this year—early enough for you to know where you stand.

Talking about money is hard, but you don't want to have your heart set on a school and have them offer you a very low figure or expect you to be a walk-on. You are going to put so much time into practicing that it needs to be worth your commitment and effort. It can be very demoralizing to put so much heart into your sport if you feel that they do not support you enough to offer you a scholarship or opportunity. I do know that there are student-athletes who have walked on a team and have earned a scholarship the next year, but it is not the norm for a team or an athlete.

Be open and cautious when going through this process. It is an exciting time. I know that when all of my children went through this progression, it was fun, but there were also some moments that were very tough for them. We had times when coaches assured us that there would be official visits or scholarships, but ended up with them either not giving much and/or not coming through with the visits that were promised. Coaches can and do change teams (we saw that a lot), and you may have established a relationship with a coach who is moving to another school. This happens more than you think, and you need to be prepared for anything. Throw the net wide until you make your official commitment. I think for us, and hopefully for you, we learned a few key things that helped get us through the process: 1) Do not get your heart set on something and be unwilling to budge when you need to. In short, be flexible. 2) There are MANY great schools and MANY teams out there. If it is not one, it could be another. If none, it is not meant to be, and you can focus on your school or other activities. 3) The school you may least likely have picked can be the best one for you. When you are young, you can sometimes idealize places and people. But when you get older, you can see why things happen and that, sometimes, they are the best things for you.

I want to be sure to stress that even if you are not recruited for a sport, you should not pass on attending college. You can attend a junior college or go the community college route and transfer later to a four year school, even if you do not play sports. But, by attending and playing at a smaller or junior college right after high school where you can show improvement, commitment, and achievement of the success that some of the larger schools want to see, it can be a fantastic way to later earn a spot on a team at a school that you prefer to attend. Many successful college and athletic careers start that way: at a junior or community college. You will just need to demonstrate perseverance.

I also want to stress that if you are a "good" athlete, but you are a "great" student, and if you ARE being recruited for sports by a "good" but not "great" school, if at all financially possible, pick the "great" school for the academics over playing sports at a "good" school. If you are academically gifted, you will probably qualify for a higher academic scholarship. I see so many student-athletes go to schools that are not challenging to them academically or don't have good name recognition just to continue playing sports and maintain the dream of competing. From parents I hear, "It is my son/daughters dream to continue playing sports, so they are attending this school to pursue their dream." This is the time I ask them, "Why?"

At that point, get a great education! If you are not being recruited seriously, chances are you are not part of the 2% of college athletes who will be able to compete professionally in sports. There is a time to turn in your cleats, mitts, trunks, sticks, balls, etc., and move on from sports to focus on a more tangible goal. Parents, at this time or intersection for your children, direct them towards the college and academics, not a sport or where they can still play and compete. There are intermural sports where students can continue enjoying their sport and there are leagues to join and participate in, even outside of college. But playing a sport just to extend the dream for four more years is putting a lot of eggs in a basket that will likely not give you anything in return. Instead, focus on the fact that you have a great student and that they will get a wonderful education—IF they attend a school that will better prepare them for their future.

Ivy League Recruiting [9]

The Ivy League is its own animal and has its own guidelines and restrictions. It still falls under the DI criteria for when a coach can contact you, make phone calls, and send out recruiting materials, but they have very different academic expectations. They also do not give out athletic scholarships, but what they do offer is acceptance into VERY tough and competitive schools that will offer you an incredible education and give you the chance to participate in a sport for their school. The Ivy League schools rate students on what is called the Academic Index.

The Academic Index is a bit of an enigma. But here is the most important information that I captured to explain it, describe football "bands," and explain why they will be important to prospective athletes.

The Academic Index (AI) is a combination of a student's class rank (it is the unweighted high school GPA, not the class rank) and SAT scores, typically calculated for high school seniors. Every prospective Ivy League student is assigned a number, which ranges from 60 to 240 (240 is a perfect score.) The AI is divided into three categories. While the first two reflect SAT I and SAT II scores, the third is GPA adjusted on the same 20 to 80 scale to round out the score (the GPA 'score' can usually be calculated by multiplying the unweighted high school GPA by 20). Although the league does not disclose its data, the New York Times estimated that the average student at an Ivy League institution has an AI around 220, with Harvard, Yale, and Princeton having slightly higher averages than their other counterparts at Brown, Columbia, Cornell, Dartmouth, and University of Pennsylvania. The Ivy League has set a minimum AI of 183 and will likely adjust upwards again in the next few years, for any student-athlete offered admission, which is roughly comparable to a 3.0 GPA and an 1140 out of 1600 on the SAT I.

However, each team's overall AI must remain within one standard deviation (estimated to be between 12–16 points) of the average AI for the entire student body. Deviations can't be calculated without knowing the exact distribution of all scores, which the Ivy League does not publish. These are just approximate. For example, if no Ivy League institution has an average AI below 200 for their whole student body, no athletic program in the Ivy League approaches that 183 benchmark.

The AI limits the pool of potential recruits from the start, which allows (or forces) coaches to focus their efforts on targeting high-achieving students. From the perspective of an admissions officer, a recruited athlete must satisfy the same standards as the rest of the class. In the Ivy League, which is a conference known more for its Nobel Prizes than sports accomplishments, the AI has helped preserve the league's high academic standards. The thought process is if a student is injured and unable to play sports (or quite frankly, since there is no scholarship expectation to meet, a student leaves the team), they would still be a good fit to the school and can meet the rigorous academics.

There is no expectation or requirement to compete once you have been accepted into the school.

Once a coach feels the recruit meets academic and athletic standards, they are offered a "Likely Letter" that is similar to a National Letter of Intent from other colleges. This is what an athlete will want and hope for from an Ivy League school. It's formal, written communication from the Admissions Office that states that you will be admitted as long as you continue your high school education as expected. (Maintain your GPA, and do not mess up!) Only the Admissions Office may give out the Likely Letter, but it doesn't always happen and recruits still are recruited. The key word is "may." Likely Letters are for athletes being recruited (and, oftentimes, offered scholarships) by other schools; this gives them a more formal method of acceptance and assurance that they will be admitted.

Football is different than other sports in the Ivy League. Football has what they call "bands," which are like levels. They will categorize athletes based on the position they play. An Ivy League football coach can recruit up to thirty players, and those recruits must fall into one of four academic bands based on their Academic Index. Band 4 is the highest.

A Band 4 athlete must have an Academic Index that falls within one standard deviation. So, if the general AI for the student body is around 220, the Band 4 guys must be around 207. Eight of the coach's thirty recruits must be Band 4. Next is Band 3, which goes down to two standard deviations off the average index. About thirteen of the thirty recruits must be Band 3 or *higher*. That's an index of around 194 or better. Seven more recruits can be in Band 2, which is 2.5 standard deviations. That's around 180. Lastly, for Band 1, the coach is allowed to bring on two players that are at or above the 183 index. Here is how it breaks down.

Band 4

Eight football players. These would be the players that may not play often, but academically, they help raise the average of the teams AI, and they can fit into this band.

Band 3 (or Higher)

Thirteen football players. The majority of the athletes will fall in this range. They are high achieving academically and are very good athletes.

Band 2 (or Higher)

Seven football players. From here, we start to see the more highly recruited athletes, but they still have a minimum academic expectation.

Band 1 (or Higher)

Two football players. These are the highest recruited athletes, and it is where the academic expectation is the lowest. These are players that are expected, and recruited, to make an immediate impact on a team. There is still a minimum academic requirement, but if you are an exceptional football player, you have more room academically.

Total: 30 Players

This will vary widely depending on the school and the year. Harvard's bands are much higher, while Dartmouth's is much lower. Similarly, the number of recruits per band depends on the previous three recruiting classes—for example, a school could take 1 bottom bander in years 1, 2, and 3 and then take 5 in year 4. Most schools don't do this but it would be permissible.

You can see that this allows the Ivy Leagues to have a bit more flexibility when recruiting athletes for football. I hear at times that it doesn't seem to be fair to have football receive this (and many other) concessions, but you have to remember that football is the main sport moneymaker for many schools, and there is a business aspect to some of these decisions. Fair or not, it is a revenue stream for schools, and they are allowing student-athletes to compete at a great institution. These can be wonderful opportunities for student-athletes from all walks of life to receive an education and play football.

Ivy League schools are an awesome place to get a GREAT education and have the opportunity to compete, but understand that the focus at these schools is STUDENT first, ATHLETE second. No Bowl games, no playing past Thanksgiving (if you play football), and even their practices are limited time-wise, to allow athletes to study. The tradeoff is that they do have higher expectations of their athletes on and off the field, pool, court, track, rink, etc.

Military Academies

I have a complete chapter on military academies, but for athletes, there are some specific things to know.

Military academies also have a strict minimum standard for recruiting, but there are also deviations allowed for those athletes that meet most, but not all, of the requirements of the academies. One of the options: Athletes can attend "prep school" (short for preparatory school) if they do not meet all of these requirements. This school year is taken after high school before you head into the actual academy, and the school is located either on, or near, the school property. It is a separate school from the academy, and it is there to help prepare athletes for the academic, military, and physical challenges they will have at the academy. Some say that it is harder to get into the prep school than the actual academy because there are only a few hundred slots for the school each year.

Not all students who attend prep school are athletes. The other students who attend are either prior service students, foreign students who do not meet a requirement, or other students who have high achievement in most areas but may need extra attention to meet an academic or other standard. It is for those students and student-athletes who meet most, but not all, of the requirements and expectations, and where the admissions board feels that they may need an extra year of preparation, hence "prep school."

However, something they don't always tell you is that there is no guarantee that you will make it into the academy after the prep school year. You still have to apply again, even as an athlete. If you are an athlete at a prep school, you will compete against other smaller schools and the other military academy prep schools. It is more casual at the prep schools, and they do an abbreviated version of the full academy experience.

One of the benefits of attending a prep school is that you receive a higher monthly stipend at the prep school, simply because you go into the school with a military entry-level classification, basically on enlisted soldier pay. This gives you a nice little bump in pay compared to the regular academy stipend that you receive. The time at the prep school also counts towards your service in the military, so right out the gate upon graduation from the actual academy, you have a year of service going towards your retirement. It does not count towards your years of service obligation to the military, but it does give you a bump for pay earlier in your career.

If you choose to stay in the military and be a career person, you will have one more year that counts towards your years of service because you attended prep school. Another benefit is that it also gives you a chance to meet 200 other potential students before even attending the actual academy. My son Jordan attended the prep school at West Point, and that was one of his favorite experiences there. His class was the first one to attend the newly built prep school that was actually on the West Point property.

Everything was brand new, and he played football for the prep school on brand new turf!

You cannot apply directly to the prep schools, but a recruiting officer or a coach will reach out to an athlete and push to have them attend the school if they do not meet the minimum criteria right out of the gate.

Camps

I would be remiss if I did not talk about camps for athletes. These are camps that colleges offer that are paid for by the athlete. The camps are opportunities to learn new skills but are mostly used as an opportunity for coaches to observe potential recruits. At these camps, athletes compete, do drills, and show their abilities. I definitely recommend attending these camps, especially at the schools you are most interested in attending. It gives you the chance to show your abilities, and it gives them a chance to see you in action. Camps are often a prerequisite for a scholarship offer to a recruit.

I recommend attending the summer before your senior year, and I also recommend you plan them strategically, so you are able to hit a few camps at a time. For example, when our boys did football camps, we looked at the areas and planned it so they could fly to the first one. Then my husband drove them to the others, hitting a few in the area or region. College camps will allow you to attend the camp just for one day, which our kids did at several of them. Camps are usually two or three days, depending on the sport. They give you exposure to some of the best college coaches, seeing you compete in person—maybe for the first time. It also allows for that next level of relationship development between the students and the coaches.

You may not be able to attend them all, but as with all that you are doing, rank which ones you want to go to the most and work your way down. Sometimes smaller colleges do not have camps, but coaches will show up at the larger camps to see who they want to recruit. If you are in touch with a smaller school, contact the coach at that school to let them know you are going to be at a camp in their area. That way, they can come to see you compete and meet you.

Some things we have learned along the way when it comes to camps:

- **After the camp, follow up with the coaches to thank them.**
  Keep the line of communication going. The next step will hopefully be a call for an official visit from them!

- **There was a time or two when my boys were tired and may not have competed at their best.**

  It can be a long circuit if you are hitting several camps. Looking back, we definitely should have limited it to just one day for each of the camps. If you are doing multiple camps, try to manage your time after the camp well. Rest up! Try to stagger it a day or two for recuperation, if at all possible. There was one time that David got the flu in-between camps. It was very disappointing. He still showed up and met the coaches but was unable to participate in the camp activities and showcase his abilities. So, be sure that you are taking care of yourself during this time.

- **Bring LOTS of fluids and snacks.**

  The camps may provide some, but it is better to bring your own food and drink to help you stay hydrated and fed.

- **Volunteer to do the drills first.**

  It shows initiative, and it shows them that you want to be there!

- **When you are at the camp, be involved, be engaged, and be your best!**

  This is not the time to relax. Think of it as an opportunity to show them what you are capable of, even if you are tired. Push through it!

- **Talk to coaches when you have the opportunity.**

  Any coach. It does not even have to be about the sport, but just have conversations with them. This helps them remember you, and if it is between you and another athlete and you have been the more "personable" one, who do you think they will recruit?

- **Be the first one there at the camp and the last one to leave.**

- **It is okay to let them know you are only able to attend one day.**

  Some kids feel uncomfortable letting the coaches know that they are looking at other camps and colleges. A lot of athletes do this. Just be honest. They will prorate the camp for the time you are able to attend. However, if a specific college is your top choice, and they are interested in you as well, try your best to attend the whole camp.

As you can see, there are so many options for an athlete and many opportunities to help pay for your college using your athletic opportunities—if you put in the time and effort it takes. It also takes a little luck and good timing. If you focus on your grades, as well as your talents athletically, it will leave you open to all the best possible options for your future.

5

SAT, ACT, SAT Subject, and AP Test Preparation

MANY PEOPLE ASK ME about preparing for the SAT and ACT tests.

This is a very important part of the puzzle for college admissions. Most colleges take into account all of the components that make you who you are. But SAT and ACT scores are definitely a factor for those upper-tiered schools, as well as an opportunity for additional scholarship money (based on your scores) at ALL colleges. Even outside scholarships will ask about your scores. It actually may prohibit you from getting into college period, if they are too low. But there are ways to help ensure you get the best possible score on these tests.

Financially, if you are in a situation where paying for the tests is a challenge or you are on financial assistance of any kind, be sure to apply for a waiver. Many people do not know that there is a waiver for taking the test, so talk to your school counselor and take advantage of it.

The SAT and ACT tests are administered on Saturdays at local high schools, and you do not have to take it at your home school. There will be options in your area, depending on the best date and location for you.

I will talk about AP and SAT Subject tests later in the chapter, but every student who is planning on attending college will need to take the ACT and/or the SAT test, while not all schools require or expect the AP or SAT Subject Test scores.

Let's first look at what each test is and what makes up the sections within them.

SAT (10)

- Critical Reading
- Writing and Language
- Math
- SAT Essay

The majority of questions are multiple choice, but there are grid questions in the math area. The SAT is made up of ten sections with the first section being the twenty-five-minute essay.

SAT Scoring [11]

- **Total score: 400–1600**
- **Reading and writing section: 200–800**
- **Math section: 200–800**
- **SAT essay: Three scores ranging from 2–8**

These sections are then combined to give you a total that is called a composite score. An average composite score for the SAT is 1050-1060, with 1180 being a good score and 1340 or higher being excellent (giving you more options for colleges).

 ACT Scoring [12]

- **English**
- **Mathematics**
- **Reading**
- **Science**
- **ACT Essay/Writing**

The ACT test is made up of seventy-five English questions, sixty math questions, forty reading questions, and forty science questions.

The ACT is out of 36 points, and they average each section together to give you your average. 20 is the ACT average, with around 26 and above being a good score and 30 and above being excellent. Because the ACT is an average, it is easier to hide or mask a weak section, which is a benefit. For example, if you get a 29 in reading, a 30 in English, a 22 in science, and a 31 in math, your average score will be a 28. That is still a great score, even though science is not your strong subject. You can do this more easily with your ACT than your SAT.

Where you want to go to school will determine what scores you are shooting for and where you fit in. I recommend making a spreadsheet. Put on one column the schools you want to attend and what their average SAT/ACT scores are. This will help you find out your "reach" schools and "meets" schools, schools that are a bit higher that you can shoot for and schools where you already fall score wise and with other academic requirements (the "meets", "reach" and" safe" schools, will be discussed in a later chapter in more detail).

Here is an ACT and SAT example spreadsheet:

School	ACT score average for school	SAT score average for school	My score: ACT	My score: SAT

What is Superscoring?

Superscoring is a process where colleges take your highest scores on each section of the ACT or SAT tests to give you a higher overall score. In other words, if you got a 25 on math one time you took the test and another time you took it and got a 27, the school will take the 27. If you got a 20 on English once and a 30 another time, you will have the 27 and the 30 for your supers-scores. Military academies super score, as do many other schools. Here is a list of some notable schools and their stance on superscoring. These were taken from their websites and condensed to make it easier to see. Things also can change at these schools concerning superscoring, so it is important to verify with the schools.

School	Official Statement from Schools on Superscoring [13]
Boston College	If you have taken the SAT more than once, Boston College will take the highest individual section scores from each date and combine those scores.
Boston University	Boston University will allow students to choose College Board's Score Choice; however, we strongly recommend students submit their scores each time they take the SAT. BU has always considered a student's highest SAT section scores in making admissions decisions and will continue to do so.
Brown	We automatically focus on your highest test scores and therefore Score Choice is a bit redundant.

School	Official Statement from Schools on Superscoring [13]
Columbia	Applicants may select the Score Choice option for the SAT. When evaluating applicants, we consider only the highest testing results reported from individual sections of the SAT. We are always seeking to give students the greatest opportunity to showcase their academic talents and hoping to make the testing experience as stress-free as possible. We encourage applicants to take these examinations no more than twice, but we do not penalize applicants for exceeding that recommendation.
Duke	Duke requires that students send their full testing record for the SAT. Duke will use the highest available Critical Reading, Writing and Math scores, regardless of the date those tests were taken.
Georgetown	Georgetown University does not participate in the Score Choice option available through the College Board. Georgetown requires that you submit scores from all test sittings of the SAT. If an applicant takes the SAT more than once, the admissions committees will consider the highest critical reading score and the highest math score from multiple test sessions when reviewing the application.
Georgia Institute of Technology	Send us your scores when you take the test – don't wait! Your scores may fluctuate with each test instance, but we will only use the highest section in our review of your application. Delaying sending us your scores could put you at risk of missing an application date or being excluded from information sent from our office.
Harvard	You are free to use the College Board Score Choice option.
Johns Hopkins	Johns Hopkins University considers your highest section scores across all SATs taken–even if they were on different test dates–in our evaluation of your application. We therefore encourage you to update your application with new test scores each time you take the SATs.
MIT	If you take the same test multiple times, we will consider the highest score achieved in each section. We do this in order to consider all applicants in their best light. Students are free to use the College Board's Score Choice option to submit the scores of your choice as well.
New York University	With regard to the SAT, NYU participates in Score Choice, enabling you to elect which tests you want to send to NYU. If you take the SAT multiple times, we will only review the highest Critical Reading, Math, and Writing scores you submit, regardless of test dates, creating the highest possible composite score for you in our evaluation process.
Notre Dame	For our evaluation we will use your highest individual SAT Critical Reading and Math subscores from multiple testing dates to compute your composite score.
Princeton	Applicants are welcome to use the Score Choice option for standardized test score submission. Princeton will consider the highest individual section results across all sittings of the SAT Reasoning. We encourage applicants to submit all official test scores as soon as they are available.
Stanford	For the SAT, we will focus on the highest individual Critical Reading, Math and Writing scores from all test sittings. We will superscore the results from the current and redesigned SAT separately.
University of Chicago	We recommend you send us all of your test scores. Only your best testing results (highest sub-scores AND/OR best result of the 2 testing options – SAT vs ACT) will beincluded/used in your admission review. Lower testing will not be included in your final/official application,so it cannot count against you.
University of Connecticut	We will accept the highest scores from your combined test dates.

School	Official Statement from Schools on Superscoring [13]
University of Miami	If you take the test more than once, you must send us all of your scores to ensure that we have your best performance on record. We will continue to superscore the SAT, but will only combine scores from like tests (in other words, we will not combine a student's best score from the new SAT with the best score from the current SAT).
University of North Carolina	If you send us scores from multiple test dates, we'll take your highest score for each section of the test and consider those scores as we evaluate your application. If you send us both an SAT and an ACT, we'll look at whichever is higher.
University of Southern California	For students who take the SAT more than once, USC records the highest scores for each section – Critical Reading, Mathematics, and Writing – even if achieved at different sittings.
University of Virginia	It has been the Office of Admission's long-standing policy to consider the best test scores submitted by applicants. When reviewing SAT scores, we use the top score from each section across all administrations of the exam. We hope you will submit all of your scores knowing that we will recombine the sections to get the best possible set of scores.
Vanderbilt	Vanderbilt University has indicated that it considers your highest section scores across all SAT test dates that you submit. Only your highest section scores will be considered as part of the final admissions decision. Each time you submit scores, Vanderbilt University will update your record with any new high scores. Vanderbilt University strongly encourages you to submit your scores each time you take the SAT.
Villanova	Candidates are asked to submit the scores from each sitting of the SAT. The Admission Committee will review the highest critical reading and highest math scores from the SAT from different dates for admission.
Virginia Tech	Virginia Tech wants to see all of your test scores. We will use the highest scores and even combine your highest test scores from multiple test dates when evaluating your application.
Yale	When assessing SAT results, we will focus on your highest individual SAT Critical Reading, Math and Writing scores from all test dates.

Superscoring isn't used at all schools, but it is great to know it is an option for some. If you do not see a school listed, ask that school when you are applying. Just give them a call and see if they do allow it or, as I mentioned, check on their website to verify.

Recent Changes to the SAT

Recent SAT changes have made it much more user-friendly. One of the best things is that they do not penalize you for guessing (there was a penalty for it in the past). This is a great benefit, since you have a 25% chance of getting it correct when guessing. So why not!

Here in a snapshot is the comparison between the two tests, reflecting the new SAT format and the ACT standard. This will help you to see the differences, what each one encompasses, and the benefits of one over the other.

The ACT and SAT tests are accepted by all US colleges and universities. Here are some comparisons between the two.

Features:	ACT	SAT
What are they testing on?	Knowledge of subjects taught in high school problem-solving abilities	Measure literacy and writing skills. Also analyzes
How long is the test?	Approximately three hours and fifteen minutes, plus the forty-minute essay section	Approximately three hours, plus the fifty-minute optional essay
Essay is Optional	Yes	Yes
Penalty for guessing	No	No
How many tests a year?	Six	Seven
Top Score	36	1600
What year did it start?	1959	1926
Reading Section	Four reading sections	Five reading sections
Science	One science section	None
Math	Arithmetic, Algebra I and II, geometry, trigonometry, probability, and statistics	Arithmetic, Algebra I and II, geometry, trigonometry, and data analysis
Difficulty Levels	For the English and reading sections, the difficulty level is random. For math and science, it generally gets harder as you progress through the sections	Math questions generally become more difficult as you move further down the line of questioning. Reading just goes chronologically through the passage. Writing and language do not get harder as you continue on
Registration	Usually required five to six weeks before the test date www.act.org	Usually required four weeks before the test date www.collegeboard.com
Cost	$50.50 or $67.50 with writing	$46 or $60 with essay test

There is no right or wrong test—just preferences. I recommend to EVERY student: take one of each and see which one you score higher on and which one you feel more comfortable taking. Usually there is one you prefer. Another really important strategy is to take it early enough in the school year (I recommend doing this your junior year) to allow you to take the test multiple times. Then you will be able to retake it if necessary or if you are shooting for higher scores. If you wait until your senior year, it puts you in a tough position where you may have to settle for lower scores. It also puts you against the wall where you HAVE to do well on it the first time, which can be counterproductive during the actual testing, instead of feeling relaxed, knowing if you don't do well this time, you will have the first one under your belt. Taking it multiple times allows you to see where you need to focus and gives you a great gauge on time management and the process.

How to Convert Between Your ACT and SAT Scores

Here is a great chart that converts the ACT to SAT and vice-versa. This will help you determine which test you take better. For example, if you got a 30 on your ACT, it will convert to approximately a 1410 (average) on the SAT. But if you took the SAT and received a 1450 on it, you know with that higher score, you do better on the SAT test since that would convert to a 32 on the ACT.

SAT	ACT		SAT	ACT		SAT	ACT
1600	36		1250	26		900	17
1590	35		1240	26		890	16
1580	35		1230	25		880	16
1570	35		1220	25		870	16
1560	35		1210	25		860	16
1550	34		1200	25		850	15
1540	34		1190	24		840	15
1530	34		1180	24		830	15
1520	34		1170	24		820	15
1510	33		1160	24		810	15
1500	33		1150	23		800	14
1490	33		1140	23		790	14
1480	32		1130	23		780	14
1470	32		1120	22		770	14
1460	32		1110	22		760	14

SAT	ACT		SAT	ACT		SAT	ACT
1450	32		1100	22		750	13
1440	31		1090	21		740	13
1430	31		1080	21		730	13
1420	31		1070	21		720	13
1410	30		1060	21		710	12
1400	30		1050	20		700	12
1390	30		1040	20		690	12
1380	29		1030	20		680	12
1370	29		1020	20		670	12
1360	29		1010	19		660	12
1350	29		1000	19		650	12
1340	28		990	19		640	12
1330	28		980	19		630	12
1320	28		970	18		620	11
1310	28		960	18		610	11
1300	27		950	18		600	11
1290	27		940	18		590	11
1280	27		930	17		580	11
1270	26		920	17		570	11
1260	26						

Below are some great quick tips for taking either of the tests.

Time Management

Watch the clock. Have a watch on your desk. If you have a section with forty questions and you have thirty minutes, you know that when you hit twenty questions you should be at fifteen minutes (the halfway mark). If not, you will need to work faster. I also recommend checking your time around the tenth question mark.

Hit the Easy Questions First

Another tip is to look through your questions and answer the ones that are easier first. Typically, they are at the beginning of the section. If you are stuck on a question, skip it and move on to the next. VERY IMPORTANT: Make sure (if you do skip forward on a question) to fill in the bubble corresponding to the question you are answering. Make a little "tic" mark next to the question on your bubble, so you easily can go back to the ones you missed. This helps you avoid filling in the wrong bubbles.

Guessing

With guessing allowed on both tests now, you have more flexibility and opportunity than previous test-takers. I have to stress that guessing is not your goal for the tests, but occasionally you will have sections where you run out of time. A good rule of thumb is when you are down to two minutes on that section, have a letter you always go with (A, B, C, or D), and fill the remaining unanswered questions out with that letter. As I mentioned before, you have a 25% chance of getting it right if you guess—but you have a 0% chance of getting it right if you leave it blank. So guess away when time runs out. Then, if you have a minute left, look over as many of the questions as you can to see if you can answer them quickly. If not, you at least have them filled in with the 25% chance of being correct. I believe it was Wayne Gretzky who said, "You miss 100% of the shots you don't take." The same goes for ACT and SAT tests.

Use Common Sense

When answering a question you aren't 100% confident in, use common sense or rule out ones that are incorrect. If you know for sure it isn't A or D, you have now increased your odds of guessing to 50%. Answer it, put a dot or tic mark next to it, and come back to it if you have time. Also, sometimes the answer seems too easy. Reread it to make sure you read it correctly, answer it, and then move on. Don't overthink it.

Come Well Prepared

Arrive early, have all the materials that they allow: paper, pencils (bring two that are sharpened and have erasers), a watch, a snack, a drink, a calculator, etc. Eat a good breakfast. It would be a long morning on an empty stomach. Bring a healthy snack and drink. Turn off your cell phone and use a watch (with no alarm or sound) to show the time. Have the watch where you can use a countdown on it if possible, so you can see at a quick glance how many minutes you have left.

Be Mentally Prepared

This is not the weekend you want to choose to go out and party. Get to bed early, be rested, and mentally prepare yourself to do a great job. Come in with a positive attitude, and do not sit by someone who does not take this seriously, as they can be a distraction during the test, or—worst-case scenario—try to cheat off of you.

Stay Close to Home

When selecting a location to take your test, try your best to select your home school or one you are familiar with. It is a small thing, but when students are in familiar and comfortable surroundings, they are more relaxed and can do better on tests instead of focusing on being in a strange place. This isn't always possible due to date conflicts, but do your best to be where you most feel the most comfortable.

Timing for Tests

Taking your test at the beginning of the school year can reflect a lower score than other times of the year. This may be the only time you can take it, but be prepared if it is. You have been out of testing mode for the summer, unless you have taken summer school or have been very diligent taking the tests available online. You also lose a bit of knowledge on basic skills over the summer, and it can take a few weeks to gain those skills and knowledge again. There are several test dates available, so I recommend looking at these early in your junior year to plan for your tests. Watch the deadlines. You can plan if and where you will have conflicts and alter them accordingly. I think taking your first real test, not the PSAT or PLAN test but the actual ACT and SAT, is best during the middle of your junior year. This will give you several options and opportunities to take it at the end of your junior year and the beginning and end of your senior year. It will also give you the whole summer to study and look at where you had your gaps on a section and study those sections, taking your scores from your first test(s) into consideration.

Deciding Where to Send Your Scores

When you register for the tests, it allows you to send the scores to several schools (up to four) for free, as part of the registration. You may not know where you want to go, but you will have an idea where to send them. Even if you send it to four schools but decide later you want to send it to another school, you can do it then for a small charge. If you truly don't have any idea where you are going, send it to the local college in your town and either leave the rest blank (though you will have to pay the small fee later when you do decide) or discuss some options or ideas with your parents.

Talking with your school counselor is a great opportunity for getting on different school radars, as well as finding out about schools you may not have considered. They will talk to you about your field of interest or areas where you excel currently, and can help direct you until you have done more research on where you want to apply.

Some students are great test takers and have no problem taking these tests. But most (yes most) students need help or practice. I feel, just like you would study for any upcoming test, this is an important part of preparing for one of the biggest tests of your life. You can go online to either of the ACT or SAT websites, and there are practice tests online to help. Some have a small fee, but they are well worth it. These practice tests are great tools and resources you definitely should take advantage of.

Some books I highly recommend for both the ACT and SAT tests are:

The Real Act Prep Guide from the Makers of the Act: The Most Recent Addition

I recommend this to all students taking the ACT. It has practice tests in there as well as tips on sections. Great resource.

The ACT for Dummies by Michelle Rose Gilman, Veronica Saydak, and Suzee Vlk

Easy to read and easy to use with quick tips and strategies for taking the test.

The Official Sat Study Guide by the College Entrance Board (New SAT Version: Do Not Borrow Someone's Old Book on This One)

This comes with a DVD option as well and has practice tests. I always feel the guides by the people who put out the test are great tools, and you can see the structure and nuances of the test that other books may not always capture.

For the SAT: be SURE not to use the old SAT study books, as they will focus on the old concepts and place a wrong emphasis on skills that have changed.

Kaplan New SAT Premier 2016 with 5 Practice Tests: Personalized Feedback + Book + Online + DVD + Mobile (Kaplan Test Prep)

This has it all, and you don't have to go to classes for it!

That brings me to taking classes or prep tutoring for the tests. If at all possible, and if you can afford it, I think you should do this as well. There are so many varying types and options, but I think it is something that gives you the benefit of having an outside person helping you and working you through problem areas. Your best resources for finding a tutor are:

- School Counselors
- Teachers
- Local Colleges
    - Many tutors are available through colleges. Check with their counselors.
- Google Search ACT/SAT Tutors in Your Area
    - Be sure to get references. There is no reason to pay good money on something this important without hearing success stories.
- Look for Private Tutoring Schools
    - These are more expensive, but can be a great option as well. The downside can be that you don't have the same tutor each time you go, and you may be in more of a group setting, with three or more students in there at a time.
- ACT/SAT Classes Offered Through your School or Community
- Word of Mouth
    - Ask around and see what other students have done or are doing. Asking older students who have graduated and are at college are great resources for what is available in your area.

Sometimes having someone hold you accountable each week for studying or taking the online test is necessary for students. It can be hard juggling all the things that you do, plus studying for the test, especially when an immediate grade or deadline is not imposed. All my children went the tutor route, as I think this makes the tests a little less intimidating. When you are taking the practice tests and working with the tutors on what to expect when taking the actual test, the first one is less stressful. It also helps having a tutor after taking the test that allows you to go through the areas and sections you did not do well in. They can help you improve.

I know many students and parents find the SAT and ACT tests limiting in its scope of determining what knowledge a student has, and they say that these tests are unfair. I agree and I disagree.

I think for colleges, it is very hard to even the playing field when a student applies. If I was a college admissions officer and I had a student coming from a very challenging private school with a 4.0 GPA and a student who attended a public school with a 4.0 GPA, their ACT and SAT scores would help me see if they are an academic fit for the school, based on their overall knowledge. The tests assess what students have retained and what their knowledge is based on the curriculum that they have been exposed to. Also, you can have a very smart student who does not always do well academically but has a higher IQ or is a great problem-solver but doesn't always apply it in the classroom. The ACT and SAT can be the determining factor when a student's grades do not reflect the student's knowledge.

On the other hand, you can have a great student who is smart but does not always do well on these type of tests—hence, making it "unfair." It is hard to satisfy everyone or every type of student or test.

For the students who do have trouble on these types of tests, I DEFINITELY recommend taking the ACT and SAT test several times to feel more comfortable and generally, it does allow for them to get higher scores if they work hard. My son Jordan took the ACT and SAT tests fourteen times. That is not a typo, he took them FOURTEEN TIMES! It was just to get into his school of choice. He raised his score 6 points from the first test to the last test. Now, I will say that improving a score by 6 points is uncommon. Generally students raise their score on average of 2–4 points (ACT) from the first time taking it to the last time they take the test, but as you can see, it is possible. Jordan never wants to see another ACT or SAT test again, but he studied, did the practice tests online, had tutors, read every book out there imaginable that was recommended to him, took a class—and eventually it paid off.

I see both sides of the ACT/SAT test debate. There is validity to the tests and how the scores come out. There is a skill to test-taking. Taking these kinds of test does not necessarily say what kind of student you are. The ACT and SAT are not the only way to judge a student and most schools nowadays do not use them as the only measuring stick.

Students (and parents) get really hung up on this and feel that they are defined by these tests. The tests are not what define you, and they do not tell you if you are smart or not. It is one aspect of your learning, how you learn, and what you know based on the curriculum you have been exposed to. Just go out there and do the best you can when you take the test. Know that at the end of the day you have exhausted all avenues, you have taken it as many times as you possibly could, and your score—and everything else combined—will help you get into college, not just one number or score on a test.

AP Tests [27]

AP tests take place after an AP class. These classes will measure your knowledge of the skills you have learned in that particular subject. It may also give you credit and a more advanced placement in college in various courses. It will depend on the college, but for those who do allow this, it is a wonderful way to save money and time since you may not have to pay or take a particular course in college if you receive a 3 or more on a test (see "How the AP Tests are Scored"). It will either allow you to advance to the next level or opt out of something completely. I will tell you that most, if not all, of the Ivy League schools will not place you out of any courses, even if you score high. They also have their own placement test that you will take online when you are accepted to help place you in the right class level.

AP Test are typically two to three hours long, so be prepared for that and do the same things you would do for the ACT or SAT tests, including eating a good breakfast, using time management, bringing snacks, etc. The test consists of both multiple choice questions and free response questions that will require a more individualized response. There are thirty-eight AP tests or classes that you can take in subjects such as art, English, history, social sciences, math, computer sciences, science, world language, and culture. Obviously not all schools have these as AP courses, but be sure to look at options on their website as well as checking with your high school on what AP courses are available..

https://apstudent.collegeboard.org/home

How AP Tests Are Scored

- 5 – Extremely Well Qualified
- 4 – Well Qualified
- 3 – Qualified
- 2 – Possibly Qualified
- 1 – No Recommendation

The AP tests are not required for most high schools. Honestly, it is more beneficial to actually just take the AP class and do well in it than to take the test, especially if you are heading to an upper-tiered college with stricter academic requirements. My son David only took the AP tests since his teacher told the class that if they took the test, irrespective of how they did, they would receive a 4.0 on their final. That was a great deal, and David definitely took advantage of that offer, even though the school he went to (Harvard) did not require them. There are colleges that do want to see how you do on the AP test, so it is also important to research when applying at the particular colleges you are interested in. The AP exams are administered at the end of the school year. For college application purposes, you would take this test or tests at the end of your junior year.

SAT Subject Test

SAT subject tests, which used to be called SAT IIs, are one hour multiple choice tests that judge a student's knowledge on a particular subject. They are more diverse than the SAT testing and have a larger range of topics than the other tests. The tests will cover such areas as:

- Literature
- US and world history
- Math Level 1 Includes Algebra I, II, and Geometry
- Math Level 2 Includes All Level 1 and Pre-Calculus and Trigonometry
- Biology (there are two types that you can take, depending on your interests)
- Chemistry
- Physics
- French
- German
- Spanish
- Latin
- Japanese

I highly recommend taking these tests at the end of your junior year when the material is fresh in your mind and you are preparing for your final exams and/or AP tests. You are allowed to take up to three subject tests on any given test day, which is great. It will be important to check out the schools you are interested in and see if they require the SAT subject tests. Upper-tiered schools generally require two or three. Also, some schools require specific ones. For example, if you are entering an engineering program, they may require you to take Math 2 for their program. You will be required to apply for these tests, just like you have the SAT or ACT tests.]

Here is the site you will use to apply:

https://collegereadiness.collegeboard.org/sat-subject-tests

There are guides and practice tests available on this site for you to view what questions are asked and which of the subject tests are more suited to your abilities. Remember, not all schools require them, only the schools with stricter requirements. Some will also not require it, but will "recommend" you take them. To improve your chances of getting accepted into the schools that" recommend " these tests, I would take them to help highlight your academic abilities in the topics you excel in.

6

Applying to Military Academies

A MILITARY ACADEMY IS AN incredible opportunity for a top-level college education from some of the most respected schools in our country.

They also offer amazing opportunities for those who wish to serve our country and become an officer. You can receive and commit to these educational opportunities at the most reputable places possible.

There are five US service academies:

1. US Military Academy at West Point, New York
2. US Naval Academy in Annapolis, Maryland
3. US Air Force Academy in Colorado Springs, Colorado
4. US Coast Guard Academy in New London, Connecticut, and
5. US Merchant Marines Academy in Kings Point, New York

I will give you relevant information for the three major ones: the Army, Air Force, and Naval Academies.

I have worked with many students who've sought to attend these academies. Most of the students I've helped haven't known the criteria and expectations for acceptance, and many started the process too late in high school.

Acceptance into military academies is truly a four-year process, in the sense that you have to have great grades, leadership, athletic capabilities, and evidence you're an exceptional citizen in your school and community. You can't afford to have one "off" year in high school; it would critically affect your overall grades and recruiting eligibility. If you are interested in attending an academy, you cannot mess around—ever. You must fully commit from the get-go and achieve greatness from the beginning. The expectations of these schools leave you no choice but to start from the first day of your high school career.

If you get into trouble your freshman year, chances are it will impact a military academy admissions opportunity. Also, the academies require a five-year commitment to one of the branches of service after college. This is a huge commitment, and one not to be taken lightly. It is a great honor to serve our country, but it is also a great responsibility—with risks attached to it. Two of my sons received appointments to military academies. Jordan attended West Point and graduated as a second lieutenant. David received appointments for both West Point and the Air Force Academy, though he ultimately chose to attend Harvard, despite accepting the potential of a service commitment when he applied to the other schools. When you apply, you need to fully understand what your commitment will entail.

Before we get started, let's define a few terms.

When you apply for an academy, you are seeking an **appointment.**

This is the golden ticket, so to speak. You receive it as an offer after you have met all the criteria, applied, interviewed, and passed all of the tests.

Before you can be considered for an **appointment**, you must obtain a **nomination** your senior year. A **nomination** does not guarantee an **appointment**. However, no **appointment** can be offered without a **nomination** . Each nominating authority: senatorial, state representative, and vice presidential has its own processes and deadlines.

Do your research!

Most congressional offices prefer that you contact them in the spring or summer of the year before you desire to enter an academy. So, it is recommended that you request nominations during the spring semester of your junior year or at the same time as you are completing your **pre-candidate questionnaire.**

Note: Regardless of when you initiate your request, the academy must receive your nomination by January thirty-first of your senior year. If they do not receive notice by this deadline, you will be disqualified.

Nominations do not carry over from year to year. So, if you wish to apply again during your freshmen year of college (many students apply later if they didn't get in the first try or aren't ready for the commitment) and you received a nomination while you were in high school, you still have to request a nomination again. Also, if you are in prep school at one of the academies, you have to apply for a nomination again at the end of your prep school year. (I will talk more about the prep schools later in the chapter.)

Securing nominations is a competitive process. To ensure your application will be complete, you should seek them in **each** of the categories for which you are eligible.

Once you determine the categories, you must contact the appropriate authority to make your request, then follow their application processes to obtain one.

Get up-to-date contact information for your senators at http://www.senate.gov and representatives at http://www.house.gov. Be prepared to identify your place of residence by ZIP code, state, or congressional district. Access each website for specific instructions on the nomination application process, including which office to contact and exact deadlines.

While some offices will accept requests through the fall, most do not accept them for nomination after October of your senior year. Members of Congress may submit their nominations to the academies as late as January thirty-first; however, the majority of nominations are received before that time.

The vice president of the United States may nominate candidates from the nation at large and is allowed to have a maximum of five cadets attending the academies at one time. For each cadet vacancy that occurs, the vice president may nominate up to ten candidates to be considered for appointment. Vacancies occur when cadets graduate or leave prior to graduation. All pre-candidates are eligible for this nomination category. Do not mail your request for a vice presidential nomination to an academy: the academies will make recommendations to the vice president based upon your admissions file. If you wish to request a vice presidential nomination, you may complete the online application found at http://www.whitehouse.gov/administration/vice-president-biden/academy-nominations. The deadline is January thirty-first. These are generally given to students who have a parent who has served in the military, but it is not limited to them.

Now that I have laid that out, to apply, you must be of good moral character and meet these basic eligibility requirements [15]:

- You must be at least seventeen years old but not past your twenty-third birthday by July first of the year you will enter the academy.
- It's typically open to United States citizens, but there are some international admissions opportunities.
- You must be unmarried, not pregnant, and not have dependents.
- You must possess a valid social security number.

I always recommend heading to the websites provided and verifying you meet their criteria. Then, follow these steps.

1) **Apply early!** January of your junior year is a great time to start a conversation with the liaison officer and to apply for summer leadership at one of the academies.

   The week-long summer leadership camp applications and information are available on each website. It will give you a taste of what to expect there. It also gives you an opportunity to talk to admission officers, take your candidate fitness assessment test (CFA), and to determine if you can meet the rigorous expectations. There is a cost to the camp, and you have to be selected.

2) **Take the ACT and SAT test early and often.** Get the minimum requirements for admissions. (Read the SAT and ACT preparation chapter to prepare yourself.)

3) **Continually improve yourself academically and physically.**

4) **Schedule an interview with your liaison officer.** Every state has someone in your area to meet with. This is available on the provided websites. After you express an interest in attending an academy, they will contact you. It is CRUCIAL you keep in communication with the liaison officer by showing continuous attention and updating them regularly. There are only a few spots from each state. The squeaky wheel (so to speak) will always be the one the liaison officers push through. If it's between you and another student with the same GPA and qualifications, the student who shares a stronger relationship with the liaison officer will likely be the one recommended for an appointment.

5) **A quick note concerning email addresses:** Change your address if it is inappropriate. If you are unsure if it is inappropriate, ask your parents. Having an email address such as onehotchick@myemail.com or numberonestud@myemail.com is the wrong first impression to relay to a liaison officer, or anyone for that matter. It sets a poor example from the beginning.

Here is a sample introduction email.

INTRODUCTION EMAIL

Lieutenant Colonel Jones,

I wanted to introduce myself to you. My name is Anne Smith, and I am currently a sophomore in Cheyenne, Wyoming at Sawtooth High School. I am very interested in attending the United States Military Academy and serving my country.

I have attached my résumé, which delineates my academic, leadership, athletic, and volunteer activities. I would love to have your input concerning focal areas to improve my chance of being accepted into the academy. Would there be a good time for me to call you to discuss this? I would greatly appreciate your help and any direction you can give me. Also, if there are any informational events in the area that you feel I should attend, I would appreciate hearing about those as well.

Thank you very much for your time. I look forward to meeting you in the near future.

Sincerely,
Anne Smith
asmith@allemail.com
555-555-5555

6) **Make sure you are keeping an up-to-date résumé throughout high school.** You will need it when you apply for nominations, and it will make it much easier to fill out questionnaires. (Read about this in detail in the Résumé Building chapter.) When creating a résumé, be sure to separate it out by section and demonstrate continuity.

7) **Military academies will give you extra points on your application for employment**. If you can work on the weekends or over the summer, it will add value to your submission. You can be creative with employment opportunities, but it is a great plus.

8) **Look into Boys/Girls State for the summer before your senior year.**

9) **Practice for your candidate fitness assessment (CFA).** Check out the CFA expectations and practice the areas that they test. (See the CFA section in this chapter for more details.)

10) **Start the application process for your nomination your senior year.**
Meet all deadlines and know where to go for your nomination. (I will discuss this more later in this chapter.)

Websites for the Application Process

United States Military Academy (Army)
http://www.usma.edu/admissions/SitePages/Home.aspx
United States Air Force Academy (Air Force) http://www.academyadmissions.com/
United States Naval Academy (Navy) http://www.usna.edu/Admissions/

The admissions process includes a review of three major academic performance indicators.

1) SAT/ACT Scores
2) GPA and Determination
    o This is based on types of classes and the level taken.
3) High School Ranking

While each academy has different standards, they all seek similar individuals who possess exceptional academic achievement and leadership potential. Because they offer one of the most prestigious and respected academic programs available, academic admissions standards are high.

Course Recommendations [16]

To be academically competitive for an academy appointment, they recommend the following high school courses:

- Four years of English
- Four years of Math, with Coursework Through Precalculus and a Strong Background in Algebra and Trigonometry
- Four years of Lab Science
- Three years of Social Studies
- Two years of a Modern Foreign Language
- One year of Computer Study

The more advanced courses you take in high school 1) the easier it will be once you are there and 2) the more competitive your application will be.

For SAT and ACT scores, the academies use superscoring (see the SAT and ACT chapters to get a more detailed explanation of this term), which is an awesome way to really bump up your score.

For a quick definition, superscoring is a process where colleges take your highest scores on each section of the ACT or SAT tests to give you a higher overall score. In other words, if you got a 25 on math one time you took the test, and another time you took it and got a 27, the school will take the 27. If you got a 20 on English once and a 30 another time, you will have the 27 and the 30 for your supers-scores. Things can change at the academies concerning superscoring, so it is important to verify on their websites at the time you conduct research.

The following requirements and allowances are all taken from the respective academy websites. Students who score lower will typically not be competitive for an appointment.

Air Force Academy [17]

SAT	Mid-50% Range	Mean
Critical Reading/Verbal	600–690	642
Math	630–700	672
ACT	**Mid-50% Range**	**Mean**
English	28–33	30
Reading	28–33	30
Mathematics	28–32	30
Science Reasoning	27–33	30

United States Military Academy [18]

ACT	Range 31-36	Range 26-30	Range 21-25	Range 16-20	Range 11-15	MEAN
English	38%	39%	44%	2%	0%	29
Math	34%	48%	44%	0%	0%	29
Science	27%	44%	28%	1%	0%	28
Reading	49%	34%	16%	2%	0%	30
Writing	18%	45%	32%	3%	0%	28
SAT	Range 700-800	Range 600-699	Range 500-599	Range 400-499	Range 300-399	MEAN
Reading	20%	44%	31%	4%	0%	627
Math	25%	50%	22%	2%	0%	645
Writing	15%	43%	36%	7%	0%	608

United States Naval Academy [19]

SAT Verbal	610–740
SAT Math	620–730
ACT English	26–32
ACT Math	27–31

Acceptance rates for military academies from *Forbes* Best Colleges [20]

Air Force Academy: 17%

Naval Academy: 9%

United States Military Academy: 10%

Ranking of military academies as of 2017 from *Forbes* Best Colleges*

Air Force Academy: 41

Naval Academy: 20

United States Military Academy: 24

*I want to stress that these rankings change each year. But consistently, these schools are always in the top fifty around the country.

Along with great grades, the academies want individuals of high moral character to further develop into future leaders of the various academies and our nation. The admissions process includes a qualitative review of character factors. Each applicant's character assessment consists of the following.

- **Admissions Liaison Officer Interview**
    - o You will meet with the officer to determine if you are a potential candidate for his or her recommendation.
    - o When you go to the interview, and any time you will be meeting your liaison officer, dress appropriately. A liaison officer told me he turned a student down before they even talked because the potential recruit was wearing a t-shirt and jeans and looked sloppy. This is the time to pull out a tie, suit, jacket, nice pantsuit, or dress. Dress for success!
    - o Keep in touch with your assigned officer often. Not weekly, but check in every time something changes positively, so you can update them. The liaison officer will be your advocate, so be sure to give them information that will make them want to recommend you.

- **Teacher's Evaluations**
    - o You need to facilitate three electronically submitted recommendations—these are separate from the nomination process.
    - o This will generally take place your junior school year, but you can ask your sophomore year teachers as well.

- **Writing Sample Submission**
    - o It will include questions such as: "Why do you want to attend the academy?" It will usually include three questions and a lengthy essay.

- **Personal Data Record Review**
    - o This include any past criminal violations. It's why staying out of trouble is critical. Any criminal record or violation can put your application in jeopardy.

- **Drug and Alcohol Abuse Certificate**
    - o This verifies that you do not use them. There also will be a drug test further along in the process.

o Sacrifices are made and decisions are important. It takes a full commitment to the process—and that means not being in the wrong place at the wrong time. My son who attended West Point never went to a party in high school. EVER. He did not want to be around alcohol and drugs. There were a few parties he heard about that were broken up and "minor consumption" tickets were issued. A few fights occurred. Drugs were taken and sold at these parties. If he had been there, who knows how that would have affected his application! If he was somewhere where he shouldn't have been, he could have been associated with what happened at these parties, even if he was not directly involved.

Extracurricular Activities

Participation in a variety of athletic and non-athletic high school activities is essential in preparing for any demanding program, and is a competitive factor in your application to an academy. Sustained participation and leadership is desirable. This includes leadership positions, such as captain of your baseball team, Student Council secretary, treasurer of Key Club, etc. Low participation in sanctioned or high school athletic and non-athletic extracurricular activities may result in a noncompetitive application. This is something you can, and should, be starting your freshmen year. Boy Scouts, school groups, varsity letters, and achievements in your sport(s) or activities are essential to making you "recruitable" and competitive. Club teams and outside sports are great opportunities and ways to fulfill the athletic expectations. Community service and involvement is crucial as well; they want to see a well-rounded individual.

Boys and Girls State chalks one up for leadership, if this is what you need for your application. It is also a great experience. Here is the website to find one in your area: http://www.boysandgirlsstate.org/

Qualifying Medical Exam

The Qualifying Medical Exam is an important hurdle. Passing it will get you one step closer to admission. This exam indicates your overall fitness and health for military duty. This is near the end of the process, after you are a potential candidate. You will receive a letter from the Department of Defense Medical Examination Review Board (DoDMERB). It will give you the location and date of your exam. You will be scheduled at a civilian medical facility or at an Army, Air Force, or Navy facility near your home. Afterward, DoDMERB will forward the test results to you. Along with this, you take an eye exam.

Candidate Fitness Assessment (CFA) [21]

The Candidate Fitness Assessment (CFA) was developed to measure and evaluate a candidate's potential to successfully complete the physical programs at the United States Naval Academy, United States Air Force Academy, and United States Military Academy.

The six test events of the CFA are administered consecutively in less than forty minutes. I want to point out that this is the current form of measurement for the CFA. However, the military can choose to change this. Be sure to check out the current CFA on website of the military academy you are applying to. Candidates should do their best on all six events, keeping in mind that the events sequentially produce a cumulative physical effect. In other words, after completing the first five events, it is doubtful that a candidate will score his or her best on the one-mile run, which is the last event.

This was considered during the development of the criterion-referenced standards that will be used to evaluate performance in each of the six events. Candidates' raw scores will be converted to scale scores (0–100 points) based upon their performance on each event. The 100-point maximum score, by event and gender, are listed in the table below. A candidate who achieves the 100-point level on any of the first five events should not attempt further repetitions, as it will not improve the score. In other words, if you maxed out on scoring, don't waste your efforts doing more. It will just tire you out without helping your score.

The CFA is an important component to determine if candidates can meet the physical rigors of military life. The test must be administered properly and standardized in order to accurately reflect a student's physical and motor fitness, and to be fair to all candidates. The CFA MUST be administered by a high school or prep school physical education teacher or commissioned officer (for military candidates). The test must also be administered according to the following directions in a single forty-minute time period. At the completion of testing, the administering official will submit the test scores via an emailed electronic module. I highly recommend having this done by someone you feel comfortable with. The whole process can be a bit stressful, but if you have your coach or PE teach administering the test, you will definitely feel better and more relaxed.

Event:	Basketball Throw	Pull-ups	Shuttle Run	Crunches	Push-ups	One-Mile Run
Male	102	18	7.8	95	75	5:20
Female	66	7	8.6	95	50	6:00

Maximum performance scores by event and gender are the same for all academies. You only have to take it once even if you are applying to multiple academies; the scores are transferable.

After you have done all of the above, as it pertains to the admissions process, then you wait. If you are a candidate, you will be given a portal for submitting forms, essays, and various requirements. Appointments are usually given in February or after—so plan for that. Be sure to have a backup plan! I have seen several students put all their eggs in one basket. Remember, the acceptance rate (for all of the academies) is between 9% and 17%, which means they are very competitive!

Prep School

A lot of times students are competitive candidates, except they are deficient in one area. Perhaps you scored a 24 in English on your ACT, but very highly everywhere else. Or you are being recruited for a sport but need a little bit of extra help academically to prepare you for the rigors of an academy. Prep school is an option you might be offered when you apply.

Prep schools are also very competitive, as there are only around 200 spots for these schools. Each of the academies have prep schools, and they offer wonderful opportunities for students to develop in school, learn a foundation for the military, and bridge the gap before attending the regular academy. The admissions process is not different than applying for the academies. However, you have to be selected by the admissions board, the same way you would if you were applying for the academy itself. If you are offered this option instead of an appointment to an academy, know that you are among a select few the school believes in. They will be preparing you for the following year. During your prep school year, you will have to do the application process all over again, even retaking the SAT and ACT one more time, as well as the nomination process. This can be very deflating to some students, but if you truly want to attend an academy and prep school is an option, it is well worth it. Many student have said it was a great year for them, helping them adapt to the rigors of the academies, as well as getting acclimated to military life. It allows students to make great friends before attending the regular academy, and it also allows a nice transition from a civilian to soldier. I love this option for students, and it was one that my son Jordan accepted. It made his experiences at the actual academy extremely fulfilling and helped prepare him for it.

Prep schools focus on the academic, military, and athletic aspect of the military academies. The courses you will take will be limited to only a few, again, to help you prepare for the academy. They will generally be focused on math and English, and you will also have some military classes that will help you get acclimated. A big portion of the prep schools are recruited athletes, but there are also students there who are soldiers or who are just missing a small piece of the admissions expectations.

The school will also help you with the application process when you have to apply again in the fall. A "prepster" will start the process at the school, as well as take the SAT and ACT onsite. If you are an athlete, you will be competing against other academy prep schools and smaller colleges. Not all sports are recruited at the prep schools, but there are several they recruit (to help athletes prepare for the academics.) Football, basketball, soccer, cross country, track and field, lacrosse, and wrestling are the sports generally recruited for or are offered at the prep schools.

The application process for the military academies is lengthy and, overall, it takes years to fulfill. You MUST be on task from the beginning of your high school career if this is where you want to land. It is a process that requires patience, and it involves a true desire to make the commitment to not only attend an academy, but to serve our country after you graduate as well. You can see that the commitment and dedication leading up to attending an academy requires this same dedication. You need to keep a faithful stance on what you do, how hard you work, and your adherence to the process. Remember that you will be serving our country as an officer, and that is a position of power and leadership. Those involved in the admissions process want to know that you can maintain this level of obligation and that you will be able to withstand the rigors of the school and the service expectation afterwards. There are many steps to this process, but if you are one of the fortunate ones to attend an academy, the hard work it took you to get to that first day of reception is only the beginning. They are all challenging schools, both academically and physically, but they are also places where you will have some of the most incredible experiences, opportunities, and friendships that you will ever encounter.

7

Determining Which College to Attend

THIS CAN BE A challenge for many families and it can be, quite frankly, overwhelming. That totally makes sense. There are thousands of schools to pick from all over the country, how do you decide where to apply? Then the big question is, "Which one do you decide to attend?" There are many questions and ways to narrow down your options when you are making that decision, and there are questions you should ask yourself in advance. I worked with a student who wanted to go to a particular school very much but didn't realize that the school was extremely expensive and didn't offer his major, which pulled it out of the mix for him. Asking and answering these questions will help you make choices that are based on facts, not just emotions. Here are some important questions to be asking:

1. **Do you want to go to a school in city (urban setting) or rural (suburban)?**
   Do you want a large or small school?

2. **GPA/ACT expectations.**
   Do you have the grades for the school? What is the minimum ACT/SAT score? Do you fit in the parameters and expectations of the school?

3. **What do you wish to study?**
   Does the school offer a fitting program? (Things change, but you need to explore this to point yourself in the right direction.)

4. **How expensive is the school?**

5. **Will you have scholarships and financial aid at this school?**
   What is the typical aid offered at the school?

6. **Geographical preference.**
   South, West, North, Midwest, East, etc. Are you open to out-of-state colleges?

7. **What are the application costs?**

8. When are the application deadlines?

9. What is the ranking by major?

Remember, if you go to an in-state college, you pay in-state tuition. For cost purposes, it can be the least expensive option. But if you can swing a scholarship (academic, athletic, or for various talents or specialties), it can be worth going to an out-of-state school. Most colleges offer financial aid, so include that when you're determining your options.

There are some great search engines to help you with researching and seeking out schools, which is the first step you want to take in this venture.

https://bigfuture.collegeboard.org/college-search
http://www.collegedata.com/
https://www.niche.com/colleges/?degree=4-year&sort=best
https://www.usnews.com/best-colleges
http://www.prepscholar.com (This site gives you average of GPAs and ACT/SAT scores for the schools of interest.)

The search engine I use quite often is: https://portal.idcis.intocareers.org/. Even though it is an Idaho-sponsored site, it is useful for students around the county. It is an easy-to-navigate tool for education searches. First, you head to the "Just Browsing" section on the opening page, then select the tab that best describes you. Your choices will be CIS Junior, CIS High School, CIS College, or CIS Adult. After you make your selection, under the "Education" tab at the top, you will select the "Where Can I Study?" drop down. From there, you search "US Colleges and Universities" for the schools you wish to view. You can either select schools by state or by name. It is extremely user-friendly and a nice one-stop-shopping website for your purposes.

Once you select a school or a state on the left hand side of the page, you can search the demographics, admissions expectations, type of community (urban or rural), see how many students attend (is it a large or small school?), majors offered, cost and financial aid, and more. I LOVE this search engine and recommend it to everyone doing a college search. If this site does not provide an answer to your questions, it also provides you a direct link to the college website for further information. I recommend you always go directly to the site to gain a more extensive view of majors and minors, but this is a great initial option and tool for researching colleges.

Selecting a Major

This can be a tough one. When selecting a major, you might not select something as an incoming college freshman that you will stick with as a junior or senior. But generally, when you do choose another major than your original selection, you will pick something that is already being offered at your school. So, more often than not, switching majors will take place within the same school. With that in mind, if you narrow it down to one or two majors as potential areas of interests, it makes your college list smaller. For example, if I wanted to attend a school that offers quantitative math as a major, but I am also interested in the possibility of majoring in finance, I would look for schools that offered both options. That way I could choose to double major or switch later in my college career.

If you are not sure what you want to major in, meet with the guidance counselor at your high school. They will help with narrowing down some options, using a series of questions and aptitude tests.

Once you have made that determination, I recommend a Google search of the best colleges in that field. I like the US News search engine, as it has a lot of other information. Also, what may not be the top school in the country overall may have the best particular program in the country. For example, UNLV (University of Nevada Las Vegas) is ranked #129 in the country for schools, but their hospitality management major is #3 in the country. It is important to look more specifically for the major you are interested in, not only the school ranking.

After you have found the search engine you prefer, make a graph with the names and locations of the schools (see the graph in this chapter). You can create a graph on your own and fill in the information that is important to you, but I started one with general areas and criteria for school determination. Look at the questions that are most important to you, and use them as your guidelines.

If you are having trouble locating a specific fact about a school, just Google it. For example, if you are looking for "average GPA for Dartmouth College," you type that in the search bar. If you're looking to see what the "Average SAT scores are for Duke," you simply type that. Pretty easy!

The spreadsheet takes a little time, but it's an easy visual comparison of the schools that interest you. For parents, this is a wonderful activity to work on with your student. You can assign areas for them to take on, and then you can do some yourself. This will help them take ownership of the process, and they are more likely to have buy-in and a vested interest in the plan. It also helps with decision-making when you are able to look at the schools side by side. It can make decisions easier when you are purely looking at the facts in one place.

Another rule of thumb is to pick a few schools from these three categories:

Reach Schools

These schools will be challenging to get into—but may be your dream school. I would go into the application process with reasonable expectations. Understand that getting in isn't the only thing you need to consider. It is STAYING there and being able to meet the academic requirements. Money may also be a factor in a reach school. If this is the reason, remember there are scholarship opportunities available at many schools, as well as financial aid. Keep that in mind before ruling them out or putting them on the reach list.

Meet Schools

You already meet all of the academic requirements for a meet school, they offer your major, and they are within your cost range. Don't always let cost be a determining factor when putting a school on this list; it is important to look at both cost and aid offered. For example, the cost may be $40,000 in tuition, but they are offering you $20,000 in financial aid. Another school may cost $32,000 in tuition but offers no financial aid. So don't allow the initial sticker shock to steer you away from a school at this time. Look into what they are offering to determine which bracket to put each school in.

Safe Schools

These are in-state schools or schools that offer a solid education and you "safely" meet the academic requirements to get into this school. They may also qualify as safe schools for financial reasons. You meet the academic requirements for these schools, and they are safe because of this criteria; you know you can get in.

Let's look at the chart, so you can see how to build it. For example purposes, we will use a high school student named Sally. Sally would like to be an engineer but is not sure which kind of engineer she wants to be. She lives in Nevada and is willing to go anywhere in the country for school, but would prefer an urban setting and to attend a large school. She has a 3.6 GPA and received a 27 on her ACT.

Here is a great way to start breaking down and understanding the questions you need to ask yourself when narrowing down your college search. Let's let Sally guide us through the chart as we go along.

School Name	Meets, Reach, Safe	Location/ Setting/ Size	GPA/ACT	Major Offered	Tuition Room and Board	Aid*	Cost after Aid	Application Deadline	Cost of App. *+	Ranking for Program
U of Illinois	Reach	Champagne-Urbana/ Suburban/ Very large	3.83/28	17 Engineering Options	$28,026 $11,000	71% $13,146	$25,880	Jan. 2	$50	#1
Purdue	Meets	Lafayette/ Suburban Very large	3.68/27	15 Engineering Options	$28,010 $3,873	83% $13,155	$18,728	Nov. 1 **Early Action	$60	#2
U of Texas	Reach	Austin/ Urban/Very large	3.71/29	21 Engineering Options	$35,796 $10,070	68% $11,685	$34,181	Mar. 15	$75	#7
Virginia Tech	Meets	Blackburg/ Small Town Rural/ Large	3.66/27	19 Engineering Options	$27,306 $8,564	64% $18,985	$16,885	Mar. 1 and Nov. 1 for ***Early Decision	$60	#8
Arizona State	Safe	Tempe/ Urban/Very large	3.49/25	17 Engineering Options	$25,784 $11,386	71% $15,885	$21,285	Oct. 3 ***Early Decision Nov. 28 Priority Consider-ation	$50	#22
U of Minnesota	Reach	Twin Cities/ Urban/Very large	3.73/28	16 Engineering Options	$24,378 $9,314	78% $13,052	$20,640	Dec. 15th	$55	#4
U of Florida	Reach	Gainesville/ Suburban/ Very large	3.73/28	14 Engineering Options	$26,755 $9,910	99% $12,522	$24,143	Mar. 15th	$30	#24
UNLV Las Vegas	Safe	Las Vegas/ Urban/Large	3.25/23	10 Engineering Options	$6,277 None-Live at home	71% $11,207	$0	July 1st	$60	#151

*Aid is the percentage of students who receive aid. The percentage AND dollar figure should be examined. The dollar amount is great (and the cost may look fantastic as a whole), but how many students actually receive this level of aid? You will want to know when researching this statistic. This factor will also give you a snapshot of the schools regarding aid and how much is actually given to students. When researching this, go onto the schools website and find the school's search engine. From there, type in "Net

Price Calculator." It will ask you a few questions regarding your family income, and it will also give you a ballpark figure of what the cost of tuition is, with any aid from the school calculated in. This is a rough estimate and doesn't always take into consideration scholarships you may be offered, but it is a great starting point on cost. Do this for all of the schools you are researching.

Early Action is an opportunity to apply early to the school and to find out earlier if you are accepted. The deadline will be earlier than the regular deadline for the school. If a school offers it and it is not binding (see **Early Decision), I recommend you do it at that time. It gives you the opportunity to find out if you are accepted early enough to start making decisions earlier in your senior year of high school. It also gives you opportunities for scholarships (some are offered first come, first served), and it also helps you determine if it is within your budget.

The Ivy League schools only allow you to apply Early Action to one of their schools. However, you can still apply for regular admissions at the others. But, the upside is that it's not binding if you are accepted. My son applied Early Action to Harvard, and MIT was trying to get him to apply Early Action there (which would have negated his application to Harvard, his first choice). Most schools don't have these restrictions but it is important to understand and know each schools requirements regarding this otherwise it can negate an application.

***Early Decision is binding. Stanford is an example. If you apply for **Early Decision**, it is binding. This means that if you are accepted, you HAVE to go to that school unless you can't afford to go. This would be very important to know since Stanford might not be your top choice. I would apply Early Decision to your TOP school but also take into consideration your likelihood of getting in. If you are applying to Stanford, and you have a 3.2 with a 23 ACT score, the likelihood is not great that you would be accepted. (It would be a reach school unless you are a highly skilled athlete.) If you have an opportunity to apply to another school where you have a better chance of getting in (a meets or safe school), I would recommend using it for that college. You can still apply to your reach school, in this case Stanford, but you would apply through the regular admissions process.

*+ Application fees are non-refundable, so before you commit to applying to ALL the schools on your list, keep in mind it can add up very fast. From this list, you will start with four to six schools. I recommend one or two reach schools, two or three meets schools, and one or two safe schools. Definitely pick more meets schools than reach or safe schools. This gives you a better selection when the time comes to make a decision.

When picking a school, there may need be flexibility concerning some of your personal requirements. For example, if you look at University of Illinois on Sally's chart, it would be a reach school based on her GPA/SAT/ACT scores. But it is #1 in the country for engineering, so it's a great option if she were to be accepted. However, it's in a suburban setting, so Sally would have to decide—if everything else fell into place—whether or not she would forgo her desire to attend a school in an urban setting. Is there a nearby city, so she would be happy living there for four years? That's where visiting the schools comes into play after you determine your "finalists." But for now, put everything on the chart that is important to you.

You may add a column for a sport. If you are a huge basketball fan, that may be important to you. Do they have a basketball team? Or you could be looking at being recruited for a sport and will need to ensure they offer it and scholarships for that sport (if it is a DII or DIII school, they will not); this could be another column. You can personalize the spreadsheet based on your preferences.

Let's look at the chart again. Based on what Sally is seeking, a few schools meet her criteria as a large school in an urban setting. However, she will have to determine a few factors:

1. **Cost**

   Out-of-state can be very expensive.

2. **GPA and ACT**

   Sally's are great, but they may not be high enough for a few of the schools.

3. **Transfer Opportunities**

   Sally may opt to attend UNLV for two years, beef up her GPA, save some money, and then transfer to one of the other schools with a better engineering program. The first two years cover prerequisite courses, so this could be a cost-effective option, as well as an opportunity to stretch herself, improve her grades, and shoot for the other schools. (Don't rule transferring out as an option.)

4. **I would recommend Purdue.**

   If Sally were dead set on attending an out-of-state school, and it has been determined she can afford it, I think Purdue is her best option. Even though it is in a suburban setting, it still meets most of her other criteria. The school also has a very high percentage rate for financial aid and a great engineering program.

As you can see, there are several criteria to consider before applying, but if you narrow it down to the reach, meets, and safe school categories, you won't be caught without acceptance to a school. Receiving acceptance letters gives you a boost in self-esteem, and it also gives you a gauge to see where you fit in.

The question after starting the application that generally comes up is, "Which school do you choose if you get into several schools?" That is where visitation can help with making comparisons, which we will discuss later in this chapter. But before that, when looking at the schools on paper, you should look at what makes sense. A student with a 3.2 who received a 22 on their ACT will not meet the academic minimum for an Ivy League college. When students apply to those types of schools and ONLY those schools, I think they are wasting their money, getting their hopes up, putting their eggs in one basket, and—most importantly—not being realistic. As a parent, this is not a time to give false hope to your son or daughter because this is their future. Talk to the counselors at school, talk to other parents, talk to your student, make a realistic plan, and start working towards it. That isn't to say you shouldn't apply to one of the schools that appears out of reach if you really want to give it a shot. But based on academic requirements, you need to have realistic expectations. Look at all the aspects of the schools and find those that fit into all the categories you desire. They will be different for each student, depending on their academic achievements. If you are a 4.0 student, your reach school will have higher academic expectations than a 3.5 student.

School Visits

I am asked about school visits almost every time I work with a family or student. They ask if they need to visit the schools, and my answer to that is "maybe." I equate this to buying a house. You can research online and look for the best neighborhoods, schools, and the lowest crime rates, but at the end of the day, you will want to visit the house and neighborhood to see how it feels. "Can you see yourself living there?" You (if you are the student) are spending the next four years at this school; it is important for it to feel like home. If you have several options to pick from, this is a wonderful way to determine which one you will want to attend. It also gives you a great opportunity to talk to the counselors there in person, and a chance to see the campuses and the students who you would attend school with.

However, let's say you are starting to look at ten to fifteen schools. Can you imagine the expense and time it would take to visit all of them? It would be a daunting and extremely expensive task. I suggest the following:

1. **Start Researching**

   Learn everything you can about the ten to fifteen schools online first.

2. **Geographic Concerns**

   From these schools, determine geographically which are closest to you and also closest to each other.

3. **Pick the Top Ones in Each Category First**

   One from each: reach, meets, and safe schools. Start with these schools first. There are overnight visits at most schools, where a student can spend the night in the dorms and attend a social function or a sporting event—or even attend classes. This is a wonderful way for potential students to get a taste of the atmosphere. One of the students I worked with went to several schools on visitation, and he was sold on one before he even got to the school. He was sure he would go there. However, when he actually arrived, he was very surprised about how it felt. He spoke with the counselors at the school and realized that another one of the schools (that he had discounted initially) had a much better program in his area of focus. Once he visited that school, he changed where he wanted to attend. He said it felt like home to him, and he knew that he could see himself there for the next four years.

4. **If Possible, Bring a Parent or Adult with You**

   When you start the tour, they (parents) can ask the questions you, as a student, may not think of. If that is not possible, parents, make a list of questions that include things such as cost, scholarships, crime in the area and campus, housing, food plans, etc. These are important factors that students may not think to question.

5. **Have Realistic Expectations about Distance**

   For the schools that are further away geographically, be practical. Look at realistic expectations of attending the schools, as well as the desire to attend them. Maybe you can plan a vacation around that area or region, where you can drive to the school to visit on a day trip? Also, these can be spread out over junior and senior year, so there isn't a rush to go on all of the visitations at once.

6. Wait Until You're Accepted

Another option is to wait until you get acceptance letters before planning visits. This is the most economical way to visit schools, but it can feel last minute to many people. My advice is to visit the schools that you can drive to junior year or the summer before your senior year. You may even decide not to apply to some of the schools you visit for various reasons, or if these schools move down on your wish list after visitation.

That is my yes answer on visiting schools. On the other hand, I do believe you can make the best of any place you attend. Anywhere can feel like home if you work at it and try. But starting college is a huge change in itself, and if anything can be done to facilitate a streamlined transition process, such as visiting the school beforehand to make it more familiar, it will lead to an easier and smoother transition. Finances may not make it easy to visit schools. If that is the case, I recommend doing as many online virtual tours as possible and wait until you are down to the last few schools in the spring of your senior year to visit.

By using the chart I have outlined for you, visiting some of the schools, having realistic expectations, and selecting colleges that are reach, meets, and safe schools, will make the process of deciding which school you will ultimately attend much easier for you.

8

The Nitty Gritty of Applications (and How Are You Going to Pay for This?)

YOU HAVE NOW NARROWED your search down to ten to fifteen schools based on your personalized graph and determined which ones are your reach, meets, and safe schools.

Now you may be asking, how many of these schools do you actually apply to? This will largely depend on how many schools you want to pay the application fee for. Remember, these fees are typically $50 to $100 each—and NONREFUNDABLE. You can request a fee waiver from the schools if you have financial need, but other than that, it can definitely add up quickly.

My recommendation is to apply to seven schools at most, making sure you have at least two in each reach, meets, and safe schools, with the extra one being in the meets category. This way, you have put it out there in all areas and can feel good about giving it a shot for the reach schools without putting all of your eggs in one basket. You are not only playing it safe but are also being wise about your selection process.

I also think it's okay for parents to help with the application process. Sit down with your student and help them walk through the process. Answer questions about the application. The process can be very daunting for students to do alone. There is a lot of information to absorb and decisions for a seventeen or eighteen-year-old to make going forward. If you, as a parent, can help with the fundamental parts of the application (name, address, basic stats, etc.), it allows them time to focus on the essays and decisions.

I know this is something you will have to determine as a family, based on what you feel in your own home. But I have heard so many things from parents such as, "My child didn't take the time to fill out the application, so they aren't going to college." There is a difference between a student who is truly not invested in the process (or even attending college) and those who are incredibly gifted, but need a little hand-holding and prodding. One student I worked with was an extreme procrastinator—an incredible student, but I finally told her mom to just set aside a time to help her daughter fill out the applications. This helped a lot. The student is now midway through a very successful college career at NYU. She even studied abroad and has done some incredible things at her school. There is plenty of time for students to do things completely on their own, but this can be a process that parent and child can share. I found this time in my children's lives to be very collaborative since we (as parents) were paying for some of the schooling and my children were looking to me for direction. I was able to remind them along the way that they were going to school for educational opportunities and ultimately a job afterwards. We shared great teachable moments together.

Sometimes kids can be shortsighted. They see the next four years instead of the next forty. It is up to us, as parents to help them with these decisions. I don't want to penalize my child if they are struggling with the application process. There is enough on their plate in terms of changes and decisions! Some of you may disagree with this point, and that is completely your choice, but my kids have all turned out to be responsible, independent people. They do everything on their own now, and they did as soon as they attended college. I just knew they needed the help before they got there. Sometimes it's just about helping them set aside time to fill out the applications and assisting them. Helping my kids understand time management and the importance of deadlines was a great outcome for all of us.

This does NOT include doing their essays though. They can ask you to proofread them, and you can offer suggestions and correct grammatical errors before submitting, but you will be doing a disservice to your children if you do the heavy lifting for them on the essays.

Once you determine which schools you are applying to, go to that school's website to apply (unless they have a common application, which we will discuss later.)

Check for deadlines and note them on your graph, on a separate document, or on a calendar.

When you are ready to apply, be sure to have these handy:

- **Most Recent Transcript**
- **Highest ACT/SAT Scores**
- **Résumé**
  - o You upload or copy specifics from it.

- **Letters of Recommendations**
  - o These are discussed later in this chapter.

- **Parent's Financial Information**
  - o You'll need it for any related questions that may arise. (This is for determining need for financial aid. It is not an official determination at this time but can give you a good preview of what you might receive. Remember to use the net price calculator discussed in the previous chapter.)

- **Essays**
  - o Each college is different. I think it is a good idea to jump onto the application section and view the topics. Get started early because each school might have a different topic. If there are similar essay topics, it is great to be able to repurpose them; that way you aren't reinventing the wheel.

If the school has the application through their website, just complete it and pay at the end when prompted. You typically set up an account that allows you to come back later if needed. Keep note of the passwords and usernames to help expedite the process when you come back to them. It isn't a bad idea for you to call the Admissions Department a week after you have submitted the application to be sure that they have received all the information needed. I have run across this a time or two where Admissions didn't receive everything, and it was a good thing we called! Sometimes these departments are too busy to send an email out, or you may be very rushed to get them the information that they require. Make sure you send them everything they need within the requested timeframe.

Common Application

This application process is used by over 700 colleges across the country. It is basically one-stop shopping. You have the benefit of applying to several colleges using the one application. There are instances, though, where you will have supplemental or additional requests from the schools, so be sure to check those as you apply. They may require additional essays or letters of recommendations along with the "universal" or common application. You also have to pay the application fee separately for each school. But the benefit of filling out one application and just checking off the schools is a wonderful advantage.

You will need to create an account by logging into http://www.commonapp.org/ using your email and creating a password. Then you select the schools where you wish to apply. There is a "requirement tracker" for all schools, so you can see the specific needs of the individual schools. The site has a downloadable worksheet as well. It's a very nice to-do list and a way to keep track of what each school needs and what you have already sent in.

You will then be prompted to provide basic information about yourself such as grades, scores, extracurricular activities, and your parent's information. You can start this process, put in what you have available, and then come back to it, using your login information. It's very simple and streamlined. When looking for applications on specific school websites, you may be directed to the "Common Application" link, so you will be able to know right away that the school participates in the program.

Early Action vs. Early Decision

I discussed this a bit in earlier chapters, but (so you have it readily available in this chapter, as well while you are applying), I felt it was worth repeating. These terms were very confusing to me initially. If you don't understand them, you could make a big mistake when applying to a school.

Early Decision plans are binding, so a student who is accepted as an Early Decision applicant **must** attend the college that they are applying to.

Here is a quick reference guide for **Early Decision**. It is important to point out that if you are unable to afford the school, they will not require you to attend.

- You can apply early (usually in November) to your first-choice college.
- You may receive an admission decision from the college well in advance of the usual notification date (typically by December).
- You agree to attend the college if accepted and offered a financial aid package that is considered adequate by your family.
- **You can only apply to one college using Early Decision.**
- You may apply to other colleges under regular admission plans.
- You will withdraw all other applications if accepted by Early Decision.
- Send a nonrefundable deposit well in advance of May first.

On the other hand, Early Action plans are nonbinding, so students receive an early response to their application but do not have to commit to the college until the normal reply date of May first. Early Action allows for these benefits:

- You can apply earlier than usual.
- You will receive an admission decision early in the admission cycle (usually in January or February).
- You will be able to consider the acceptance offer, but you do not have to commit upon receipt of offer.
- **You can only apply to one college using Early Action.**
- You can apply to other colleges under regular admission plans.
- You will give the college of choice a decision no later than May first which is the national response date.

The key to remember is you can only apply to one **Early Decision** or **Early Action** school, not both, so the school for either one should be your **top choice school.**

For example: you REALLY want to go to Yale, and they are an **Early Decision** school. This means that you can only apply to **Yale Early Decision**, but you can apply to other schools using the regular admissions process. Or you can apply to a school that is **Early Action** (only that school) and the others using the regular process. So either one **Early Action** or one **Early Decision**—not both—and all the other schools will follow the regular admissions process.

Some positives and negatives to these selections.

Positives

- You find out early either way, reducing the stress of waiting.
- You can plan for what and where you are going. You have more time to prepare after being accepted, including time to look for housing and otherwise plan.
- It will save the time and expense of submitting multiple applications.
- You will be able to look at other options and apply elsewhere if you are not accepted.

Negatives

- If you do not get accepted, it can feel like you wasted the early application option on that school.

- Most colleges do not notify **Early Decision** and **Early Action** applicants of admission until December fifteenth. Because of the usual deadlines for applications, there are only two weeks left to send in other applications if you are rejected.

  I recommend preparing other applications as you wait to receive admission decisions from your first-choice college. You do not have to submit them yet, but if and when you must, they are ready at a push of a button.

- Senioritis. Some students who gain early acceptance into a college may feel that they have no reason to work hard for the rest of the year (since they are already accepted). Students who apply early should know that colleges may pull back offers should grades drop during the rest of their senior year. Be sure to finish strong!

I recommend determining if an Early Decision or Early Action option is appropriate by researching extensively. If you know the school is your number one choice, early application is a great option. I also recommend it to students who have determined that they meet the academic expectations. If it's within your reach, you should apply. If the school is a strong match for you, and you meet or exceed the profile for ACT/SAT scores, GPA, and class rank, this is a solid choice for you.

However, I usually do not recommend Early Decision and Early Action for students who haven't researched colleges and may be applying early to avoid the stress of the process. I also don't recommend it for students who don't meet the academic requirements of the school. If it's a serious long shot, it will be a waste of time that could be spent on better opportunities.

Many students I work with believe applying early means competing with fewer applicants and increasing their chances for acceptance, though this is not always the case. Some of the Ivy League schools have a higher percentage of students accepted during the Early Decision process, though it could be related to meeting the academic rigors of the school.

These are all important things to weigh in on when determining your options. I think it is a decision that needs to be considered, then decided. But generally, I think applying to one school early, if it's the one you want and within your reach, is a good plan.

Letters of Recommendations

These are almost always requested by colleges, and they are a wonderful way for the Admissions Office to get a glimpse of you from other people's perspectives.

I recommend asking the following people for letters.

- **Teachers**
- **Coaches**
- **Group Leads**
    - o Work with Boy Scouts, Girl Scouts, 4H Leaders, advisors for extracurricular groups, or Honor Society advisors.
- **Principal or Vice Principal**
- **Employers**

It's important to select people with whom you have a good rapport. I also recommend asking the individuals in person first. Then follow up with an email that gives direction on where and how the letter needs to be submitted. Some applications must be sent electronically, so be sure to have that information available for them. I also recommend including the résumé of your accomplishments with the follow up email to help them with writing the letter. Most people you ask to write recommendation letters for you do not know all the things that you do! This is a great opportunity to help them determine what can and should be included in the letter, and it also helps them expand their content to include things that will be important to a college. I have heard from several students that the teachers they sent their résumés to had no idea they did so much—outside of not only the classroom, but also the school! This gives the person you are asking a broader view of you to draw from.

When following up, be sure they know the deadline—and give them enough time to meet it. They are busy people, and you want to honor their time. I recommend asking for these letters at the beginning of the school year because semester-end seems to coincide with the application due date timeframe. You don't want a teacher to write a letter at the last-minute or feel rushed. On most of the applications that require an electronic version of the letter, it shows you if the school has received it. I also recommend requesting a copy of the letter of recommendation to use for scholarships. That way you don't have to ask anyone for another letter; you can reuse the same one.

Essays

Most applications will require an essay. This is a very important part of the process and can definitely be the most stressful part of the whole application. But here is where you can draw upon your own life experiences, challenges, and highlights—and even people around you that have had an impact on your life.

I always tell students to allow their true feelings to come through in the essay. It can be hard to make yourself vulnerable or expose how you feel or think, but this can be a great opportunity to let the college admissions board see who you really are, and it can make the difference when decision time comes around. Many times the essays ask you to share things about experiences that have molded you or people who have made a difference in your life. Do not be generic.

Ask Yourself Some of These Questions

- **What hardships have you had to overcome?**
  How did you do it, and what did you learn from it?

- **If looking at someone you admire, why do you admire them?**
  What is it about them that you want to emulate? Are they a role model and why? How have they impacted you and others in your community or family?

- **What difference/impact would you make at their college?**
  What have you done in your current community/how can that translate into the future? What do you want to do at their school when you get there? Remember, colleges don't want you sitting in your room studying 24/7; they want to know you will make an impact on their college and community. They want you to be involved and engaged at the school. How will you do that? What will you give back or start at the college that would be beneficial to other students and people there? This is twofold because it gives you an opportunity to highlight the things you have done already—and also expand upon it at a college level. If you started a fundraising drive for a group in your high school, how can you do the same at the college level? If you are an editor for your yearbook in high school, write about how you want to work on the college newspaper concerning current events and their impact on students. Think about your current world and how it can fold over to the future and to college!

- **Favorite Book/Movie**

  This is one that can seem very easy, but I am thinking colleges do not want to hear about your favorite Harry Potter movie. This is one where you would look to a thought-provoking book or movie—something that had more meaning and purpose or affected you—and why it did. However, there is room for a lot of creativity! You may remember that *Charlotte's Web* was the first book you ever read and write about how it made you feel. Maybe there was a childhood event that you associate with that book. Be creative, but also try to be thought-provoking. Do not pick this essay (if you have a choice of subjects) just because it seems easy.

Be yourself, but be creative. Think like a person who looks at hundreds of applications a day. What makes yours different (in a good way)? What sets your essay apart from other applicants?

I remember when my son David was heading over to Harvard, and he was getting set up with housing. They asked that the parents send an essay to the school describing their child. This was used to place them with roommates, as well as a counselor (or mentor) for their freshman year to help them get acclimated. I sent a three-page essay describing David in great detail and how I felt about him leaving. I described what kind of person he was and what kind of friend he was to those around him. I put in the essay that he was so friendly that he "could make friends in a paper bag."

Later, after I sent it in, I seriously questioned what I wrote, thinking that this was "Harvard" and I should have sounded more proper, not so frivolous. I thought it was too "real." After it was sent in, I worried and stressed that he was going to be put with some strange kids, and I was responsible for starting him off on the wrong foot. Well, when we did receive placement for his counselor during his freshman year, he was assigned the dean of the freshman class. My first thought was, "Great, it was because of my stupid comments and details on my essay!" I thought that they must be worried about him, thanks to me! Well, I went to the school a few months after he started there, and the dean wanted to meet me. I was very nervous about meeting him.

One of the first things the dean said to me was how much he enjoyed the essay and especially the "friend in a paper bag" comment I made about David. I couldn't believe it! I was shocked that he 1) remembered and 2) LIKED what I said! He said it made him chuckle! 3) He said he picked David as one of his students because he wanted to get to know him, as he sounded like someone he wanted to meet. That dean turned out to be an incredible mentor to David all through his college years and a great friend of the family to all of us. I visited him almost every time I was in Boston. This was a bit of an epiphany for me going forward, especially when I work with students. It made me realize that when writing an essay, sometimes exposing yourself, your feelings (and even vulnerabilities) can really open the admissions panel to something that is real and true, and it can tell them a story about who you are. It could be the very thing the board is looking for. So, do not be afraid to open up! You have a lot to share, and this is not a time to hold back. Be you—and let them see who you are. Let them know your story.

I recently worked with a student on her essays, and she is a very gifted writer. Her essays flowed and were incredibly interesting and passionate. But one of the things that resonated in her writing was a clear political lean in a particular direction. This brings up a very important part of the essay process. Try your best to be neutral on a position or topic. This can be difficult when you have very strong feelings towards a particular thought or current event. You never know who is looking at your essay, and if they would be swayed on a decision based on a particular bent that they have. This is not to say that you shouldn't have strong opinions or thoughts, but when writing your essay, work towards offering something that anyone from any walk of life, religion, political view, race, sex, etc., would not be offended by. Keep very divisive current events out of the essay.

I'm not saying that those on the admissions board would ever rule out a student because of what they write, but I believe in caution. Use this opportunity as a platform for your writing style and ability to speak to ALL people. Human nature being what it is, someone may have a strong opinion or feeling based on personal events in their lives. They might not be able to help but draw a negative opinion about you.

In addition, the admissions board will be looking for students who are inclusive, passionate, and worldly—not divisive. If you want to write about a particular hot topic and you are set on it, I recommend that you write from both points of view. Don't come to a conclusion about what you feel or think about it, just present the facts from both sides. This allows you to demonstrate your ability to listen and see what others see, whether or not you agree with them. You are simply presenting a discussion and making observations based on what others may believe or think.

I also recommend having someone else, even a few people, read over your essay(s) before you submit them to make any corrections on grammar or structure, as well as content. I worked with one young man who was incredibly gifted, smart, kind, and talented. But his essay was very stilted and unemotional the first go-around. It lacked depth, and it did not capture who he really was. I had him rewrite it several times. The last one was absolutely beautiful and truly gave a brilliant picture of him and what a wonderful young man he is. He was accepted into a great school and was also offered admissions into several of the Ivy League schools.

Another important thing when writing an essay: You are instructed to write as essay with a specific word count (for example: 100 words or less or 500 words or less). Do not go over on this! Doing so can actually disqualify you from the application and those on the admission board love it when you are under the word count as they are reading a lot of essays! On some of the essays, you will have no choice. It won't allow you to submit it if you do go over. However, if it gives you an option to submit it directly from Word or another source, be sure to stay within the guidelines.

Using active verbs will help you keep it within your word count.

For example:

Instead of writing, "Mom is sewing" write "Mom sewed."

It removes some of the small words. Also remove unnecessary words.

Instead of writing, "The thing I am most proud of during my high school career is participating in the chess club," write "I am proud of my participation in the chess club."

Proofreading is very important; several times in fact. The first go-around, do not worry about limiting it to the number count. Just write it all down, as you can pull out redundancies and correct it after—just get your initial thoughts down. When you are done, go over it and start pulling out unnecessary words and sentences that you do not need, and replace sentences using active verbs, etc. This will help pull it into the structure of whatever work expectation they have, but it also helps to keep the content of the essay intact. Have someone else proofread it, which will give you a different perspective on it as well as catching any errors you may have missed.

Lastly, for essays, if you have a choice on the topic, pick one that you enjoy and have something to say about—not the one that seems the most challenging. It will come through in what you write. If you do not have a choice, start asking people for ideas when you're stumped. Talk to your school counselor, teachers, parents, etc. They can come up with different ways for you to think and write about it. It doesn't always have to be the obvious answer, and it can be a new creative way for you to look at something. As I said before, the admissions counselors are looking at TONS of applications. If you write something outside of the box, it can be what interests them—and sets you apart.

Weighted and Unweighted GPAs [25]

This comes up often, and I know that these can also be confusing terms. Some schools or scholarships will ask for one or the other. Simply put, **unweighted** is based on a scale of 0–4, with no allowances for AP or honors classes to help inflate your GPA. AP classes and some honors classes "**weigh**" their grades at a higher level since they are harder courses. So students who have an A (or what typically would be a 4.0), would receive a 5.0 in that class, thus increasing their overall GPA. That would then be included in your **weighted GPA**. I believe that a weighted is a better representation of a student's academic achievement, as it takes into account harder classes. However, when you are asked for one or the other, this will help you to determine which one they are looking for.

Last-Minute Charlies

This may be you!

You may be someone who leaves things to the last minute. If you are, I have to stress that this is something that can affect not only the next four years of your life, but possibly the REST of your life! If you neglect filling out applications on time, or you do not ensure everything is submitted properly, you may not just sacrifice your first choice. You might not be attending college at all! This is where I recommend parents help, as this is a time with deadlines that can impact many things. I find that a lot of times students procrastinate out of fear. A little bit of "analysis paralysis" sets in—and they just freeze. Here is where you, as parents, can talk them through it and work with them during the process. It also is wonderful for them to receive some good time management training from you, as I have mentioned before. Even if you set aside a specific time each day or week to have them fill out the applications, it helps keep them on track.

Scholarships

Scholarships are a wonderful way to supplement, or even pay for, college. The great thing about scholarships is that they do not have to be paid back—they are given and go towards paying for college. They can be given for many different things, but mostly they are given for a specific talent, skill, or academic achievement.

There are some strange ones out there as well. I have seen scholarships offered for students who are over 6'2". I know—crazy, but a true fact.

Take a look at these unusual scholarships, or just Google "unusual scholarships": https://www.scholarships.com/financial-aid/college-scholarships/scholarships-by-type/unusual-scholarships/

I also have seen scholarships offered that are based on creativity and your essay submission. Most are not just exclusive to an application, except those that are need-based, meaning those who have a financial need and those with a minimum household income. However, even need-based scholarships have a minimum expectation on GPA. As a rule, most scholarships require a minimum GPA and ACT/SAT score. This is where working hard throughout high school pays off. All the extracurricular activities you have participated in throughout your high school career can actually work towards helping you pay for your college. One of my sons completely paid for his freshman year of college with scholarship money he received!

The best thing to do when applying for scholarships is to start early and choose the scholarships you want to apply for. All of them have different deadlines and criteria. You may be able to use an essay for several of them, so planning ahead is the best thing when applying. I suggest starting a spreadsheet, similar to this one, to keep on track. The dates are not accurate, as they are purely for example purposes. When you find a scholarship you are interested in, put it in the chart to keep track of what it is, the dollar amount, the deadline, what type of scholarship it is, and if you have completed the application. Many of the websites have their own tracking system, but you may be going through several different websites, and this is a great way to avoid overlapping.

Scholarship	Website	Deadline Amount	Dollar	Type	Completed
You Deserve It!	https://scholarshipowl.com/awards/you-deserve-it-scholarship	06/27/18	$1000	Application	X
Wyzant Scholarship	https://www.wyzant.com/Scholarships/	08/15/18	Up to $10000	Essay	X
Delete Bullying	http://endcyberbullying.net/scholarship/	09/21/17	$1000	Essay	
Order Sons of Italy in America National Leadership Grant	http://www.osia.org/students/scholarships.php	09/28/18	$4000-$25000	Application	

I would put the dates and deadlines in chronological order to help with planning purposes, as well as checking off those that have been completed and submitted.

You may be asking where to find these scholarships. There are so many out there; you will most likely never be able to apply for all of them. But I will say this, the more you apply for, the more opportunities you have to get them! Here are a few major scholarship engines:

https://www.fastweb.com/college-scholarships
https://bigfuture.collegeboard.org/scholarship-search
http://www.collegescholarships.org/financial-aid/

I recommend the following steps in searching for scholarships:

1. **Google "scholarships."**
   See what else pops up besides the scholarship sites that I have mentioned. There are tons of places that offer them. You may find one on a particular website and another that was not on the first one. So scour the web thoroughly.

2. **Open up accounts on the scholarship sites.**
   They will do the work for you! Once you fill out an initial questionnaire based on interests, talents, academic achievements, etc., they can determine which ones you qualify for.

3. **If you qualify, look for scholarships based on ethnicity.**
   There are scholarships offered to people with Hispanic, Asian, and African-American backgrounds. There are many that are specific to ethnicity.

4. **Look for scholarships based on skills.**
   Are you a duck caller? Yes, there is a scholarship for that. Are you in The National Honor Society? Yes, they have scholarships. Google search scholarships for your specific gift, talent, hobby, and skill—you will be surprised at what pops up!

5. **Look for scholarships based on your potential degree or department.**
   For example, women who are heading into mathematics or engineering are offered several scholarships.

6. **See what the schools offer.**
   Search on all the school websites. There may be more scholarships that aren't

noted in the application process. Call the schools directly if you have any questions about the requirements.

7. **Rolling admissions.**
If you are accepted on a rolling basis, as the applications come in and you meet the requirements of the school, some scholarships and financial aid are offered "first come, first served." There is a definite benefit to applying early, even if it's through the regular admissions process (and not Early Action or Early Decision). The early bird DOES catch the worm when it comes to money at many schools.

8. **Look for scholarships specific to your city and state.**
There are groups and programs in cities and states that give scholarships for the rising students in the area. You have a higher chance of getting local scholarships because the pool of students is smaller.

9. **Check with local businesses and your parents' place of business.**
Many banks, stores, and companies offer funding as well.

10. **See if your local YMCA, scout groups, leadership groups, and military groups (like the Jr. ROTC) offer money.**

11. **Ask your high school counselor.**

12. **There are many regional scholarship programs.**
They help you pay in-state tuition, even if you live out-of-state but are located in a particular region. This is not for all programs, schools, or degrees, but it's definitely something to investigate. It can open up options in other states as well. As you can see, most states are covered under these options which, in turn, creates huge financial savings for you. The theory behind this program is that most students will settle into the region where they attend school. These programs are a way for schools to keep students in that area.

> **Western United Exchange (WUE)**
> Students who are residents of designated states are eligible to request a reduced tuition rate (150% of resident tuition at participating two and four-year college programs.) Alaska, Arizona, California, Colorado, Hawaii, Idaho, Montana, Nevada, New Mexico, North Dakota, Oregon, South Dakota, Utah, Washington, Wyoming, and the Commonwealth of

the Northern Mariana Islands participate in WUE. If you want to attend school in Montana but live in Hawaii, you can qualify for in-state tuition for the school in Montana—even though you don't live there. For example, out-of-state tuition for University of Montana is $22,720. However, in-state tuition is $4,604. That is a huge savings! http://www.wiche.edu/wue

New England Board of Higher Education (NEBHE)
Similar to the WUE, this New England-area program serves those living in Connecticut, Maine, Massachusetts, New Hampshire, Rhode Island, and Vermont. http://www.nebhe.org/programs-overview/rsp-tuition-break/overview/

Academic Common Market
If you live in the Southern part of the country, the Southern Regional Education Board offers a program similar to WUE and NEBHE for Alabama, Arkansas, Delaware, Florida, Georgia, Kentucky, Louisiana, Maryland, Mississippi, Oklahoma, South Carolina, Tennessee, Texas, Virginia, and West Virginia. https://www.sreb.org/academic-common-market

Midwest Student Exchange Program
This tuition co-op includes Illinois, Indiana, Kansas, Michigan, Minnesota, Missouri, Nebraska, North Dakota, and Wisconsin. http://msep.mhec.org/

QuestBridge Scholarship [23]

The QuestBridge scholarship is one of the best opportunities out there for low-income students. The objective and mission of the agency is to increase the percentage of talented low-income students attending college. This helps the college but also gives opportunities for students to attend the nation's best colleges (by offering them financial help). They also work with students to help them find the right information—to make this a successful "bridge."

The application deadline changes yearly, so be sure to verify the dates on their website. It's typically in the latter part of September.

It's open to permanent US residents who are currently attending high school in the country.

They are looking for students who:

- Have primarily A's in the most challenging courses
- Are in the top 5–10% of their class
- Achieve one of the following:
- SAT or PSAT score of 1310
- ACT score of at least 28
- They recommend submitting AP, IB, or SAT Subject Test Scores see chapter on SAT and ACT preparation).
- Strong writing ability and determination to succeed, which can be displayed through essays and recommendations.

Students typically come from homes with an annual income of less than $65,000 for a family of four. If you are awarded it, this scholarship could pay for all four years of college.

QuestBridge also looks for students who may have personal circumstances that will warrant them earning this scholarship. Some include:

- First generation to attend a college.
- Student with a high level of responsibility in the family, such as earning wages to help support their family, taking care of siblings when parents are at work, etc.
- Accomplishments in extracurricular activities.

Application requirements include a National College Match application, letters of recommendations, a counselor's report, a transcript, and standardized test scores. Over forty schools participate, so it is a great opportunity to get your schooling funded. If you are from a lower income family, this is a great option!

Gates Millennium Scholars (GMS) [24]

The Gates Millennium Scholarship was founded by Bill and Melinda Gates in 1999. This scholarship is for minority students with significant financial needs. It is renewable for all students who maintain satisfactory academic standing. The scholarship will be awarded based on the needs of the students determined by GMS, and (as an applicant) you will be evaluated based on your nominator, community service, academic achievement, and leadership potential.

http://gmsp.org/

I know the scholarship search can seem daunting, as there are so many options and opportunities out there. I recommend when you are applying for scholarships, set aside one to two hours per week to apply and check on deadlines in the coming weeks. It can be overwhelming to do more. If you do more in a week, the applications generally become more of a checklist. This is where completing essays beforehand (if at all possible) comes in handy, as you can alter one essay to fit several scholarship application requirements. On your computer, have an electronic folder with all of your essays. If the scholarship asks for an essay about yourself and what you have done in the community, you may be able to combine two essays you have already written instead of starting from scratch. Keep your résumé handy and the letters of recommendations scanned and saved on your computer to upload.

Parents, you can help by encouraging your student to set aside the time and help them stick to a schedule. There is a great sense of accomplishment in this for both parents and kids. Remember, the more scholarship money you receive, the less you have to pay. Don't be discouraged if you get few or no positive responses back on the scholarships. The more scholarships you apply for, the more opportunities you have for receiving them. Exhaust all options and leave no stone unturned.

Lastly, I have to stress that you can lead a horse to water (so to speak), but from there, it is your choice. You, as the student, have to take ownership of the application process. If you are having an adverse reaction to filling out applications and/or scholarships or are not engaged at all in the process, remember that you will be the one who doesn't receive the benefits of an education or scholarship money. As a parent, if you are receiving push-back on the whole process, ask your child about their thoughts. See if there is something that they are struggling with. There could be a concern they're hiding from you, or they might not be ready. Some students may even benefit from a "gap year."

A gap year (or semester) is time taken off between high school and college. It can be used to travel, work, volunteer, intern, or even study abroad before entering college. Some colleges allow you to apply, get accepted, and then hold off your attendance for one year. Some students need some time. Many people encourage this year, as it can be a time to earn money or travel before hunkering down. You can do things that you may not do later. Studies show that many students who have taken a gap year find they are more satisfied with their college experience when they do attend. My only recommendation: Be sure to develop a plan for when that gap year is over. This is especially true for those students who are directionally-challenged or have a harder time with decisions or follow-through. This type of student can allow one year to turn into two and so on, without a plan. It can create a snowball effect. Don't escape the inevitable—and turn a "gap year" into "gap years."

You may want to travel down a different path altogether. You may be concerned with how your parents, family, friends, or teachers will take this news. This is the perfect time to address all of these concerns. Some students may want to go into technical school, trade school, straight into full-time employment, or into military service. There are many roads for all students, and there is no one "right road" for everyone. You may even want to attend a junior college before jumping into a traditional four-year school. This could be the best route, especially if you are not ready to go to college just yet. For parents, if you are involved in the process, you can help direct your student to the path they wish to take. Use this time with your student to help them build their future, whatever it may be. But help guide them on the path during this process if college is the road they want to take. We can offer invaluable assistance to them while they weather the changes, challenges, and options available to them.

9

It's Go time! The Admission Process, the Waiting Game, Decision Time, and Finishing Strong

YOU ARE DONE! YOU have done your research, taken your ACT and SAT tests (maybe several times), filled out applications, submitted essays, and applied for scholarships. Now what?

You can breathe for a little bit and wait! This is, quite frankly, one of the hardest steps of the whole process—even though everything is done. But you can look back knowing you have done all that you could and that the rest is out of your hands.

If you have applied for Early Action or Early Decision on any of your college applications, you will probably hear back from the school you have selected by the end of December. Either way, whether you made it in or not, they will let you know the status. For regular admissions applications, some schools have rolling admissions, which means they continually are admitting students as the applications come in (if you meet their qualifications). For these schools, it pays to apply early (as mentioned in previous chapters) as it can help 1) with knowing earlier and 2) gaining the first come/first served scholarships, and 3) it can help you make a decision sooner and look for monetary opportunities. You have more wiggle room to call the schools and see what they can do for you. A lot of times schools will give you a blanket amount monetarily when they offer you admissions. However, if you are early enough (with the possibility of them losing you to another school), there is a chance they will offer you more. I think that it is always worth a shot. But irrespective of them offering you more funding, you will find out whether you did get accepted earlier, making it easier to plan. Most schools report admissions between January first and the end of March, with a May first deadline for commitment from you.

For Early Action, you will need to let the school know on May first or before. That gives you a lot of time to compare packages, including financial aid and scholarships.

I recommend using a spreadsheet (see the sample below) to compare and keep track of the schools that have made their decisions regarding your application.

For this example, the student I used in the sample spreadsheet applied for Early Decision to Yale but did not get accepted. The sample student also resides in Wisconsin, where they will receive in-state tuition for Wisconsin schools only.

College Name	Accepted	Deadline to Commit	Financial Aid* Offered/ Scholarships	Loans Offered- included in Final Cost**	Tuition and Other***	Final Cost per Year not including Loans**	Owed after 4 Years
Colorado School of Mines	yes	May first	$17,827	$3,500	$49,149	$31,322	$125,288
University of Washington	yes	May 15th	$32,000	$5,500	$47,055	$15,055	$60,220
Florida State	yes	May first	$19,583	$3,500	$32,977	$13,394	$53,576
Yale	no						
University of Wisconsin	yes	May first	$10,259	$5,300 (would not need)	$11,688^	$1,429	$5,716

*I based the financial aid for this example on average aid, scholarships, and grants offered. This will be sent from the school that has sent you the acceptance letter or email. But if not, contact the school to help you determine cost comparatives and know your options.

** It is important to point out that the final cost is after financial aid, scholarships, and LOANS are included in the package. However, you still have to consider the loan as part of your repayment. I did not pull it out in the final cost, as it is still something that should be taken into consideration when determining what you will owe. The amount they show you is only for one year, so keep in mind that this amount will be four times larger, unless you are given a scholarship spread over four years. If you are unsure, ask the school to clarify.

***Room and board, books, fees, etc., which are very important to consider when making a decision. These can end up being quite expensive, so be sure to look at the whole picture.

^*Lives at home, so no room and board.*

As you can see from the spreadsheet, it starts to make sense why you should use this format or something similar to make easy comparisons. It will help you visualize the amount you will need to pay, not only for the first year but during ALL four years of college. It makes your decision easier. If I were the parent of this student, I would encourage them to attend University of Wisconsin and live at home for at least the first year of school. Even if the student selected this option for two years of college, and then decided to attend Florida State for the last two years of school, they would be saving an incredible amount of money. They still receive the benefit of graduating at their top school, but they can get the underclass courses done in the first two years at University of Wisconsin. They would then owe approximately $29,646 after four years if they finish the last two years at Florida State, giving that student a huge savings—of approximately $24,000 at the end of their college career!

Also, I want to point out something else on the spreadsheet. For example, if you look at the financial aid/scholarship money that Washington State is offering: it can be very misleading when you see such a huge amount on offer. Washington State offered $32,000 in aid, and initially, it can be very exciting to see such a large amount of money. However, the tuition at Washington State is so much higher than the other schools that it ultimately ends up being comparable to Florida States cost-wise, even though Washington State is offering more in scholarship. It is very important to look at the whole picture—not just the money on offer. How does it all play out, and is it ultimately still a good value? What is the cost of tuition before the aid, and what will your amount be when you are done with school?

I think of it like buying a new car. The car salesman can tell you that they will take 70% off the sticker price, and you think you are getting a great deal. However, the initial sticker price of the car is inflated or extremely expensive to begin with. This can give you a false sense of savings when ultimately, you need to find the final cost, plus what you will owe as the interest accrues. If I am being shown a $20,000 car with 10% off the sticker versus a $50,000 car with 40% off, the $20,000 car now becomes $18,000—while the $50,000 car is $30,000. So now, the 40% deduction does not look as appealing. Be sure you are asking the right questions to see what will get you the most for your dollar.

Many students make the mistake of selecting a school for the wrong reasons. Unless someone, such as a family member, is completely paying for your school, money is no object for you, or you receive an athletic/academic scholarship that will pay for all of your schooling, the cost of the school should definitely be a determining factor in your decision. I know students who graduated college with $80,000–$90,000 in debt. Unless you are going into a field where you will be making a boatload of money, such as a doctor or lawyer, you could be paying that off until you're fifty years old. I see graduating college students being forced to pick a job right out the gate that they really don't want because they need to make their student loan payment. If you are looking at this extremely important decision when selecting the best school, keep this in mind: it can be a life-changer.

If you could talk to your forty-year-old self, I guarantee your older and wiser self would greatly appreciate you putting thought into how this can and will affect you in twenty years. You will not regret giving thought to cost, no matter what age you are at the time. This is a great discussion to have with your parents. Find out what they are planning on paying towards your education, if they are planning on that at all. Discuss what your options are. I also think it is beneficial to look at what your payments will be and how long it will take you to pay the loans off, comparing all of your options from the schools that have accepted you. You will look at what each school is offering and what you will be responsible for at the end of four years.

There are many websites out there that offer this calculation, but I like the one offered on Nerdwallet. Almost all of the student loan websites will have this function. https://www.nerdwallet.com/blog/loans/student-loans/student-loan-calculator/

I know it is hard imagining life four years down the road, but this is where you should ask for guidance from your parents. It is important to be open to compromise, but also be open to receiving some wisdom from your parents on fiscal responsibility. If they are paying for a portion of your college, truthfully, they should have some say in the decision. Parents have had experiences that you, as a young adult, have not had. They have learned their lessons the hard way or have seen people make decisions that have impacted their lives negatively. Be open to discussion and help from them.

I have come up with some compromises to help with negotiations, whether you are the student or the parent.

- **Parents**
  Offer to buy something of importance for your child if they are willing to compromise on where they are going to school. If you offer a trip to Europe upon graduation, which costs you $3,000, and in turn have saved $25,000-30,000 for you and your child, that's a good trade! How about a used car—

something that would be meaningful to a student, so they feel they have received something from the trade-off.

Students

Determine what would be a motivating factor for you! Discuss these options with your parents and, again, be willing to compromise.

- **Parents**

Set new rules if they live at home. Be willing to bend. It makes it easier for everyone if your child lives at home while they attend college, if a local college has been selected. This will obviously be a more cost-effective option for all of you, but your child may not be willing to select this option, based on a desire to be more independent. Set parameters on what they can now expect from you. They may need to do their own laundry and cook for themselves, but should now have a looser curfew and not as many rules because they are moving into adulthood. This will help make the transition easier for them, and it will also help them transition into them becoming adults with more responsibilities—as well as more freedom. It takes the burden off of you as a parent on many levels, but they need to see some benefit in the compromise as well.

Students

If you were to live at home to help defer the cost of housing at an in-state dorm, what do you need from this living arrangement? You will need to be willing to help out more than you have in the past (you are a young adult now), but you may be able to ask for more freedom. Initiate the conversation if this is an option for you.

- **Parents**

If your child is truly set on a particular school, compromise by selecting the option of attending an in-state school for the first two years (as mentioned earlier in the chapter) to get their underclassman courses out of the way. Then they can attend their dream school the last two years. This will save a great deal of money and will allow them to plan for the last two years at a higher cost.

Students

Choosing this option is a great deal—why pay more for the same thing? You will still be able to attend the school you want, but you will be able to save money that you can never get back.

- **Parents and Students**

  If living at home is not an option for either you or your student, it may be time for the student to be on their own. This could just be time for this to happen, or maybe there is no meeting of the minds as far as what the expectations are at this time. I recommend the compromise of attending the more cost-effective in-state college, but you, as the student, move out to your own place or with a roommate. It will still be less expensive if parents are helping with the overall cost of college. Both of you can split the cost, and students can take a part-time job or work out a way to help with the expenses. If this keeps the peace in the family and keeps down the amount everyone is paying, this is an awesome compromise. It is a win/win situation!

Students, I recommend talking with your parents all along, not only during the decision process. Seek your parent's help on this from the very beginning, as it will make this part much easier. Start talking to them when you initially look at schools. Make a plan with them so it is not a surprise, and find out what to expect from them financially. This gives you the proper expectations for college. Be sure you are all aligned on what you will be responsible for and what they are contributing. Many students make assumptions, and when it comes to this point of decision-making, they are surprised by what their parents are NOT paying for. Then, commonly, that student makes a rash decision and picks a school they will not be able to afford. They may not even go to college at all. If you, as the student, are paying for college all on your own, this is a very important decision. You will want to seek guidance from a trusted adult if your parents are not part of the decision or are absent from the process.

Ultimately, it is your choice. But I cannot stress enough that seeking help in making this decision is extremely important. At times, as human beings, we make decisions based on short-term rationale. Your parents have "been there/done that." How many of us have made errors that were very much in the moment? Probably all of us, but parents want to help avoid years of living with the consequences when the wrong choices are made. I am talking about extreme debt and/or selecting a school that will not help your future.

The positive side to this whole timeline is that, at this point, you have submitted your applications. You are slowly getting responses back from colleges. You will be able to start these discussions and decisions way before the May first deadline.

When you decide which school to attend, it's a great time for visitations. I discuss that more in-depth in the "Determining the College You Want to Attend" chapter. If you have not gone on any visitations yet, this is a great time to select a few that are at the top of your list. You can arrange to stay over and see how it feels to be there.

After you have chosen the college to attend, and you have a plan in place for it all, then you are set! You will submit a deposit, fill out any additional forms, and submit any insurance requests and immunization verifications. You can now enjoy the rest of senior year, knowing your future is set.

So, what is next for you as a student during your senior year? Many students get what is affectionately called "senioritis." It is almost inevitable to have this set in at some point. The decisions are made, the burden is lifted, and all you can think about is "PARTY!" I would say you can definitely relax more, but it is extremely important to finish strong, stay in it, and be mindful that things can be lost if you don't. I heard of one student who was heading into college after high school and decided to have fun his senior year. He ended up getting a DUI after hitting a mailbox and had to wait a year because of trials and hearings before he could attend. I am sure that was a very scary time for him, and he was unsure whether he would get there!

I used to worry about this possibility probably more than I should have with my kids. Not necessarily that they would get a DUI, per se, but that something extreme would derail their chances of going to college. It could be a fight at school or being in the wrong place at the wrong time. I stressed to my children that the wonderful opportunities that they were given could be taken away from them—due to just one wrong decision. I really kept on top of their grades, whereabouts, and activities for the last few months of school and summer. They probably do not know how much I was concerned about them, but I was definitely "involved" from the background. This is where communication is key.

As a parent, tell your children that no matter what: no drinking and absolutely no drinking and driving. You, as the parent, are the "go to" person for them. They should not fear calling you if they made a decision that they need help with. Assist them in setting parameters and talk—A LOT!

We, as a family, planned a lot of activities to do together during my kids' senior years: things that kept them busy but also created memories that we will always have, no matter where they ended up. This is a great time to get them involved in something new or take on a part-time job. The summer is good for this, as well as helping make some extra money for savings and expenses for the following year at school.

This can be a tough year for both kids and parents. I know this, as I have lived and experienced it firsthand. Remember that the tough times you may go through during senior year, for both parents and kids, are just a process that is very normal. But you will also have some amazing times and growth. Going through adversity is a way for students to separate and become responsible adults. Everyone involved may be struggling with the impending change and transition which, in turn, can cause anxiety. Be patient with each other, and parents, help your student move into adulthood by showing them that you will always be there for them, but allow them to find themselves in the process.

10

Don't Forget FAFSA, Financial Aid, Loans, and Your CSS Profile

AS IF FILLING OUT applications and scholarships for college isn't enough—you have more things to complete!

I could not call this book complete if I did not mention the Free Application for Federal Student Aid (FAFSA). This application will be filled out to determine eligibility for student financial aid. Even if you think you do not qualify, it is important to fill this out each year. It can also help with student loans. Nearly every student is eligible for some form of financial aid. Students who may not be eligible for need-based aid may still be eligible for an unsubsidized Stafford Loan regardless of income or circumstances. Some private financial aid providers may use your FAFSA information to determine whether you qualify for their aid.

You will need to submit the FAFSA every year when attending college. The FAFSA includes questions regarding household income, student income, financial obligations, whether there are other students in the household attending college, dependents, and other relevant information.

A student who meets all of the following criteria may be eligible for aid:

- Has a High School Diploma or GED
- Is a US Citizen, a US National, or an Eligible Non-Citizen
- Has a valid Social Security Number
- Has Registered with the Selective Service System Between the Ages of Eighteen and Twenty-Five, if Required to do so (Females are Excluded from this Requirement)
- Maintains Satisfactory Academic Progress (SAP)
- Signs the Certification Statement
  - o They are not in default on a federal student loan and do not owe money on a federal student grant.

o Their federal student aid will only be used for educational purposes.

o They have not been found guilty of the sale or possession of illegal drugs while federal aid was being received.

You can apply for the FAFSA between October first and June thirtieth of the year before you attend college. However, state deadlines are different for their financial aid, and you will need to look on the website to determine their deadlines. Many of the state's application deadlines are "as soon as possible," so be sure to check with them to not miss out.

https://fafsa.ed.gov/deadlines.htm

You will also need the previous year's tax returns. There is also a great feature offered on FAFSA called the data retrieval tool (DRT). This is used to import your tax information directly from the IRS website. It doesn't work for everyone, but it is a nice tool when it does work. However, if it doesn't work, have the previous tax returns handy for inputting all the information, as the tax returns are definitely required for the FASFA.

According to the US Department of Education's website, you have three preparation options for the FAFSA:

- Online at fafsa.ed.gov
- By Telephone at 1-800-433-3243
- By Paper—Mailing it in

Types of Financial Aid

This is an area that can be confusing to many students and parents, as there are several types of financial aid offered. It isn't always free. Here are the four most common types of aid offered by the federal government. Be sure to check your local government for financial aid as well, as each state offers options for in-state college students and other opportunities.

- **Pell Grant**

  A grant of up to $6,095. (This can change each school year, but for the 2018/2019 school year, this is the amount.) This is for students with a low expected family contribution, and they will have exceptional financial need. A 2016 Nerd Wallet study found that students missed out on $2.7 billion in free federal Pell grants by not completing the FAFSA. That is huge! This money doesn't need to be repaid, unlike other types of aid. As long as you maintain satisfactory academic progress (SAP), you can receive this grant. Depending on your family contribution, income, and other determining factors, you can receive quite a bit of help. Copy this very long link to see what you will receive through the Pell Grant program or head onto the Federal Student Aid Website to find out more about Pell Grants.

https://ifap.ed.gov/dpcletters/attachments/GEN1804AttachRevised1819Pell PaymntDisbSched.pdf

- **Stafford Loans**

  This is the most popular student loan program, where the government offers loans with a flexible repayment option. There are usually lower interest rates on these loans. It is the first option you will want to apply for because of this reason. There are two types of Stafford Loans: subsidized and unsubsidized. You can be eligible for one, or both, depending on your household income.

  o **Subsidized**

  Need-based loans under the Stafford Loans. What is great about this one is that the government pays the interest while you are in college and during the grace period before repayment begins. (This is generally a six-month period after graduation from college before employment.) You can receive $9,500 for the first year, $10,500 for the second year, and $12,500 for the third and subsequent years. (This is for the 2018/2019 school year and can change depending on the program.) But, either way, free money and worth applying for! No more than $3,500 for the first year, $4,500 for the second year, and $5,500 for the third and subsequent year may be subsidized loans of the maximum amount offered.

  o **Unsubsidized**

  These loans are not based on income and not all students are eligible for the maximum amount of $3,500 for the first year, $4,500 for the second year, and $5,500 for the third year and beyond. These amounts can change depending on the program. (This is for the 2018/2019 year.)

  While the federal government backs unsubsidized loans, the government does not pay for interest at any time. You are responsible for paying the interest throughout the life of the loan. While you're attending school, or during the six month grace period after you graduate, you have the option not to pay interest. However, the unpaid interest will be added to the principal, or the final balance that you owe. This can definitely add up!

- **The Federal Work-Study Program**
  A program where students can receive part-time work up to a certain amount of pay. In most cases, the federal government pays half of a student's wage and the school pays the other half. This program is provided for students with financial need. It is administered by the schools that participate in the Federal Work Study Program, and you will need to check with the school you plan to attend to see if they offer this program.

CSS Profile

The FAFSA should not be confused with the CSS Profile. CSS is short for scholarship service profile, and it is also required by some colleges. You can apply for financial aid through this profile. This "profile" is much more detailed than the FAFSA, and it can take up to a few hours to fill out, so grab a snack and drink and settle in. This profile is mainly used by private colleges; state and public colleges generally do not require it. Once you fill out the questionnaire, it will be sent to the colleges and universities that you request and that participate in the program. There is a small fee for this application, but you can apply for a waiver online. The College Board will waive the fee for low-income, US-based students who are applying to college for the first time. This will be a supplemental requirement, and students will need to fill out a profile and submit it, if and when the school requires it. You will fill this out through College Board at this website. https://cssprofile.collegeboard.org/

There is also a link on the CSS website page for you to see updated colleges that participate in the CSS profile, and it will have separate document and application requirements. If your school is not on the list, I recommend looking at financial aid on the school's website to be sure that there are no extra forms or criteria for dispersing of funds or other financial-need grants. There are approximately 400 schools that participate in and use CSS.

Student Loans/Parent Loans

I have a feeling I am going to be opening a can of worms on this one. Such a tough subject! You've probably heard the statistics that you can research online, but I found a recent one on the Student Loan Hero website that says, "Americans owe over $1.48 trillion in student loan debt, spread out among about forty-four million borrowers. That's about $620 billion more than the total US credit card debt. The average class of 2017 graduate has over $39,000 in student loan debt, up six percent from last year." You can look at some other statistics on this website at https://studentloanhero.com/student-loan-debt-statistics/.

That means it could take you up to twenty-five years to pay off a student loan, as there is an extended repayment option for student loans exceeding $30,000. This also means you are paying a substantial amount of interest over time, and the average student loan payment is $351 per month. These can be some scary statistics, for sure.

First, I need to say that people need to look at the whole picture when applying to schools. Many times students and parents get turned off by the high tuition costs and do not even look at how much financial aid the school offers. There is a bit of sticker shock that turns many people off without doing a little research to see how much it will actually cost them. Let's look at Harvard for example, and I use Harvard as an example simply because they ARE one of the most expensive schools in the country, or at least that's what most people think and assume. However, they also have one of the biggest endowments offered of any school in the US. Here is the information directly from their website (https://college.harvard.edu/financial-aid/how-aid-works/fact-sheet) regarding aid offered:

- 55% of our undergraduates receive the Harvard Scholarship.

- 20% of our parents have total incomes less than $65,000 and are not expected to contribute.

- Families with incomes between $65,000 and $150,000 will contribute from 0–10% of their income, and those with incomes above $150,000 will be asked to pay proportionately more than 10%, based on their individual circumstances.

- Families at all income levels, who have significant assets, will continue to pay more than those in less fortunate circumstances.

- Two-thirds of students work during the academic year.

- 16% of the roughly 6,600 current undergraduate students are Pell Grant recipients.

As you can see, if you fall in the range of $40,000–$65,000 in 2018, you most likely will not be paying anything to go to the school!

First, you will have to get in (of course), but you can see that financially, they offer aid to those who need it. So, before we even look at loans, you should evaluate the financial aid options from the school you are looking at, apply for all possible scholarships, and then make the determination of how much you are willing to borrow. Most financial analysts recommend between $21,000 and $24,000 of debt when you leave school. With this being said, at the average payment of $351 a month, a student can pay this off in a little over six years. While having a degree is no guarantee for a future job, it definitely gives a person better opportunities and options. Ask these questions, as well, when you are deciding and looking at schools.

- Can you work in the summer to help pay towards your college and not have the need to borrow?
- Can you work part-time during school?
- What are Mom and Dad willing and able to help?

We, my husband and I, usually paid half the cost for our contribution as a guideline for our children. Our thought process was that we wanted our children to have ownership in their college experience. If it was completely free, and we paid everything, they would not feel vested in attending college. It would not have as much value to them. It will depend on the student, but that was a rule of thumb for us. We also made it so that all of our children did not graduate college with more than $21,000 in debt. We were fortunate with this, and I know it can be a tough one. But I recommend that you strive to look at all the options before making a decision that exhausts all of your scholarship and financial aid opportunities. Come up with an amount that is comfortable to your family, and agree to have that figure be your guideline, whatever it is.

I also think it is very important to weigh in on the school itself. If you are looking at a school with a hefty price tag, ask the school these questions before making the final determination.

- What is the schools placement rate upon graduation?
- What is the average salary of those who graduate?
- What is the graduation rate?

- What percentage of students do they give financial aid to? How much is that aid dollar-wise?
- How much debt does the average student have upon graduation at that school?
- Is the school a "name," either in its field or by reputation? In other words, is it really worth the money?

I know the previous questions seems harsh, but if you are planning on attending a small, private college (for example) that no one has heard of, it costs $58,000 a year, and virtually no financial aid is given to you, what do you get at the end upon graduation? A golden pony? No: heavy debt and a degree that may not end up making you more money in the long run than say a state school. These are all things to question before you look at student loans, parent loans, and what debt you are willing to incur.

We also have found success with paying monthly for our portion of the college tuition. With three children in school at the same time, these were hard overlapping years. But we always took advantage of this option with at least one of our children each year, so the debt did not accumulate for us. We also took advantage of making payments earlier than they were owed, generally in the summer months when we did not have monthly payments to the school.

Students have to start paying their loans back six months after they graduate. I know my children started making payments each summer when they had money from working, even while they were in school: not all the money they earned, but generally a few hundred dollars, which helped bring their balance down each year. My children are only a few years out of college, and I only have one child right now with a small amount of student debt—and he just graduated a few months ago! So I definitely see that this method works.

This leaves you open to more opportunities to take a job you really want after graduation, or you will be free to travel before starting your career. When you aren't as driven by the fear of making monthly payments, you can be more flexible with opportunities that will come your way.

I also recommend that when paying back loans, you pay more than the minimum amount. If you get a bonus at work, a tax return, etc. (even though it may be tempting to buy something fun or spend it on a vacation) making payments towards a student loan will help bring down your balance and decrease the amount of time you will make payments.

As a rule of thumb, the first thing to start with is the government-issued loans. There is a difference between a grant and a loan. Be sure to recognize that when accepting them. Grants are given to you with no requirement to pay back, while loans must be paid back. The government loans are offered at a lower interest rate. That is your first step.

Next, contact the school directly for other options; even see if they can adjust the financial aid they previously offered you. Some schools allow you to petition for higher financial aid based on hardships or things that you cannot quantify on an application.

If all else fails, apply for a student loan online or through a bank. But shop around, read the fine print, and—just like anything you buy—do not spend outside of your means. I know someone who left college with $91,000 in debt! After this person graduated, they unfortunately started working at a job that paid only $28,000 a year, which is very common when you are just starting out. However, when you look at it in real terms, you would figure that if you have a payment of $539 a month (which is close to what it would be) at 6% interest, it will take at least thirty years to pay off $90,000. Yes, 30 years! That means this student will be over fifty years old before they pay off their loan. It will take a long time to pay that amount of student loan debt and make any headway, especially earning only $28,000.

However, if you are attending school to become a doctor, a lawyer, or an investment banker, or to work in some field where the expected income offsets the loan, it would make more sense to expect a higher amount of debt after you graduate. You will also be making a higher incline on your salary over the years. Look at what the industry you will be going into offers for salaries and what you feel you can afford to pay when you are employed after you graduate. If you are going to school to become a teacher, it may not make sense to graduate with a huge amount of debt because teachers are not expected to receive an income comparable to a doctor. A doctor could make upwards of $90,000 for a starting salary, and a teacher's average starting salary is $38,000. This is when you look at the possibility of attending a state school or junior college for two years before transferring to another school. This is a great option for many students who have limited means or who do not fall in the financial need category, but may not have the means to write a check and pay for college.

This is also when the benefits of doing well academically in high school pay off. You can potentially receive academic scholarships to offset the cost of the school, which generally are very generous. Be sure to look on the school's website or talk with their counselors about the opportunities for these types of scholarships. Where my daughter attended college, she increased her ACT score by one point (yes, only one point!), and she received $2,500 more for that school year in scholarship money.

For those who are athletically gifted, you can receive athletic scholarships (see my chapter on recruiting). Even if it is partial, this can be a great benefit from the school. You also can receive scholarships for activities that do not fall under sports such as speech and debate, band, choir, cheerleading, etc. These are discussed more in my chapter on scholarships, but it's definitely worth mentioning when discussing aid. The whole package will be important to look at as you put it all together.

Getting these type of scholarships or aid are not always an option for all students, so let's look at some quick tips to help with student loan decisions.

- **Look to keep the average borrowed aid at $5,000–6,000 per year as a rule,** unless you are heading into a field that is expected to have a higher rate of return (a higher income will be expected)

- **Parents: Make monthly payments instead of extending out longer term.**
    - o Look at the option of receiving loans from the school or through the government at the school. Many schools also have options for student loans and parent loans through the school. They sometime offer it at a greatly reduced rate, so this is something to definitely look into. Ask what they offer. At some schools, there is a payment schedule if you want, or need, to make monthly payments instead of a lump sum at one time. You can also set up quarterly payments or semester payments, depending on what is offered at the school, I have found that most schools offer this option if you ask. Even if you do not see it available on their website, call the Financial Aid Office to ask if they can set this up. They also may be able to offer other options that you are unaware of.

- **Determine the school tuition value.**
    Are you getting back some bang for the buck? Is it a school that is top or high in the field of study? Does it have the name recognition that will help with a good job after school? Example: Colorado School of Mines, one of the top schools for engineering, is known for its program, even though you may not

know the school itself. So, it's a good pick (depending on what is offered to you financially) for recognition purposes in its field. This is a good choice. Stanford, no matter what your degree is, is a highly recognized school and will have a name value that will help after you graduate. Not all students can get into these schools, but look for these factors when making the determination of value to you. If you are unsure where the school stands or ranks, search the programs on the web to see their ranking, and if the program is valued in your field, even if the school is not necessarily recognized. People in that industry will be aware that the school is well-known and that it is a solid program.

- **If you are set on a certain school, look at attending a less expensive school for two years.** Attend a state or community college for your first two years, and then transfer to the preferred school for your final years.

- **Keep in mind a dollar figure you do not want to exceed.**
  What you plan to pay back after you graduate should be based on the potential in your field or career path. For example, look at the starting salaries in your expected industry. Based on national averages, this is what you can expect when graduating in these fields [22].

    o Teacher: $38,617
    o Investment Banker: $82,424
    o Engineer: $67,860
    o Nurse: $56,678
    o Physical Therapist: $66,545
    o Lawyer: $150,327
    o Producer: $51,392
    o Public Relations: $43,184
    o Pharmacist: $104,730

With this in mind, if you are getting paid $32,000 a year for a public relations degree, how long will it take to pay off your student loan? Is your college investment worth the outcome?

- Exhaust all avenues for grants and scholarships, and talk with the school you want to attend (and your high school) about other options before applying for loans.

- Discuss options with Mom and Dad (or grandparents) and decide on a fair amount for them to help with the cost of college, if at all possible.

- If all else fails, shop around: talk with your bank, college, etc., reading the fine print on fees and costs associated with it as well as the interest rate before applying for student loans.

I know that it's a lot to take in. But if you have a plan beforehand, it makes it so much easier. You most likely will not make a rash decision. Be prepared to adjust your course of action if it ends up being too expensive for you. Be flexible knowing that this decision could impact you for several years (or even decades), and you don't want to make an easy decision now that will end up costing you more in the long run. Maybe you will have to take a semester off and work or do something different than you expected. In the long run, you will definitely benefit from it. Think about saving yourself from making student loan payments when you have grandkids! Plan for your future now, and it will benefit you IN your future.

Take your time and research your options before committing.

11

Letting Go: A Chapter for Parents

THIS IS A HARD part for us as parents: the letting go process. I wish I could tell you that it was super easy, but it was not. I cried after each one left for college, even though I promised them I wouldn't. When my daughter left for college, and her school was only twenty minutes away, I still cried all the way home after dropping her off. I mean, like hard-core crying, not the pretty trickle-down-the-cheek crying.

For me, when they left, it was about change. It was about feeling they did not need me anymore or that we would grow apart. It was about me feeling that I had lost my purpose and identity as a parent. Especially when senior year is, or was, a struggle with your child, it can definitely be hard on us. We envision this as a time when we and our kids are feeling exactly the same thing—and not wanting it to end. I have to tell you, as parents, we definitely do not feel the same as our children do about this process. They are experiencing many feelings: fear, excitement, happiness, sadness, anticipation, and a whole mix of other things—sometimes at the same time! It's a very scary time for them, but it is also a time where they are so ready to get on with their lives. They are unsure about letting go of what they know, love, and what feels familiar. We have to be patient with them and help them go through this process so they don't feel alone. It is also a time to allow them the space to work through everything on their own and to be able to find that happy balance.

Wow, you have to be a mind reader AND a genius! Generally we, as parents, can tell when we need to pull back and when we need to step in. We can usually sense it, but it isn't always easy, and you may have to tread lightly.

Some things that helped me, and I believe helped my children, with the process.

- **Start buying things for their dorm or college apartment early on in their senior year.**

  Buy items like bedding, decorations, posters, etc., even. This gets them excited about moving on to their new life, and it will also help you feel like part of the process. I think it kept me busy, as well, looking for things for them to have in their new place.

    o I bought them picture frames for their special pictures and put one of our family in them so they can always think of us. I filled the others with their friends and even their dog!

- **Be part of the move-in process (if possible).**
  I did this with two of my four kids, and it was wonderful to see where they would be in their room and their school. I felt more comfortable after helping them find things and places around campus. Such as: Where is the laundromat? Where do they eat lunch? Where are their classes? Where do they buy groceries? This isn't always possible and each child is different. Some want to find it on their own, and as soon as you drop them off, they want you gone! But even if this is the case, you can drive around and keep a mental note of things. You can see where he or she could get their hair cut and in a month or so, you can mention it to them. Or look for a church in the area or on campus for them to get plugged into. Again, you don't have to do that with them, but it can be a great point of reference and conversation with your child if they mention they feel disconnected or lonely or in need of direction. It also made me feel better knowing where things were distance-wise, so I could visualize it. It made me feel more connected somehow.

- **Be there for them when they call—just to talk.**
  They WILL be lonely and homesick at some point. Listen—but do not make them feel bad by telling them you feel the same and want them home. They need to go, and you need to let them go. This is a normal process for all kids (and parents), but they need to know it is okay and normal, and that they will get through it. Remember when your kids left for their very first day of school and how hard it was for them and you? This is much bigger and much more important of a transition. Each child is different and may need more encouragement, so when they call and say they hate it or want to come home, tell them it will get better. Tell them once they settle in and get acclimated, it will feel like home. It can take up to two years for this to happen, unless they are involved in a sport or group that may allow them to connect faster. Encourage them to get connected and work through it. If not, it could set them up for quitting

things and not working through adversity. It isn't a bad thing for them to work through the challenges they will face.

- **Before they even leave for college, suggest looking for clubs or groups to join.** Have them email the organizer of the groups, find them on social media, or communicate in some other way, so they will feel more comfortable as soon as they get there.

- **Encourage them to be in communication with their future roommate(s).** This way they have a friend before they get to school. This can be very exciting for them, and it can also help with splitting up things to buy for their room such as a microwave, small refrigerator, fan, etc.

- **Take them out and spend time with them before they go.** Even when and if you are not getting along, this means more to them than you know. They will appreciate it, and it will be something to reflect on later.

- **Take it in stride if you are NOT getting along at this point in time.** This is common, and it will pass. Just be patient with your child and allow them some latitude. For you kids out there, try to be aware of what your parents are going through. I know this is YOUR time and it is about YOUR move and it is about YOUR change, but be mindful that your parents will miss you when you go.

- **For parents: Start planning for a vacation, project, job, or creative expression.** Pick something that you can sink your teeth into when they leave. I got a dog, Brutus, and he was a wonderful distraction and is still a great buddy to have around and give attention to. This is a wonderful time to reconnect with your husband or wife and do things that you did not do before. If you have more kids at home still, it can change the dynamics, and you can now focus on the next ones in your house. I was the Team Mom and president of my kid's sport's teams. This was a great way for me to channel my energy and focus on the kids left in the house. I also got a wonderful job that helped me focus my creative energy, and it was nice to be around other people and to feel productive.

For me, each child has brought the same feeling of change. But now, having gone through it with all of my children, I have to tell you the spoiler about the light at the end of the tunnel: it all ends up okay! In fact, I think once I worked through my own feelings, I found another layer and level of connection with my children. It allowed for a wonderful and more adult-like dynamic in our relationship that was, and is, fantastic. This time of letting go is about letting them achieve things, experience things, and learn things—all on their own. The feelings we are having at this time is the desire to be part of their transition and experiencing it along with them just like we have been doing for the last eighteen or so years. Truth be told, this probably will not be about experiencing those things first-hand like we have in the past, but it is where we see all the things we have poured into them be put to the test and realized by them. I remember hearing a parent tell their child that the world is their oyster as long as the world is within forty miles from their home! I think, as parents, we should not limit the opportunities we expect or want for our children. No matter how hard it may be for us, it is not our life they are living, and our children are not extensions of us. They are their own individuals who should experience everything in life. We would want the same for us if given that chance. Now is the time to give your children your blessing to go forward and accomplish all the great things you have trained them for. This is their time, and you can be a great cheerleader from wherever you call home. So be strong for your kids, and enjoy this time in your life as well. Find a way to embrace this new phase. You have done a great job, and you can watch the fruits of your labor right where you are, no matter where they go.

"Sometimes love means letting go, even when you want to hold on tighter."

12

From the Mouths of Babes: College Student's Perspectives

MUCH OF THE TIME when I am working with students, their parents have given advice similar to mine. But, for some reason, human nature as it is, they will listen to a stranger's advice (mine), but not always those closest to them. We all do it, even though our loved ones know us the best and want the best for us. Go one step further. Have these same students talk to kids their own age, who have gone through similar experiences—then they REALLY listen. This chapter is completely dedicated to advice from current, recently graduated college students to adults who have been in the world a bit to students heading in the direction of college. My son David recommended doing this chapter, and I am really grateful that he suggested it. These students have a lot to say and offer some VERY good advice, suggestions, and hopefully, you and your parents can learn from them. These students are from schools across the country, from all walks of life, and have so much to say. A shout out and thank you to all of these incredible young men and women who have helped contribute to this chapter. I truly appreciate it. I have even learned a thing or two about these students who I have watched mature and grow throughout the years. The minds of young adults are invaluable, and I hope you will find the same treasure in their words of advice.

What Advice Would You Give to Other Students Entering Their Freshman Year?

"I would tell incoming freshmen to enjoy college and make the most of your opportunity there. Take advantage of absolutely everything that you can. Try new things and meet as many new people as possible. College is a place where you have the ability to learn as much or as little as you want, so make the best of your time. Especially if you are going to school far from home, there will be an amazing collection of people at your college. Take your time to get to know people and learn from this as well because college is just as much about people as it is about what you do inside the classroom. Lastly, I would tell freshmen to know that everybody is in the same boat. The adjustment to college life is difficult, but everybody is going through the same process as you are. Be confident in yourself and always remember that you do belong at your school just as much as anyone. This will be difficult at times throughout your freshmen year, but remind yourself to be confident and that you do, in fact, belong."

– David Trompke, Harvard University, Cambridge, Massachusetts

"I would tell students to take advantage of every opportunity that is presented to them, even if it might be out of their comfort zone. Get involved with your major, join a club, run for a leadership position. For example, I have always wanted to study abroad in another country but was beyond nervous to leave school for an extended period of time. I eventually found the courage and left the spring of my junior year to study abroad in Italy. I am so glad that I pushed myself to learn and grow in a different culture and gain independence."

– Brielle Dennison, Washington State University, Pullman, Washington

"Make sure you have a structure to your week. There's a lot of free time in college. Once you lose that structure it's hard to get back on track. Include clubs, sports, or call-outs in your structure and make sure you commit to their events like they're paying you to be there. It allows you to become a more rounded person, as well as giving your week a structure."

– James Nguyen, Purdue University, West Lafayette, Indiana

"Accept and approach any aberrant situation with excitement; embrace the weird. Comfort at this stage should be rare; otherwise, you're not testing yourself and the virtues you believe you possess. Also, you're not right—about anything—you just have an opinion."   *– Mitch McConnell, University of Oregon, Eugene, Oregon*

"Come ready to have your world turned upside down. Don't ever come in expecting that it's going to be like high school and I can do what I did then and be fine. This is not high school, this is college. Come ready for the next four years of your life that will ultimately be the first time in your life where you have no one guiding you and it's mostly on your back what you do. That being said, get involved, join clubs, go to sporting events and, most importantly, keep your grades up."

– Alex Trompke, Michigan State University, East Lansing, Michigan

"Upon my initial arrival on campus, I was afflicted with what many would call 'impostor syndrome.' Throughout all of my social interactions, I quickly came to realize that I was among many other students who had taken college courses, attended elite science and technology magnet schools, and prestigious East Coast prep schools, whose alumni included but weren't limited to presidents and world leaders alike. There I was, a bright-eyed and (not even) relatively naive college freshmen from a state people often thought was located in the Midwest without a single physics Olympiad title to my name, attending orientation events on diversity amongst a host of geniuses.

At first, I thought that passing and surviving at college was a feat unto itself, but now entering my junior year, I realize that that perspective was more of a handicap than an enabler. Freshmen, you are at the top of your game having trumped through the puberty and accompanying social and academic expectations of your hallowed high school hallways.

Though it's no secret that college is, so to speak, an "entirely different ballgame," take the impetus from your graduation to your first year. You realistically are not going to be the top student among top students, but you can certainly act like a top student until you are. Because you are a freshman, your first year is as good as any to branch out and become an opportunist within the realm of reason. Sign up for clubs, classes, and volunteer for opportunities aligned with your interests. Talk to upperclassmen, but make sure to take their advice with a grain of salt: in the end, your experience is what you (and only you) make of it. Above all, invest in your relationships with your classmates and professors.

Most, if not all, of my major involvements can be attributed to my relationships with professors and students alike, though I didn't start talking to professors until my sophomore year. Anyone can make it in college regardless of one's starting platform, but what can set you apart is how you approach and maximize the potential in your environment."

– Vanessa Wong, Massachusetts Institute of Technology (MIT),
Boston, Massachusetts

"There are so many things I wish I could say to freshman, but a lot of the reality of it (and this is part of my advice too), is that it is so valuable when you live, make mistakes, and learn for yourself. I see it so many times within our freshman on the team: that they just make mistake after mistake and our older kids try to be a good example and even have these talks with them, but they won't really learn it until they feel it and learn it for themselves. So, I guess my first piece of advice is, it's okay to make mistakes, but try your best to be a good person. Words don't teach, experiences teach. Mistakes follow you sometimes for a very long time and no one likes that. So pick and choose your mistakes. But also, memories follow you forever and those are times you can never get back. I look back on some of the things I did my freshman year, and I will probably never do them again, but I also learned a lot of the decisions I made, good and bad. So another piece of advice I have is, yes, make mistakes and learn for yourself, but don't hurt others in the process. Don't burn your bridges so quickly.

My second piece of advice is: take advantage of all the opportunities. College can be so fun, but it's what you make it. Your college years go by so fast and you'll regret every opportunity you didn't try to take advantage of. My next piece of advice is a little contradictory to the second, but it's something a professor told me this year. Delayed gratification is OKAY. So many students have this fear of missing out all the time and, therefore, they do things they don't want too or they do too many things and can't find a good balance. It's okay to not go out with friends sometimes so you can sit home and study and get a really good grade on your test. But I wouldn't suggest making it a regular thing because there are things that you will get to experience in college and only if you put yourself out there. Fourth, find balance. Seek advice from older students on how to genuinely manage your time with school, sports, clubs, friends, etc. I see so many of our freshman fall off the bandwagon so early because they were too eager to get to all the 'fun college stuff' they forgot the real reason they were here—to get an education.

That leads to my next piece of advice: remember you are here to get an education. I have had trial upon trial in my college years, a lot of them having to do with friends or relationships. I don't judge myself for being upset or anything like that, but some-times I do look back on things I went through my freshman year and wish I would've remembered that as long as I was being the best person I could be, which I was, and I still had friend issues/relationship issues, that's not my problem. My problem and where I needed to focus, was on SCHOOL. Because that's the ultimate goal. Four years of college isn't very long, therefore, a lot of these people/things won't matter after you graduate. But what will carry with you for the rest of your life is your education and how you took advantage of that. Next, this is something I have just recently learned and it is so important. Only try to control the "controllables." They are so many things that happen in college, good and bad, but it's how we react to them that shows who we really are as an individual. Represent something good and worthy. I was having a hard time with something this year and I was talking to one of my senior friends and I said without even thinking, 'I'm so jealous that you are graduating.' He looked at me and said 'Alex, no you aren't. You are letting the conditional things around you that change all the time, dictate your happiness. People, places, things don't make up your happiness. If you want to be happy, change your own story and only worry about the things you have control over.' That piece of advice changed my life.

Next, I advise students to learn how to study properly. Seek the guidance of older students and really get on top of it from the get-go. Next, leave your high school past behind. Even if high school was awesome for you, come to college with a clean slate— it'll help you make the right friends. Next, learn that you don't have to be a partier, but if you want to be that's awesome too. Find your limits and your balance. Going out is a good time, and even if you go out regularly, sometimes you just don't want to drink, etc. So learn how to say no without having any fear of missing out. Or learn how to say yes if you need to get out of your comfort zone. Either way, find a balance. Stay in touch with your family.

Next, this is something my school really struggles with and I think it might just be a small school thing, but I'm not sure. But remember that you are an adult. This is college. An adult that is having a super awesome fun time, but still, this isn't high school. Handle things to the best of your ability as an adult, meaning don't hold grudges, forgive, don't gossip, don't cling to a hundred of your girlfriends like high school. Be an independent person and you will find the genuine experiences that you are supposed to get out of your college experience.

Next, get off campus sometimes. Explore the city you are in, go on hikes with friends, see what's out there.

Lastly, build a good relationship with your professors. They are such an amazing source of knowledge and you would be silly to not take advantage of their academic and life wisdom."

– *Alexander Koga, University of Puget Sound, Tacoma, Washington*

"Be sure to enjoy it but not too much. Follow the motto, 'Some play and mostly work makes Jack graduate.' Get as much exposure to different majors so you can truly find what will be fulfilling for you later in life."

– Rachel Trompke, College of Idaho, Caldwell, Idaho

"Get involved. College opens up an opportunity to expand your interests and friend groups, so don't be afraid to try new things and visit clubs and groups that interest you." *– Hayden Cross, United States Military Academy, West Point, New York*

"I would tell incoming freshman that first semester is much different than high school: professors don't give second chances, you have to spend at least twice as much time on an essay then expected to surpass your standards, and school should always (ALWAYS) come before social life. Don't get me wrong, try and have a great social life, but get what needs to get done in the classroom first."

– Tanner Schelling, Seattle University, Seattle, Washington

"Make sure you know that school is right for you. Don't rush to try and figure out what you want to major in because your mind will change three or four times within the year. Don't focus on the parties because at the end of the day those won't help you pass finals. It's easier than it looks to make friends, especially in college because chances are the friend you're making generally doesn't have many friends at the same college as you so you are both new in a way. Also don't feel pressured to join a frat or sorority because that's the cool thing to do, it's very time-consuming and not to mention a lot of extra money for random things in the program; a lot of people join hoping it's the greatest thing ever but then soon realize that's their first commitment now, so make sure to take time and read about all the clubs and groups to join in case you change your mind."

– Keisha Oliver, Oregon State University, Corvallis, Oregon

"The number one thing I would recommend is to get involved in everything and anything you possibly can. Along with that, definitely live in the dorms your first year with a roommate(s) you didn't previously know. This will automatically force you to start creating new relationships and to get outside your shell. Go to as many events as you can: this includes, but is not limited to, sporting events, welcome week events, social gatherings, etc. Join a club or sorority/fraternity—whatever may pique your interest. College and school are very important, but it's also important to maintain a life outside the books. Find something that allows you to rest your brain and escape from studying and school. And, most importantly, don't go home every weekend if you are close to home. If anything, going to a school out of my home state was the best decision I made. It forced me to become independent and become more adaptable to new places and people. In addition to this, study abroad if you can. It was honestly the best decision of my entire life and opened up my mind so much to the world around me. Not to mention getting the opportunity to study and learn in a foreign country is a huge asset to have on your résumé and for future employers."

– *Jenna Julianno, University of Minnesota, Minneapolis, Minnesota*

"The advice that I would give to a freshman would be to know your priorities and don't sacrifice who you are for what everyone else is doing. Be an individual. I believe in the saying 'be yourself, everyone else is taken.' People are coming from all over the country or world and will have different morals and beliefs, and you need to make sure that what you believe in is grounded appropriately. Next, I would say to know your limits on what you can take on and be respectful of that, it's your first year. This goes along with the next advice I have, which is energy management. Energy management is equally as important if not more important than time management. Make sure you are eating and focusing on the task at hand. Lastly, I would say you're away from home now so if you get in trouble Mommy isn't going to save you."

– *Jordan Trompke, United States Military Academy, West Point, New York*

"When I first got to college, I was only seventeen years old. I had always been young for my grade but never felt it as much until I actually got to college. One of the biggest things that held me back at first was thinking that everyone around me was in some way more prepared socially and intellectually (especially at a school like Harvard). Obviously I couldn't have been more wrong, but nonetheless, my peers intimidated me. What I did not realize was that college was not just a brand-new experience for me; it was a brand-new experience for every single person in my class. No matter how smart, how athletic, or where we were from, we all had a purpose and a right to be going to school where we were—or else, the college wouldn't have admitted us. Once I got my head around the fact the fact that these people on campus were my peers and not my superiors, I was able to be myself more, fit in, and find a group that I was comfortable with. I was able to participate more in class, make my opinion heard rather than listening to everyone else, and I was able to confidently walk through The Yard like I belonged. It was not easy to convince myself that my new home was a new home for everyone and that everyone was struggling to find his or her way as much as I was. Once I settled down and started to embrace the challenge of change rather than wish I could skip through the entire transition period and wake up a senior the next day, I found life at school much more enjoyable.

I left school shortly into my sophomore year—this brings me to another point. Don't be afraid to step away from everything. It doesn't necessarily have to be in the form of completely withdrawing from school (although I would recommend a gap year to a lot of people going straight from high school to college—in the end, I probably wasn't the most prepared for college life), but get away, go visit a friend in the area. Often times I felt refreshed and even more excited to be at school when I got away for a weekend. Lastly, for me, I have learned that you can never try too much. It is much easier to drop a student organization or an activity that you are doing than to get into said group or activity. Usually to join a group you have to put a lot of time and energy to prove to the leaders of that group you will be a dedicated and supportive member. It would only take a minute to go up to those very people and respectfully say, "My schedule is too busy, and I don't feel like I can put enough effort into helping this organization, so I have decided to focus my time elsewhere." For me, it feels like experimenting begets more experimenting, and keeping an open mind snowballs into more and more possibilities. Once you begin saying no to a few things, you begin to say no to everything and get very stuck. Eventually, I feel you will find yourself trapped and wishing you had opened up to more ideas earlier on, but by that point, it will have been too late."

– Matt Weissman, Harvard University, Cambridge, Massachusetts

"I would tell them that starting off right is only going to help you later on—that not having the typical college freshmen year is best because the fun times will come."

– Khalil Oliver, University of Oregon, Eugene, Oregon

"If you have a high school girlfriend/boyfriend, make sure you think long and hard as to whether the relationship is worth continuing. Your first year at college is your best opportunity to meet new people and make good first impressions, and sometimes having a significant other from high school can get in the way of focusing on your new life at college. Get involved with as many things as possible. This gives you more opportunities to meet people and network when everyone is in the same position of being around so many new people. Once you figure out the people you like and the activities that you enjoy the most, then you can drop the other ones that you didn't benefit from as much, but it's much harder to join late than it is to join early and drop activities later."

– Anthony de Vera, United States Naval Academy, Annapolis, Maryland

"I would advise incoming freshmen to get comfortable with being uncomfortable. You're immersed in a totally new environment. It could be one of (if not) the biggest adjustments you will make in life—no parents, no one holding you accountable, and an almost daunting sense of autonomy. With sudden change and movement away from what's always been comfortable, some of us try to find solace inside our shells. But this experience will only happen once, so get out there, meet new people, try new things, and push yourself beyond that safe zone. Every incoming freshman is likely to experience some similar feelings, so embrace those people and get uncomfortable together. Secondly, I think it's important to note that once you get here, everyone is smart. It's not high school, where it might have been easy to cruise off your innate intellect without cracking a book and somehow getting an A. That doesn't work in college. You will meet some extraordinarily intelligent people, and if you are the smartest person in the room in any of your classes, you are probably in the wrong place. However, don't let that be justification for poor academic performance. Those who do well in college are the ones who are willing to put in the work. Intellect will only get you so far; so trust me, the A students are those who opt for the library instead of the rager on Wednesday nights."

– Tanner Johnson, Duke University, Durham, North Carolina

"My first piece of advice is when searching for advice about college, ask multiple sources. Each person giving advice is most likely talking through personal experience. Just because certain tactics helped them does not mean it is suited for you. Everyone will find out what their individual needs are as they start attending college. Secondly, and most importantly, college is a commitment. I say this because you cannot do this for someone else, and this doesn't mean you need a game plan going into college, but it is an experience you partake in to get something out of it. And no, I don't mean just the degree. If you plan on joining a college, make sure it is something you want and not just something to pass the time. You are only wasting your own time in that case. College is a great time to try and figure out what kind of career you want to build through multiple programs and community activities, so take advantage of it."

– Michael Asciutto, University of Nevada, Reno, Nevada

"I would advise students entering their freshman year to develop some kind of plan. What I mean by that is not a plan as far as what career he or she wants to pursue but more of a plan geared towards what exactly the student wants to get out of his or her college experience. Rising freshman should set goals, whether they be academic, physical, or social goals, before setting foot on campus. If a student wishes to go to a top-tier grad school, for example, he or she should set goals early on in their college experience to work towards that end state. However, a balance must be achieved between doing academic work and enjoying a social life. In college, you will develop relationships that will last a lifetime. You mature a lot in college, so it makes sense that it is more practical to hang on to your college friends, as opposed to high school friends."

– Michael Ross, United States Military Academy, West Point, New York

"You do not have to decide right away what it is you want to do/major in. Don't be afraid to take different types of courses. You never know what might actually interest you."

– Tyler Manu, Yale University, New Haven, Connecticut

"My advice is to be outgoing and not afraid to go out and make new things; also be sure not to get behind in school. Try and stay on top of everything."

– Kristian Almberg, University of Utah, Salt Lake City, Utah

"The advice that I would give to other freshman students is to get involved in as much campus activities and socials as much as you can so that way, you are stretching yourself in new ways that will benefit you in terms of making a new friend group and just seeing what your college/university has to offer you."

– Joshua Taylor, Central Kansas Christian College, McPherson, Kansas

"Advice to students entering freshman year... Take everything in stride, these four years go by much faster than you think they will. So get involved in as many clubs/organizations as you can and that you are passionate about! Also, don't be afraid to try new things. You will learn so many things about yourself and meet the best people this way; chances are they will be your friends throughout college. Learn to balance school, studies, clubs, and a job early on so you can keep up everything through the four years, but also know when to take a break for yourself and don't push it too far. Doing everything is impossible and you need to take time for yourself and don't forget to have some fun during these four years. Call your parents! Chances are, you miss them, and they miss you too. I know my mom sure missed me, probably more than she let on. STUDY and go to class (it's cool to go to class in college!) You/your parents/the government/your school is paying a massive amount of money for you to attend this university, study hard and go to class because there are many others who would kill to be in your position at a university."

– Samantha Guinn, Colorado State University, Fort Collins, Colorado

"My advice would be to approach it with an open mind and realize that it will take at least a semester to get used to college. Be excited because it a major step to your development as a person and not to worry because homesickness goes away quickly."

– Anthony Ross, United States Military Academy, West Point, New York

"As a freshman entering college, I would definitely just encourage everyone to keep an open mind and to shamelessly try everything that they can. Even if you think you know what you want to major in or what types of things you want to be a part of outside of the classroom, I would branch out and take a class or two in anything that interests you. The same goes for your extracurriculars and the people that you meet. Keep an open mind and try as many things and meet as many people as you can. College is about your academic education, sure. However, what is incredible to me looking back, as a recent college graduate, is realizing how much I learned and how much I grew up in every aspect of my life. I hated some classes, and I loved some classes—and I was fortunate to combine a degree in business administration with my pre-medical studies.

As for the other classes—I still got the opportunity to acquire a baseline knowledge of so many subjects (and even a baseline knowledge can offer so much for your perspective moving forward). I tried countless extracurriculars that ended up being poor fits for me, but in doing so I found a few that I loved. And don't be afraid to quit the ones that you know are a bad fit for you! I know at least for me, personally, 'quitting' is not something I do well. But when it comes to extracurriculars, it really is all about quality and not quantity. Focusing on the ones you love will allow you to personally give and receive 100% from them. Also, future employers, graduate school boards and scholarship committees really will be able to tell that you genuinely jumped all-in and cared about the things you spent your college years doing, instead of trying to get a toe wet in a large quantity of things just to fill your résumé. I would also encourage you to keep an open mind socially. I met so many wildly different people in college, and some of the ones that helped me through the toughest times and became some of my lifelong friends are people that I would never have thought I would befriend so closely. College is an amazing time to throw yourself out of your comfort zone and expose yourself to as many things as possible. You'll be amazed at how much you learn and how much you grow into yourself doing so."

– *Kelsey Richardson, Washington and Lee University, Lexington, Virginia*

"My biggest advice to students entering freshman year would be don't be afraid to ask questions and push yourself out of your comfort zone to meet new people and establish early relationships. Freshman year you are entering into a completely different world, meeting tons of new people, in an area that you may or may not be familiar with. You quickly learn that your study habits that you may or may not have had from high school quickly have to improve. Don't be afraid to go in and talk to your professors and build relationships with them. That's what their office hours are for, and that's why they decided to become educators. They want you to ask questions and get to know you because they want to see students that are making an effort to go above and beyond outside of the classroom. Join a club or social group. Whether it's a fraternity/sorority, a sports club, or an organization through your individual college, GET INVOLVED! You will meet incredible life-long friends as well as develop great résumé material."

– *Ty Prince, University of Idaho, Moscow, Idaho*

"I would give two pieces of advice to students entering into their freshman year. First, to be as open to everyone and everything as you can. The beginning of college is one of the only times you'll be somewhere where everyone knows almost no one. The second thing is to never be afraid of asking questions. Professors love it, and it's a great way to get them to notice you."

– *Maddie Eyolfson, University of Denver, Denver, Colorado*

What Do You Wish Someone Had Told You Before Your First Year Started and About College Life?

"I wish that someone told me that the first year isn't super easy to adjust to, especially in the beginning. I loved high school and the friendships I had during those four years, and it was super difficult to have to 'start over' in a sense. Change doesn't come easy for everyone and it takes time. It takes time to form relationships and gain a sense of belonging in a new place, but once you do, it's worth waiting for."

    – Brielle Dennison, Washington State University, Pullman, Washington

"Ever an opportunist, I was so excited during orientation week with the sheer number of opportunities that I was able to access. Having come from a relatively small town where I'd had to research or create my own opportunities, I signed up for anything that sounded like music to my ears. And because I'd been able to do so many things in my hometown, I thought that I could handle it all with some mastery at time management. However, such was not the case. In high school, I could take seven classes, be a captain on the swim team, manage my own non-profit, travel to conferences, and manage to have both personal time and a social life. Such was not the case in college. Somehow, in high school, I could survive on an average of six hours of sleep, yet in college, I found myself falling asleep in classes with that same amount, even more exhausted at the end of the day. Thus, I've found it imperative that I get a reasonable amount of sleep every night (seven or eight hours).

In college, the classes are harder, the tests are more intense, and the fact that you still have to respond to over fifty emails a day on top of your schedule can be overwhelming. You could calculate all the hours you need to devote to classes, sleep, and attend your extracurricular activities down to the very last minute, but that a) doesn't leave room for spontaneity and b) makes it super easy for you to burn out.

Knowing that I'm a devoted adherent to my Google Calendar, my advisor wisely suggested that I schedule in specific time blocks for both social and personal time. Without these, it's very easy to get into a productivity rhythm that quickly loses its momentum because you'll burn out and lose motivation and efficiency. After implementing these tips, it was easier to manage everything and earn better grades, although I wish I'd been able to use this tip earlier. Less really is more when you're able to get quality over quantity. Though it can be easy to imagine that your environment resembles a 'dog eat dog' world, it's both healthier and more effective to concentrate on what you want to do (versus what you see others doing), and devote your time to what you want, but simultaneously, to do so within a realm of self-control and self-care."

– Vanessa Wong, Massachusetts Institute of Technology (MIT),
Boston, Massachusetts

"I wish somebody had informed me on the vast amount of opportunities college has to offer. Some of these opportunities seem unattainable, but if you want them bad enough, it's amazing the doors that will open for you. Talking to the right people and being aware that certain opportunities exist is a big step in experiencing some amazing things. Always be proactive."

– Michael Ross, United States Military Academy, West Point, New York

"The biggest thing I wish someone would have told me about entering freshman year would be the amount of freedom that opens up to you and how to prioritize your time with that freedom. Your whole life there's always been someone there to hold your hand through the process and tell you what you need to do and when you need to do it. When you're in college it's up to you to choose whether or not to wake up for that eight a.m. class, or instead sleep in and play video games all day. It's up to you to choose to get yourself down to the library to study for that exam or attend that big party instead. It's up to you to get to the gym and stay physically fit and eat right or stay at home and quickly get that freshman fifteen. Hold yourself accountable and remember why you're there. There will always be a party, but you have one shot at an education."

– Ty Prince, University of Idaho, Moscow, Idaho

"I wish when I started my freshman year I would have had a little more guidance to where I wanted to be exactly and help me choose my career path. Also, SAVE SAVE SAVE your money before going out of state for college, especially if your parents can't give you an allowance every week. You always need extra spending money or a part-time job when in college because all your friends will want to go out or buy stuff every weekend or go out to eat 'cause the food on campus gets old fast. I also wish someone would have told me that sharing a dorm gets tiring after a while and you wish you had your own room to have some peace and quiet."

– Keisha Oliver, Oregon State, Corvallis, Oregon

"Attend career fairs. They are usually the first two weeks of school. Most companies will recruit a vast majority of their workers/interns during this period. There are other times, but the fall season will have more offers and opportunities."

– James Nguyen, Purdue University, West Lafayette, Indiana

"I wish someone would've told me the right places to go to for my major to get more synced in. It took me some digging and a lot of grunt work to find my place."

– Alex Trompke, Michigan State University, East Lansing, Michigan

"I wish I would have known how many opportunities exist in college for tutoring and assistance centers, etc. exist for when you're struggling with academics."

– Hayden Cross, United States Military Academy, West Point, New York

"I wish that someone had prepared me for how personally challenging college is. It is hard to try so many different, new things and to not feel overwhelmed. And it can be a bit disheartening not to be good at everything (or sometimes to feel like at that current moment you really aren't awesome at anything). Because everything is pretty new! It is also uncomfortable to feel a little lost because you aren't sure where your fit is, what your capabilities are, or where you want your life to end up. I wish someone had told me that when you are uncomfortable you should know that you are becoming better. 'Comfort is your enemy,' so to speak. But everyone feels self-doubt and that is normal. I just wish I knew that all the times that I was lost and self-doubting, I was getting better.

Also, it sounds lame, but don't be embarrassed to ask for help. Call your parents, confide in your friends, ask your professors, advisors, and peer tutors for their advice. I could not have made it through college without shamelessly asking for help from the people around me even when (especially when) I felt like a failure or a crazy person. You will learn how to not be as hard on yourself, to ask for help, to ascertain when to quit or try harder, and how to just keep pushing with the knowledge that everything will work out. It will be personally challenging, but don't be too hard on yourself because everyone else is going through it too, and college will be an absolutely amazing four years."

– Kelsey Richardson, Washington and Lee University,
Lexington, Virginia

"I wish that someone had told me about the importance of managing my energy.

There will be all-nighters or workouts that destroy you to the point you just want to sleep, but you always have something to do, so manage your energy so that you can be successful. I would also say people are a great resource and should be the emphasis on social networking. People are a resource that can help you to understand on a personal level a topic; they can point you in the right direction, or any variety of helpful things. Lastly, I would say academics will set you up for the future, and you need to learn the system quickly."

– Jordan Trompke, United States Military Academy, West Point, New York

"I wish someone would have told me how to study in college. It takes a semester to figure out the best strategy. For example, if your school offers tutors (free ones are the best) or study groups, GO TO THEM! After my first quarter, I made it a habit to go to the library for at least an hour and a half each school night; even if I didn't have homework due in the next couple of days, I would study and study and study. I would say I have high expectations for myself, but if you want that higher grade, you have to study more than you think. Another thing I wish I would've been told is to go to professors' office hours. You wouldn't believe the connections you can make with your professor if it's just him and perhaps a few other students in a small room, rather than a couple hundred in a lecture hall."

– Tanner Schelling, Seattle University, Seattle, Washington

"Focus and be intentional in anything you do. My first year was spent floating without much determination. It felt undefined. After that it was over. I looked back and was underwhelmed. I became determined to approach everything with resolve. Confidence will naturally ensue: a trait that cannot be overstated."

– Mitch McConnell, University of Oregon, Eugene, Oregon

"Before I started college, I wish someone had told me to not worry so much about others but to just worry about what I can control myself. I cannot control what others say or how they act or think, but I can control how I react. One of the beautiful parts about college is the diversity that you are faced with. Everybody has different skill sets, study habits, routines, and everybody is great at different things. This is very important to understand in college: there is no single or best way to do things. On that note, don't be afraid to be different. Accept that you are unique and excel at it."

– David Trompke, Harvard University, Cambridge, Massachusetts

202 | Getting Into College Made EASY

"I wish someone would have told me that college isn't a game, it is a footstool to either give you a disadvantage or advantage in life. Academics should be your #1 priority and overachievers do GREAT in college/life—so be an overachiever."

— Joshua Taylor, Central Kansas Christian College, McPherson, Kansas

"My freshman year I struggled with accessing the resources that were at hand for me. Don't be afraid to go to office hours with your professor or to go to a writing tutor. You aren't going to know everything. Also, don't be afraid to ask a question. Odds are that somebody else has the same question."

— Jordan Drexler, University of Idaho, Moscow, Idaho

"Meet and get to know as many people as possible. You will never be around as many peers as you are when you're at college. Once you get to know a lot of people, find the ones you click with the most and invest your time into them. The best friends you have while at college will be the strongest friendships you'll ever make. Don't get involved in the typical 'college lifestyle.' There are a lot of opportunities for parties, alcohol, drugs, and other things that, if abused, can take away from the benefits of college and might even jeopardize graduation. Spend as much time with your professors outside of class as possible. Building relationships with them other than time spent in class can be valuable when you're in a situation where you need to make a grade. Take classes that are fun and that you're interested in, but are also practical. Don't waste money on easy credits just so you can get good grades. Be willing to work a little harder for the classes that will end up contributing to your profession once you graduate and enter the real world."

— Anthony de Vera, United States Naval Academy, Annapolis, Maryland

"Don't stay too close to home. You need to spread your wings. Get into the mentality that this is your life now, and there is no going back."

— Rachel Trompke, College of Idaho, Caldwell, Idaho

"That you still won't know what the heck you want to do by the time your four years is up—and that it is perfectly normal and totally okay! I used to think twenty-one/twenty-two-year olds had it all figured out—until I became one. If you have your entire life set up and planned out by the time you graduate, then that is awesome and good for you! But if you're still trying to figure out what the heck you're going to be doing, where you will be in the next five to ten years, it's okay. It doesn't mean you've failed or done anything wrong. Everything will work out how it's supposed to, and you will end up where you're meant to be. Just don't freak out or stress yourself out about not having your crap together by the age of twenty-one/twenty-two."

– Jenna Julianno, University of Minnesota, Minneapolis, Minnesota

"I wish someone would have told me that I didn't need to have it all together. It is completely understandable to fall apart and have bad days. It took me until almost the end of my senior year to understand that it is alright to not be perfect. I had this idea in my head from high school that I always needed to keep up the image of being perfect, and (the fact of the matter is) no one is perfect. It is more refreshing the older we get when people are real, rather than pretending to be perfect. This comes with time, understanding, and appreciation, but remember that you are doing the best you can, and don't be too hard on yourself."

– Samantha Guinn, Colorado State University, Fort Collins, Colorado

"What helped me overcome everything my first year was prayer. I prayed every day for something great to happen or to help me get through my classes; all I had in college was my roommates, so really all I could turn to was God when I was struggling, trying to figure out how to be an adult on my own."

– Keisha Oliver, Oregon State University, Corvallis, Oregon

"I wish I knew how critical time management was and how to better manage my time. I also wish I knew how much more work there is in college and how important developing as a writer is."

– Anthony Ross, United States Military Academy, West Point, New York

"I wish someone had told me to not always worry and stress so much about school and to have fun. Tests aren't everything and although it's important to do well it's also important to make good memories."

– Maddie Eyolfson, University of Denver, Denver, Colorado

"Just because you have all this freedom and free time does not mean you can't still stay on top of your work. It is easy to get behind, and there is nothing wrong with staying ahead of due dates. You need to find that balance between enjoying college and remaining focused."

– Tyler Manu, Yale University, New Haven, Connecticut

"I wish someone had told me not to go into college with preconceived notions about what college is and isn't like. It can be really stressful, depending on how seriously the individual approaches college. Exercising good study habits helps, but college is not the only thing in your life; make sure you are able to balance a social life with college activities. Otherwise, you will find yourself unhappy and consumed with the workload you place upon yourself."

– Michael Asciutto, University of Nevada, Reno, Nevada

What Did You Struggle with Your Freshman Year?

"Being a freshman, you are exposed to so much, whether it be girls, new classes, a new school, or even a weird roommate. The hardest thing for me was to adapt to a new area of the country and getting comfortable being away from home. It helps a lot to get involved. Never, I mean ever, be that kid who just stays in your room and doesn't embrace the freshmen experience. This is your life—take it for what it can be and what you want it to be."

– Alex Trompke, Michigan State University, East Lansing, Michigan

"Time management was a killer for me freshman year. Distractions are so readily available, and it's way too easy to procrastinate and get your proprieties out of line. To overcome this, I always carried around a sticky notepad and wrote what I needed to turn in the next day and estimated how long each assignment would take me to ensure that I always set aside enough time."

– Hayden Cross, United States Military Academy, West Point, New York

"The biggest thing I would say I struggled with my freshman year was time management. Like I mentioned in the last question: you have all of this freedom now available, and it's up to you to decide what to do with it."

– Ty Prince, University of Idaho, Moscow, Idaho

"I had too much of a social life. Didn't manage the whole doing college thing with all the parties and new friends."

– Rachel Trompke, College of Idaho, Caldwell, Idaho

"The biggest struggle I probably had freshman year was meeting new people. Granted I was on a sports team, so I automatically had great friends there for me. But as far as meeting people in classes or the cafeteria or around campus, it was hard for me to get out of my comfort zone. It wasn't until sophomore year until I realized that people are actually nice! I have some great buddies that I met in my classes and study groups that approached me, and what would you know, we are great friends now. I just wish I could've made more friends in my classes, had I known that people actually want to make friends."
– Tanner Schelling, Seattle University, Seattle, Washington

"Time management, getting along with different people, and optimism."
– Anthony de Vera, United State Naval Academy, Annapolis, Maryland

"I struggled with purpose. It's hard learning generalized topics while watching upperclassmen contributing to projects with a purpose. Insignificance is a mindset that can definitely cause barriers to achieving potential."
– Mitch McConnell, University of Oregon, Eugene, Oregon

"My freshman year I struggled with accessing the resources that were at hand for me. Don't be afraid to go to office hours with your professor or to go to a writing tutor. You aren't going to know everything. Also, don't be afraid to ask a question. Odds are that somebody else has the same question."

– Tyler Manu, Yale University, New Haven, Connecticut

"My first semester I was homesick a lot and often wondered if I made the right decision."
– Brielle Dennison, Washington State University, Pullman, Washington

"One thing that I found difficulty in was making myself go to class. The first semester of my freshman year I went to class every single day. Although they were easier freshmen classes I do believe that this really helped my 4.0 that semester. However, as second semester rolled around, I started to learn what classes didn't take attendance and got lazy because (unlike high school) most classes aren't mandatory. Another issue I came across was the teaching. Some teachers are better than others, and I have had some great teachers here at the University of Idaho, but moving from a small classroom in high school to a huge lecture hall full of students in college was difficult. The professors aren't as concerned about making sure you learn the material as they are in high school, and on top of that, some can be very hard to understand. I had a math teacher who had a very strong accent and was extremely hard to understand. These big lecture halls are also different than high school classrooms because asking questions in front of that many people is scary, and the teachers can't take extra time to explain things for just one person, like in high school."

– Jordan Drexler, University of Idaho, Moscow, Idaho

"The most difficult part about my freshman year was acclimating and adapting to my new environment. After living in the same area my whole life, and having the same routines and same friends and same home with cooked meals, it was definitely difficult completely leaving that and starting over. It is important to understand and recognize the struggles you might be faced with your freshman year, even though they are not all the same for everyone.

For me, I had difficulties in three areas: social life, academics, and extracurricular activities (i.e. football, track, and field). Socially, it is difficult making new friends that I fit in with and enjoyed spending time with. Also, not having my family around was tough to deal with. I didn't have my parents politely encouraging me to do homework, and I didn't have home-cooked meals, so this responsibility was on my shoulders. Academically, it was obviously an enormous jump from a public high school in Idaho to Harvard. I was forced to work much harder in the classroom than I ever had before, and my study habits dramatically changed as well. Athletics, or any extracurricular you might be involved in, is just as much mental as it is physical. Obviously, college sports are much more time intensive than high school sports, but they challenge you mentally just as much as they do physically. Everyone was their high school superstar, and it was difficult adjusting to being on the bottom of the food chain. Overall, the culture shock was very difficult to deal with as an eighteen-year-old kid, but ultimately, I believe, made me better off in the long run."

– David Trompke, Harvard University, Cambridge, Massachusetts

"I struggled with time management and adapting to the culture here at West Point. Time management was huge in being successful here. I seemed to be overwhelmed with work to do."

— *Michael Ross, United States Military Academy, West Point, New York*

"What I struggled with my freshman year was my early classes, having roommates who wanted to do stuff every night and stay up all night and then having to get up eight a.m. while they had eleven a.m. classes. I never struggled to go to the gym, surprisingly, because that was something I had been doing by myself for a long time. I also struggled to memorize my schedule and where the buildings were, so I always looked lost. I also struggled with math lol. The hardest was going to study groups and tutoring at night, and I never fully got that one-on-one help that I needed, so I had to call my dad and do math over the phone with him."

— *Keisha Oliver, Oregon State University, Corvallis, Oregon*

"I struggled with home. In the beginning, I was so ready to be independent and get away from the relentless rules of being an adolescent. But I promise you, at some point, you will miss home. It comes with acknowledging you will (probably) never be a permanent resident in your family's home again. College is your home—for now—and that's hard to come to terms with. Eventually, everything in college will become astoundingly familiar, and it will become your new home. In the meantime, it's okay to call your family and tell them you miss them. Stay in touch, even though it's hard with everything going on in your new life. They will keep you grounded during your lows and celebrate with you during your highs."

— *Tanner Johnson, Duke University, Durham, North Carolina*

"I think it was hardest for me (and many of my close friends as well) to find a good balance. As I said before, college really is about all different types of education. I felt like I learned so much in my academic, physical, personal, social, spiritual, and adult life. We go to college to get an academic degree and to acquire the skills necessary to excel in the professional world. But at the same time, most of us would lose our minds if we never left the library to have fun, get a workout in, spend time working on our personal relationships, etc. Each of us needs an outlet for our stresses and people to support us when we succeed and when we feel like we are failing. It is a hard thing in college to find the time to fit in your workout, studies, applications, grocery shopping, friends, meals, and what feels like everything else."

– Kelsey Richardson, Washington and Lee University, Lexington, Virginia

"My struggles in the first year of college was obtaining a healthy social life that I now look back upon and wish I could have done better. I don't regret my choices, and I had a lot of fun. The truth is, surround yourself with people you believe you can trust to be there during hard times. Making new friends in college is quite easy; a lot like high school, it is just finding the right social group you fit into minus the overall status quo and isolation that can occur in high school."

– Michael Asciutto, University of Nevada, Reno, Nevada

"Luckily for me and all other similarly overwhelmed freshmen, the first semester of MIT is conducted on a grading system of pass/no record. However, second semester, we had to adjust from a semester of mistake leniency to regular grades. I struggled to overcome this grading bulwark, as (for the first time), I had to reconcile with grades lower than an A. There were many tears in the process, but going to office hours and soliciting help from professors and TAs really helped me find the loopholes in my understanding. Attending important sessions such as these also helped me really appreciate the faculty at MIT, for both wanting to ensure their students' success, and for being patient in facilitating my comprehension of the material at hand. Gone were the notions that I had to do things by myself. While it is important to make sure that you understand the material individually, office hours and group studying really helped me solidify my own understanding and broaden my perspective of the material at hand." *– Vanessa Wong, Massachusetts Institute of Technology (MIT),*

Boston, Massachusetts

"I struggled with time management my freshmen year with sports and class."

– Khalil Oliver, University of Oregon, Eugene, Oregon

"Honestly, I think the hardest thing for me was the size of my classes. And this is because I chose to go to a very large public university, so my freshman classes were upwards of 300 students in a lecture hall. It makes it difficult to have that one on one with the professor or instructor."

– Jenna Julianno, University of Minnesota, Minneapolis, Minnesota

"I struggled with the workload of classes that I was taking, particularly due to my personality; academics are not my strong suit. (I will do my best, study for a week straight for a test and still only get a B+ on the test), but also I was doing soccer, basketball, and was on the leadership team for FCA. But my work ethic kept me in the game."

– Joshua Taylor, Central Kansas Christian College, McPherson, Kansas

"I struggled with failure. Straight from high school I never failed, I balanced everything, I maintained straight A's without studying, and I kept up the image of having it all together. Failing multiple exams during the first two years of college was really hard on me mentally and emotionally, and took a hit on my classwork. It took me a long time to learn how I needed to study to do well, but once I understood the way I needed to study to succeed, it really took off. On top of studies, I struggled financially. All through college, I struggled to pay my tuition, books, bills, rent, insurance, etc. It is a major stressor for many people, and it does cause more worry, but it needs to be clear that your studies come first and class is extremely important."

– Samantha Guinn, Colorado State University, Fort Collins, Colorado

"Academics are much harder than I had expected coming to school at West Point. Even with a year of prep school to adapt to the changes in workload, I still was not ready to take on the rigors of a top ten school."

– Jordan Trompke, United States Military Academy, West Point, New York

"Asking for help. College is hard."

– James Nguyen, Purdue University, West Lafayette, Indiana

"The biggest thing I would say I struggled with my freshman year was time management. Like I mentioned in the last question, you have all of this freedom now available, and it's up to you to decide what to do with it."

– Ty Prince, University of Idaho, Moscow, Idaho

"I struggled a little with homesickness freshman year, but I mostly struggled with branching out from the swim team, which doesn't apply to a lot of people I know. But it's good to make other friends that aren't swimmers."

– Maddie Eyolfson, University of Denver, Denver, Colorado

"I struggled with defining myself (what I wanted to do in life, what career options I wanted to pursue, what interests/hobbies I wanted to develop, what beliefs I hold, how I think, etc.). I guess that this is a major internal struggle in growing up, and it seems to hit you in college more so than any other period."

– Anthony Ross, United States Military Academy, West Point, New York

What Helped You Overcome Your Struggles Freshman Year?

"Being a part of clubs, sports, and meeting new people really helps. When you finally make those bonds with people and get to know them (and they get to know you), it makes it all homier."

– Alex Trompke, Michigan State University, East Lansing, Michigan

"I would advise having different social groups; you don't have to hang out with the same people every day or every weekend. College is hard. Academically, socially, even physically (you have to pull some all-nighters, it's inevitable). But I enjoy the challenge because I know it's bringing me closer to my goals in life."

– Tanner Schelling, Seattle University, Seattle, Washington

"Going out in the real world and working. Then you realize you have to work in order to 'survive,' so you learn to balance more effectively."

– Rachel Trompke, College of Idaho, Caldwell, Idaho

"I used the older people around to help me organize what to do."

– Khalil Oliver, University of Oregon, Eugene, Oregon

"Finding a balance is hard, and I found it by just trying to focus on what my priorities were at the exact moment that I needed to decide where to spend my time (sometimes with the help of running it by my close friends for a third-party perspective). And you will choose wrong sometimes! Sometimes taking a break from studying to relax with some friends or work out makes you feel better mentally and makes you more productive when you return to the library. Although other times you may just feel stressed that you hadn't studied another two hours. But eventually, I figured out the balance and learned what I needed and when I needed it. Unfortunately, balance is learned through trial and error—but be mindful that although your academics are undoubtedly very important, college isn't necessarily all about studying all the time. There are so many other parts of your life that are important and your studies will thrive the most when you find a healthy balance between all of the things that are important to you." – *Kelsey Richardson, Williams and Lee, Lexington, Virginia*

"I had to set short-term goals for personal development. The institution is only half of your college experience. As lame as it sounds, I actually became more involved in the community and loved it."

– *Mitch McConnell, University of Oregon, Eugene, Oregon*

"What helped me overcome ineffectively managing my time was joining my fraternity. The house that I joined was first in grades amongst all Greek houses, which meant that the members of that house held each other very academically accountable. Our house has a 'study table' system that requires all freshmen to study at the library from six to nine p.m. Sunday through Thursday. This was extremely beneficial for me in developing good study habits and setting a designated time every day outside the classroom to get my work done. It also helped in a sense that within your fraternity there are typically at least four or five guys who have already taken that class or are in that class who would be able to help you with any struggles you have in that particular subject. I now have designated a portion of my day and developed a routine where I can finish all of my work and still maintain a social life."

– *Ty Prince, University of Idaho, Moscow, Idaho*

"Sometimes you just have put your pride aside. Ask for help—it will make college much easier (also make sure you attempt the problem first)."

– *James Nguyen, Purdue University, West Lafayette, Indiana*

"I highly recommend dorm life. To this day, six years after starting college, I have friends I can depend upon that I met through a highly social dorm. A lot of the friends you make you will eventually grow apart from as they start their new life after college or the following years to come. You must be aware of that when making new friends, but don't let it define who is and isn't worth being a friend. You would be surprised the kind of people who end up sticking around. To be quite honest, I feel it is impossible to complete college alone. Socially isolating yourself only hurts in the long run; college is the start of your life, so enjoy every second you can while it is available. My friends that have stuck with me through my ups and downs are even more valuable than my degree because without them I wouldn't have made it to this point. Conclusion: College has every outlet that you can exploit and grow as an individual. Take those opportunities and run with them. You might not ever be able to seize them again. Most of all, have fun and explore the possible career options you want and not what someone else expects of you."

– Michael Asciutto, University of Nevada, Reno, Nevada

"I overcame my time management issue and adapting to the culture at my school by seeking help from others. I reached out to people who were willing to help, whether it was teachers or other students, and I recognized a major change. Additionally, I began to develop a weekly plan that kept me organized while mapping out my entire semester of my major events."

– Michael Ross, United States Military Academy, West Point, New York

"The more I got involved with school events and my sorority, the better it became. Now, starting my senior year, I couldn't imagine being anywhere else."

– Brielle Dennison, Washington State University, Pullman, Washington

"I was able to overcome this simply by swallowing my pride and talking with my professors when I didn't quite understand and had questions. Realizing that I am not going to have all the answers and will need to ask for help."

– Tyler Manu, Yale University, New Haven, Connecticut

"You may get the impression that you shouldn't ask questions or get to know your professor, but that is the complete opposite of what I would suggest! Go talk to them during office hours. Ask as many questions as possible—both in and out of class. Because chances are, someone else in the class is wondering the same thing. If there is something you don't understand, then get it clarified right away. Not by a student or friend either. Because down the road, when you're studying for finals the night before the exam and don't understand something, it's too late and you're going to wish you would have said something. Another benefit to this is that the professor knows who you are. He/she can put a face to a name and is more likely to grade you in a more forgiving way. Seriously though, it's true. College professors don't give a crap about you from the very beginning. This isn't like high school where they need a certain amount of students to attend a certain amount of days. You are paying for that credit, so take full advantage of the source and get to know your professors! This will help you so much along the way if you start doing this your first year. And you'll become more and more confident with your courses."

– *Jenna Julianno, University of Minnesota, Minneapolis, Minnesota*

"Before I started my college career, I had always thought I had worked hard. College eventually taught me how much harder I could actually push myself. Though this did take a lot of time for me to understand, hard work was what helped me overcome my freshman struggles. To help me stay focused and motivated, it was very useful for me to always have my goals in the back of my mind, pushing me and forcing me to work hard."   – *David Trompke, Harvard University, Cambridge, Massachusetts*

"What helped me A LOT was getting tutored and going to our Student Success center and being willing to ask for help and accepting it. Yes, it is a competition to get into college, but once you make it in, everyone there is wanting to help you stay there and be successful."

– *Joshua Taylor, Central Kansas Christian College, McPherson, Kansas*

"In order to do better in class, I joined multiple study groups—universities have free ones, you just need to look for them. If those don't work, there are plenty of tutors and other tutoring options that are offered. Also, use the class teaching assistant, it is their job to help you! And it's free because it's their job as graduate students to teach those in class with them. Also, finding a good group of students in classes with you to study with is very beneficial because group study is a great way to bounce ideas off one another and teach each other different sections of the course. In order to pay for everything and stay in college, I worked two jobs throughout school. On average, I worked in between sixty-five and seventy hours a week to pay for school and all my bills. I understand that is not the norm for people, but the main message is you need to do what is best for you. For me, it was staying in school, and the only way I could stay in school was to work enough to pay to stay. This situation motivated me to keep moving forward in life and graduate school quickly. Throughout school, I realized sometimes life doesn't work out like you imagine it will, but you need to do everything you can to keep striving for more and attain the goals you have for yourself. In my opinion, there is nothing more valuable than education and the opportunities that arise from it. 'Education is the most powerful weapon which you can use to change the world.' - Nelson Mandela.'"

– Samantha Guinn, Colorado State University, Fort Collins, Colorado

"I overcame this by being outgoing. I constantly looked to hang out with different friends, read and learn more, find professors to look up to and build a strong relationship with, take on different perspectives from a wide variety of people with different backgrounds, tried to travel and experience new things, etc."

– Anthony Ross, United States Military Academy, West Point, New York

"I overcame my struggles with developing friendships outside the swim team just by branching out in class and in the training room."

– Maddie Eyolfson, University of Denver, Denver, Colorado

"What helped me was to understand the system and work to truly manage my time. Every school has their own way of handling academics, and it's up to you to figure out the nooks and crannies of your curriculum. You will have to make sacrifices wherever you go to school from going out with friends, working out, drinking, or whatever, but to excel, you need to dedicate time and make sacrifices in other areas for academics. This is ultimately what will set you up for the future, and don't waste an opportunity to improve your GPA for a night out with the bros drinking and singing karaoke of Taylor Swift at some dive bar in Baltimore. Maybe on that, enjoy your time; college is great, even if you are going to a military academy. All work and no play leads to a depressed individual, and there will be times that the juice is worth the squeeze. Additionally, you always have to find that person or teacher who is willing to help you. There is always that one person in class who has awesome notes, a brother who took the course or has the in factor with a class. Find yourself the smartest kid and eat some dessert with him or her. It's your job to find them and get some help to boost your grades, and if you are that person, help out your classmates. We had a saying at West Point that is: 'Cooperate to graduate.' You don't want to be known as the person during graduation who screwed over your classmates.

Social networking after graduation can help you get a job or information on some very important things.

Also, you should get your assignments done as early as possible and get eyes on it so that you can see if it is egregiously wrong or spot on. The 'whole wait until the last minute and it only takes a minute' mentality doesn't work at high-caliber institutions for most people.

Lastly, sacrifice sleep if you aren't willing to sacrifice any other aspect. You will live, just get coffee or pour Tabasco sauce in your eyes.

So, a rundown of what can help you tackle academics would be:

1. Understand the system and adapt.
2. Make sacrifices for everything.
3. Find the smart kid/the willing teacher.
4. Social networking is important not only in college but in the future of working the night shifts at Denny's with your number four side brethren (help people if you can and help will come to you in various forms).
5. Get your assignments done early.
6. Play hard (you can only accomplish so much locked away in your room until you start realizing there is more to college than that twelve-inch monitor).

Being away from your family is something I struggled with because I had never been away from them for an extended amount of time. What helps is to immerse yourself in activities and the new family that you have around you. I guarantee that unless you are the existential equivalent of a yellow starburst (the outcast) that you will know the majority of the people who will be at your wedding from freshman year. Here I have been lucky enough to feed into a profession where the men and women I go to school with will someday give their lives for not only the protection of this great country but may also give their lives to protect myself or anyone else I walk the halls here with. I can genuinely say that I have brothers and sisters that I have had the pleasure of being with for the past five years of my life and am overjoyed to see what they will go out and accomplish. So, if you are struggling with this try a club, rush a frat, tryout for a sport, and definitely get to know the people around you.

Lastly, being away from friends/girlfriend. Make new friends and break up with your girlfriend; you are in college, so enjoy it. I know this sounds blunt, but if they are truly your friends, they will still be there. If you are supposed to be with your girl or guy, cool, but I still think you should enjoy college."

– *Jordan Trompke, United States Military Academy, West Point, New York*

"Entering my freshman year, I was in a unique position, as I was not just entering my freshman year of college. I was also entering the Army. I came to college with a mind-set that I would have a million hours in the day. I thought I would be able to take the maximum credits allowed per semester, be part of every club possible, have a fun social life, study, and fit in all of my ROTC classes. I also thought that I would be able to bring my horse to UVM's co-op barn.

A couple weeks into my first semester, I realized how overwhelmed I was and called my mom in a complete panic attack. I had to withdraw from a class due to simply being fifteen minutes late every day and smelling like horse manure. My typical days started at 4:30 a.m. where I walked 1.5 miles to the gym, where I had my Army physical training. Physical training ends around seven a.m., and from there I would walk another 1.5 miles to the barn to do my morning chores. I would then have to run back to my dorm (three miles) to get ready for my 9:30 class. Being at a co-op barn, I had barn duty two hours a day, so instead of a lunch break I was sprinting back to the barn, doing my other chores, and then sprinting back to class (the class I was always late to). I would then be in the library until midnight or later, just trying to catch up on all my studies.

Moral of the story: Don't overextend yourself your first semester. Come to college, see what your very bare bone schedule is going to be like, and then start adding in the sports, clubs, extra classes, and other extracurricular activities. I am not saying don't get involved, because you absolutely should, and that's how you will make your best friends, but time management is the biggest skill you will have to learn."

– *Grace Harrison, University of Vermont, (ROTC) Burlington, Vermont*

"Time management is crucial while in college. You have to be able to balance schoolwork, friendships, extracurricular, rest, and staying in shape. Have a planner, try to get as much sleep as possible, put away social media, and take study breaks by working out and spending time with friends. College is also a place where people with different personalities and backgrounds come together and have to live together– understanding that everyone isn't like you and being able to tolerate and see the best in people makes for a much more positive college life. Optimism is also important because the stresses of college can cause a bad attitude. What helped me the most was investing in my spiritual life by doing things like finding a good local church that I could go to with my friends every week, joining a men's bible study, and opening up to friends when problems arose or I was going through a difficult time. Most colleges offer plenty of resources other than religious groups that can help with stress and a negative attitude as well. More importantly, though, a good network of solid friends can help you overcome anything."

– Anthony de Vera, United States Naval Academy, Annapolis, Maryland

* * * *

Isn't this great stuff? It really gives you insight into what is important and what you need to prepare yourself for. The common threads of advice I found from all of these students were:

1) **Get involved:** It helps you acclimate and find your place, as well as make new friends. Find the group, sport, church, organization, fraternity/sorority, etc., that fits you.

2) **Time management is key:** Be sure to prioritize right away. Have a planner and use reminders, sticky notes, and eraser boards—whatever it takes for you to be on top of things. Be sure to be mindful of sleeping too! You may have to even manage this in college.

3) **Study and devote time to your schoolwork.** I cannot stress this enough. THIS is why you are at school, and THIS is your first priority. Set aside a time each day for schoolwork and homework.

4) **Ask for help from others:** Don't be afraid to do this. Most of the time others have, or are, going through the same things. Talk to teachers and professors if you do not understand or need help with the transition to college life. I cannot tell you how often I have heard from kids that have asked for help from their teachers, and the teachers have even cut them some slack on the work because they now know the student is trying and asking for help.

5) **Homesickness:** This won't matter whether you are across the country, across town, or in the next state over. You are not home now, period. So expect this, and know and plan for the transition when you start school. Even if you live at home, it is still a change and a time to adapt to a new school, schedule, friends, culture, freedoms, etc.

6) **Be sure to come prepared for this next phase of your life.** Whether you are a parent or a student, you can be ready to face it head on and know what to do when you are there yourself. As a parent, you can know what your student is going through and help guide them through this time and process. Many kids give up on college their freshman year and don't allow themselves time to go through this change and transition. This can be a big mistake for their personal growth and for potential opportunities that college can afford. Being away from home can be tough. It can be tough watching your child go through it as well, but it is very important to allow for this time in their lives.

Therefore, look to the advice of those who have gone through the same things and have come out the other side as wonderful, self-sufficient, incredible adults. In the end, that is what we as parents want for our children and what each young adult wants for themselves. So embrace it—embrace all of the challenges and even embrace the tough times. It will make you a much better person and one who can face anything in this world. Good luck with all of your endeavors, and remember to be strong and focus on all the challenges and opportunities you will have. You've got this!

13

Worksheets and Charts

Recruiting Spreadsheet

School	Coach Name	Phone Number		Date/Left	Date/Left (I M)	Notes

Determining Best Official Visit and Prioritization

School	Date Offered	Date Offered	Date	Date Offered	Date Offered	Date Offered	Rank

GOAL SETTING WORKSHEET

ACADEMIC	ATHLETIC	EXTRACURRICULAR	VOLUNTEER	FAMILY/PERSONAL	COLLEGE GOALS
				No alcohol in high school and no drugs or smoking EVER!	
				Never get into a car with someone who is drinking	

Goal Setting Worksheet

ACADEMIC	ATHLETIC	EXTRACURRICULAR	VOLUNTEER	FAMILY/PERSONAL	COLLEGE GOALS
				No alcohol in high school and no drugs or smoking EVER!	
				Never get into a car with someone who is drinking	

Recruiting Spreadsheet

School	Coach Name	Phone Number	Date/Left Message (LM) or spoke to them	Date/Left Message (LM) or spoke to them	Date/Left Message (LM) or spoke to them	Notes

Official Visit Spreadsheet

School	Coach Name	Date Called	Official Visit Offered	Date(s) Official Visit Offered	Notes	Ranking

Determining Best Official Visit and Prioritization

School	Date Offered	Date Offered	Date Offered	Date Offered	Date Offered	Date Offered	Date Offered	Rank

ACT and SAT Comparatives

School	ACT Score Average for school	SAT Score Average for school	My Score ACT	My Score SAT

Determining the Right College

School Name	Meets, Reach Safe Schools	Location/ Setting/ Size	GPA/ ACT	Major Offered	Tuition, Room and Board, and *Aid	Cost After Aid	Application Deadline	Cost of App. *+	Ranking for program

Scholarships

Scholarship	Website	Deadline	Dollar Amount	Type	Completed

Deciding on Colleges-Final Determination

College Name	Accepted	Deadline to Commit	Financial Aid* Offered/ Scholarships	Loans Offered- Included in Final Cost*	Tuition and Other Costs	Final Cost per Year Not Including Loans	Owed After 4 Years

*Do not include this in your final cost per year, as this is already factored in what you will owe. It is just a nice visual to see what you will need to come up with each year.

Endnotes

(1) "Boys State Web Sites." n.d. The American Legion. Accessed November 1, 2018. http://www.boysandgirlsstate.org/index.html.

(2) "Congressional Award." n.d. Congressional Award. Accessed November 1, 2018. http://congressionalaward.org/.

(3) smeyers@ncaa.org. 2018. "Estimated Probability of Competing in College Athletics." NCAA.org - The Official Site of the NCAA. April 23, 2018. http://www.ncaa.org/about/resources/research/estimated-probability-competing-college-athletics.

(4) smeyers@ncaa.org. 2017. "Division I Academic Eligibility." NCAA.org - The Official Site of the NCAA. February 14, 2017. http://www.ncaa.org/about/division-i-academic-eligibility.

(5) "Want to Play College Sports?" n.d. NCAA Eligibility Center. Accessed November 1, 2018. https://web3.ncaa.org/ecwr3/.

(6) jcoleman@ncaa.org. 2018. "Recruiting." NCAA.org - The Official Site of the NCAA. October 3, 2018. http://www.ncaa.org/student-athletes/future/recruiting.

(7) "NCAA Eligibility Center." n.d. NCAA Eligibility Center. Accessed November 1, 2018. http://www.ncaaclearinghouse.net/.

(8) Home. "ARE YOU READY TO COMMIT?" National Letter of Intent. Accessed November 1, 2018. http://www.nationalletter.org/.

(9) "The Harvard Crimson." Taking on the AI | Sports. Accessed November 2, 2018. http://www.thecrimson.com/article/2013/5/30/harvard-academic-index-explanation/.

10) "Inside the Test." SAT Suite of Assessments, Last modified December 18, 2017. https://collegereadiness.collegeboard.org/sat/inside-the-test.

(11) "Interpreting Your Scores." SAT Suite of Assessments, Last modified July 16, 2018. https://collegereadiness.collegeboard.org/sat/scores/understanding-scores/interpreting.

(12) "What Is the ACT?" What Is the ACT? | The Princeton Review. Accessed November 2, 2018. https://www.princetonreview.com/college/act-information.

(13) Safier, Rebecca. "SAT / ACT Prep Online Guides and Tips." Which Colleges Superscore the SAT? Accessed November 2, 2018. https://blog.prepscholar.com/which-colleges-superscore-the-sat.

(14) "ACT / SAT Concordance." ACT. Accessed November 2, 2018. http://www.act.org/content/act/en/products-and-services/the-act/scores/act-sat-concordance.html.

(15) "Application Steps." Air Force Academy. Accessed November 2, 2018. https://www.academyadmissions.com/admissions/the-application-process/application-steps/#checkeligibility.

"Application Steps." Air Force Academy. Accessed November 2, 2018. https://www.academyadmissions.com/admissions/the-application-process/application-steps/#checkeligibility.

"Apply to USNA." U.S. Naval Academy Seal. Accessed November 2, 2018. https://www.usna.edu/Admissions/Apply/index.php#fndtn-panel1-Steps-for.

(16) Admissions - FAQ_Admission. Accessed November 2, 2018. https://www.usma.edu/admissions/SitePages/FAQ_Admission.aspx.

(17) "Academic Performance." Air Force Academy. Accessed November 2, 2018. http://www.academyadmissions.com/admissions/the-application-process/academic-performance/#SAT_ACT.

(18) Admissions - Class Profiles. Accessed November 2, 2018. https://www.usma.edu/admissions/SitePages/Class Profiles.aspx.

(19) http://www.usma.edu/classes/SiteAssets/SitePages/2015/2015profile.pdf

(20) "America's Top Colleges." Forbes. Accessed November 2, 2018. https://www.forbes.com/top-colleges/list/.

(21) "The Candidate Fitness Assessment." U.S. Naval Academy Seal. Accessed November 2, 2018. https://www.usna.edu/Admissions/Candidate-Fitness-Assessment.php.

(22) "2016-2017 Average Starting Teacher Salaries by State." NEA. Accessed November 2, 2018. http://www.nea.org/home/2016-2017-average-starting-teacher-salary.html.

"Salary: Investment Banking Analyst First Year." Glassdoor. Accessed November 2, 2018. https://www.glassdoor.com/Salaries/investment-banking-analyst-first-year-salary-SRCH_KO0,37.htm.

"Salary: Entry Level Engineer." Glassdoor. Accessed November 2, 2018. https://www.glassdoor.com/Salaries/entry-level-engineer-salary-SRCH_KO0,20.htm.

"Average Entry-Level Registered Nurse (RN) Hourly Pay." Entry Level Registered Nurse (RN) Hourly Pay | PayScale. Accessed November 2, 2018. https://www.payscale.com/research/US/Job=Registered_Nurse_(RN)/Hourly_Rate/b6142914/Entry-Level.

Strauss, Eric. "Starting Salary of a Physical Therapist." Chron.com, Last modified November 9, 2016. https://work.chron.com/starting-salary-physical-therapist-8447.html.

"Salary: Attorney, 1st-Year." Glassdoor. Accessed November 2, 2018. https://www.glassdoor.com/Salaries/attorney-1st-year-salary-SRCH_KO0,17.htm.

Salary.com. "Salary for Producer." Salary.com. Accessed November 2, 2018. https://www1.salary.com/Producer-Salary.html.

"Average Average Entry-Level Public Relations (PR) Specialist Salary Public Relations (PR) Specialist Salary." Average Entry-Level Public Relations (PR) Specialist Salary Public Relations (PR) Specialist Salary | PayScale. Accessed November 2, 2018. https://www.payscale.com/research/US/Job=Public_Relations_(PR)_Specialist/Salary/6082444e/Entry-Level.

"Average Average Entry-Level Pharmacist Salary Pharmacist Salary." Average Entry-Level Pharmacist Salary Pharmacist Salary | PayScale. Accessed November 2, 2018. https://www.payscale.com/research/US/Job=Pharmacist/Salary/8fe870fa/Entry-Level.

(23) "About." QuestBridge | About. Accessed November 2, 2018. https://www.questbridge.org/about.

(24) "Gates Millennium Scholars Program." GMS. Accessed November 2, 2018. http://gmsp.org/.

(25) Lindsay, Samantha. "SAT / ACT Prep Online Guides and Tips." What's the Difference? Weighted vs Unweighted GPA. Accessed November 2, 2018. https://blog.prepscholar.com/weighted-vs-unweighted-gpa-whats-the-difference.

(26) Lyon, Anne. "SAT Subject Tests 101: What To Take When." Welcome to Local Betty. Accessed November 2, 2018. http://www.localbetty.com/about-town-articles/3-schools/386-sat-subject-tests-101-what-to-take-when.html.

(27) "SAT Subject Tests." SAT Suite of Assessments, Last modified October 25, 2018. https://collegereadiness.collegeboard.org/sat-subject-tests.

(28) "FAFSA®: Apply for Aid." Federal Student Aid, Last modified October 17, 2018. https://studentaid.ed.gov/sa/fafsa.

(29) "Federal Pell Grants." Federal Student Aid, Last modified September 18, 2018. https://studentaid.ed.gov/sa/types/grants-scholarships/pell.

(30) "Subsidized and Unsubsidized Loans." Federal Student Aid, Last modified September 18, 2018. https://studentaid.ed.gov/sa/types/loans/subsidized-unsubsidized.

(31) "Federal Work-Study (FWS) Program." Home. Last modified April 17, 2014. https://www2.ed.gov/programs/fws/index.html.

(32) "Apply for College Financial Aid – CSS Profile – The College Board." CSS Profile, Last modified November 1, 2018. https://cssprofile.collegeboard.org/.

(33) "Fact Sheet." Harvard College. Accessed November 2, 2018. https://college.harvard.edu/financial-aid/

About the Author

Sari Trompke resides in Eagle, Idaho and was born and raised in Chicago, Illinois. Sari has been married to her husband, Ron, for over thirty years.

Sari Trompke grew up in the suburbs of Chicago, Illinois. She headed west to Los Angeles to pursue a career in the financial services industry, where she earned her a management position at the age of twenty-one. While in Los Angeles, she met and married her now-husband, Ron. They have four wonderful children, Rachel, Jordan, David, and Alex.

As a stay-at-home mom (and after homeschooling her own children for several years), Sari discovered her passion for learning and developed her desire to teach and help others with the knowledge that she obtained. She believes that the key to success for children is involvement and help from parents, coaches, counselors, and adults in the community who are willing to help navigate students through the college and recruiting process. In much of Sari's spare time, she helps students and families in her community through the college admissions and recruiting process.

After a twelve year absence from the workplace, Sari stepped back into the workforce, working at Horizon Air/Alaska Airlines as a trainer for five years. When her children hit their teens, she chose to step back out from the workplace again to help them with the day-to-day structure at home. She volunteered at their school, overseeing the Speech and Debate Program, football, basketball, track and field, and the swim team as a President and/or Team Mom. When her children were out of high school, she worked her way up to Manager of Training and Development at Bigelow Tea, where she is able to utilize her desire to help and develop the people who work for the company.

Forever
ELVIS

Forever ELVIS

John Alvarez Taylor

SMITHMARK

This edition published in 1992 by SMITHMARK Publishers Inc., 112 Madison Avenue New York, New York 10016

SMITHMARK books are available for bulk purchase for sales promotion and premium use. For details write or telephone the Manager of Special Sales, SMITHMARK Publishers Inc., 112 Madison Avenue, New York, NY 10016. (212) 532-6600.

Produced by Brompton Books Corp., 15 Sherwood Place Greenwich, CT 06830

ISBN 0-8317-3469-8

Printed in Hong Kong

10 9 8 7 6 5 4 3 2 1

Photo Credits

All photos courtesy of American Graphic Systems Archives except those listed below:
© RE DeJauregui 63 (bottom)
Las Vegas News Bureau 42 (bottom), 49 (bottom)
Mississippi Department of Economic Development 11 (bottom)
Tennessee Tourist Development 60 (all), 61 (all), 62
© Bill Yenne 63 (top)

Page 1: Elvis stares sincerely to camera left, on the set of one of his many Metro-Goldwyn-Mayer motion pictures.
Page 2: Elvis thrills his fans during the famous 'comeback special' of 1968.
These pages, left—In an all-out dance number from the movie *Jailhouse Rock*, Elvis cut a flamboyant figure—and *right*—with a coterie of fans, circa 1956.

Designed by Ruth DeJauregui

CONTENTS

Introduction	6
Elvis on the Rise	9
The Soft Light of Home	11
Elvis Meets Television	13
The Hillbilly Sophisticate	14
On the Silver Screen	17
Jailhouse Rock	19
King Creole	20
In the Army Now	23
World's Most Famous GI	24
Flaming Blues	26
Wild in Hawaii	28
Many Elvises	30
Viva Las Vegas	33
Three Light Films	35
Double Trouble	36
Charro!	39
Sweet Memories	40
Three of Them	42
The Good Old Days	44
Elvis Comes Back	47
On Stage Again	49
Celebrity	50
The Way It Was	53
Aloha	54
How Great Is Great	56
He Gave It All	59
Graceland	61
In Memoriam	63
Index	64

INTRODUCTION

Born on 8 January 1935, in Tupelo, Mississippi, Elvis was one of a set of twins born to Vernon Elvis Presley and Gladys Love Presley. From the very beginning, Elvis Aron Presley was a survivor: his brother, Jesse Garon Presley, died six hours after birth. As a boy, Elvis enjoyed singing in the East Heights Assembly of God Church. He first performed publicly while in fifth grade, singing 'Old Shep' on WELO radio, as a reward for taking second place in a talent contest.

The family moved to Memphis, Tennessee, where Elvis attended OC Hume High School. While driving a truck for the Crown Electric Company, Elvis stopped by Sun Records' Memphis Recording Services, where he paid four dollars to record two songs—'My Happiness' and 'That's When Your Heartache Begins.' He returned there in January 1954 to record 'Casual Love Affair' and I'll Never Stand in Your Way.' This time, Sam Phillips, the head of Sun Records, liked what he heard, and a legendary singing career began.

His recordings mounted up, and he became a regional phenomenon, then a national and an international phenomenon. After television appearances on the Dorsey brothers' *Stage Show* and the *Milton Berle Show*, Elvis signed a contract with Hal Wallis of Paramount Pictures to star in three motion pictures. Elvis was to make further television appearances on the Steve Allen, Jackie Gleason and Ed Sullivan variety shows.

Among his early hit songs were 'Mystery Train' (1954) and 'That's All Right, Mama' (1954) (both with Sun Records); 'I Got a Woman,' 'Money, Honey,' 'Heartbreak Hotel,' 'Lawdy Miss Clawdy,' 'Shake, Rattle and Roll,' 'Tutti Frutti' and 'Blue Suede Shoes' (all January of 1956, with RCA Records); 'Jailhouse Rock,' 'All Shook Up,' 'Let Me Be Your Teddy Bear' and 'Too Much' (all 1957, with RCA); plus RCA renditions of 'All Shook Up' and 'It's Now or Never.'

In fact, Elvis recorded three dozen tracks in late 1956, many of which were released during his two-year tour of duty with the US Army at the end of the decade. These included 'Love Me Tender,' 'Don't Be Cruel,' 'Ready Teddy,' 'Rip It Up,' 'Long Tall Sally' and his greatest hit *ever*: 'You Ain't Nothin' But a Hound Dog.'

His acting future lay in motion pictures, however, and since Paramount had no immediate project for Elvis, Hal Wallis arranged a deal with the Twentieth Century-Fox studios, and thereafter handled many of Elvis' 'movie deals.'

Elvis' first film for Fox was to be *Love Me Tender*, co-starring Richard Egan and Deborah Paget. Released on 16 November 1956, it was a smash hit. Through the years, he would star in 30 motion pictures, among which were *Loving You* (Paramount, 1957); *Jailhouse Rock* (Metro-Goldwyn-Mayer, 1957); *King Creole* (Paramount, 1958); *GI Blues* (Paramount, 1960); *Flaming Star* (Twentieth Century-Fox, 1960); *Wild in the Country* (Twentieth Century-Fox, 1961); *Blue Hawaii* (Paramount, 1961); *Follow That Dream* (United Artists, 1962); *Kid Galahad* (United Artists, 1962); *Girls! Girls! Girls!* (Paramount, 1962); *It Happened at the World's Fair* (Metro-Goldwyn-Mayer, 1962); *Fun in Acapulco* (Hal Wallis Productions, 1962); *Kissin' Cousins* (Metro-Goldwyn-Mayer, 1964); *Viva Las Vegas* (Metro-Goldwyn-Mayer, 1964); *Paradise, Hawaiian Style* (Paramount, 1966); *Spinout* (Metro-Goldwyn-Mayer, 1966); *Easy Come, Easy Go* (Paramount,1967); *Double Trouble* (Metro-Goldwyn-Mayer, 1967); *Clambake* (United Artists, 1967); *Stay Away, Joe* (Metro-Goldwyn-Mayer, 1968); *Speedway* (Metro-Goldwyn-Mayer, 1968); *Live a Little, Love a Little* (Metro-Goldwyn-Mayer, 1968); *Charro!* (National General Productions, Inc, 1969); and *The Trouble With Girls* (Metro-Goldwyn-Mayer, December 1969); *Change of Habit* (NBC-Universal, January 1970).

There were also documentaries such as *Elvis: That's the Way It Is* (Metro-Goldwyn-Mayer, 1970) and *Elvis on Tour* (Metro-Goldwyn-Mayer, 1972), plus a number of television specials, including *Aloha From Hawaii* (1973).

With the revival of his live performance career in 1968, Elvis again began turning out the hit records, as is discussed later in this book. When he died in 1977, Elvis Presley was 42, and yet had lived a life that would require most men several full lifetimes to live. In his worldwide community of fans, he lives on.

Facing page: Elvis Aron Presley had an impoverished childhood that was rich in his parents' love. When he died a wealthy man on 16 August 1977, the world lost one of its greatest entertainers.

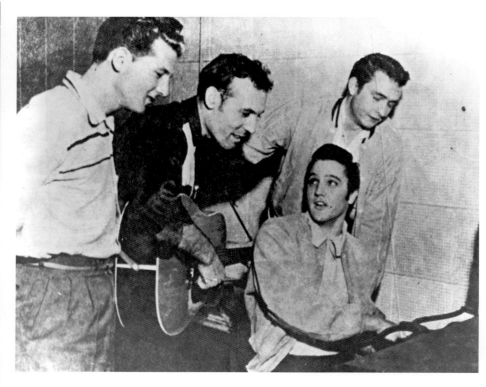

Elvis on the Rise

After signing a three-year contract with Sun Records on 19 July 1954, Elvis began his climb. *Above left:* Elvis with his beloved mother, Gladys Love Presley. *At far left:* In full swing as the 'Hillbilly Cat' on the local variety show, *Louisiana Hay Ride*, in 1955.

Elvis' peers were also legendary. *At left:* In the Sun studios—(left to right) Jerry Lee Lewis, Carl Perkins, Elvis, and Johnny Cash. *Above:* The rising star maintains his image. *At right:* The clothes were a part of it all—not to mention blue suede shoes.

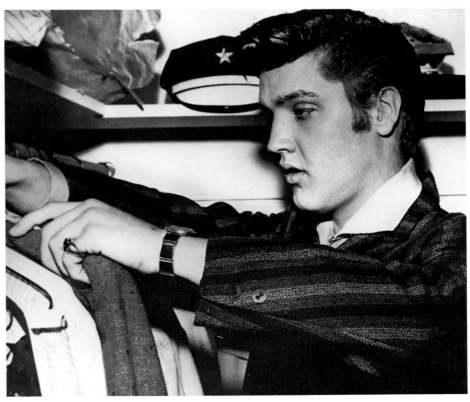

The Soft Light of Home

Elvis' face was tailor-made for soft-lit promotional photos: he seemed so at home in them. *At left:* Elvis lambent, with guitar.

As a performer, he was brilliant in any light *(above)*, but in his heart remained one true home *(at right)*, the little house his father built in Tupelo, Mississippi.

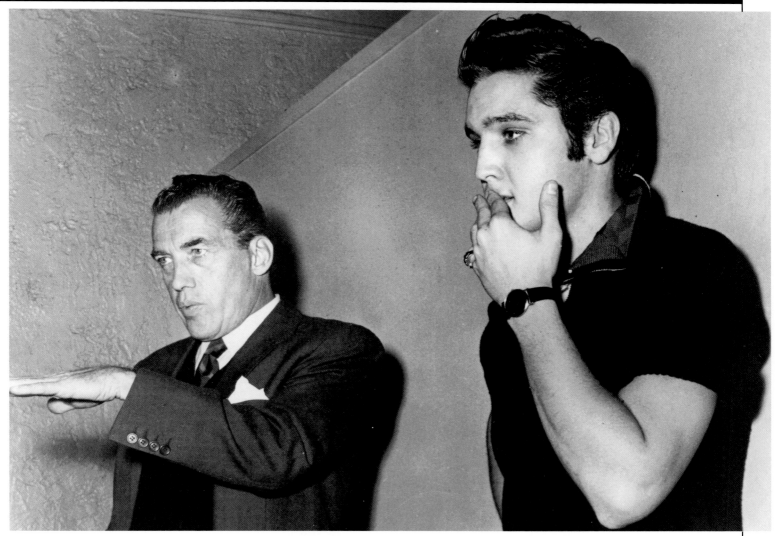

Elvis Meets Television

Elvis was a sensation during a western skit on the *Steve Allen Show* in 1956—*at right*, left to right: Andy Griffith, Imogene Coca, Elvis and Steve Allen. He was downright controversial in his appearances on Ed Sullivan's *Toast of the Town (above)*; but seemed to swing with those 'Kings of Swing,' Tommy and Jimmy Dorsey *(above left)* on their *Stage Show* in 1956.

He went from riveting to wild in his live performances *(at left, both)*.

The Hillbilly Sophisticate

By 1957, Elvis Presley was internationally acclaimed, yet the publicity was both a source of pride and meditative wonderment for him. *At left and above:* Elvis at the microphone, and in a thoughtful mood.

His wealth was such that in March, 1957, he gave his mother a $100,000 mansion where the Presley family could live together. This mansion was to be called Graceland. *At right:* Elvis at Graceland.

On the Silver Screen

Elvis starred in 30 motion pictures. *At left:* Elvis and Deborah Paget in *Love Me Tender* (1956). *At right:* Elvis solo, and with Lizabeth Scott *(above)* and Dolores Hart *(above right)* in *Loving You* (1957).

Jailhouse Rock

Elvis, as Vince Everett, slays a bully (*above left*), and is arrested (*at left*). *Above and top right:* 'Everybody in the whole cellblock/ was dancin' to the jailhouse rock....' Elvis/Vince was convincingly surrounded by adoring fans (*above right*), and found true love with co-star Judy Tyler, as Peggy Van Alden (*at right*).

King Creole

At left: Elvis as Danny Fisher and Carolyn Jones as 'Ronnie' in *King Creole* (1958). *Above:* Elvis/Danny in a fighting pose.

Above right: He wears an 'eat your heart out' look as he is kissed by costars Dolores Hart and Ms Jones.

At right: Elvis/Danny confronts Walter Matthau, as the notorious Maxie Fields, in an electrifying scene.

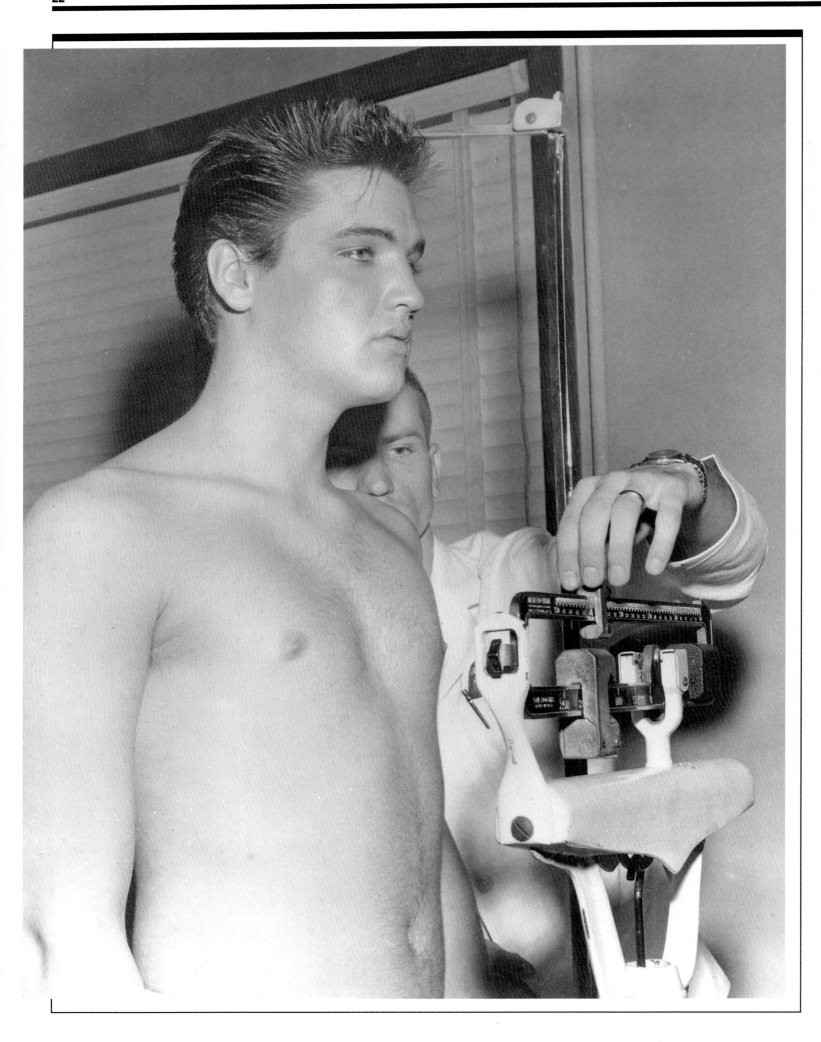

In the Army Now

On 24 March 1958, Elvis was accompanied to the Memphis Armed Forces Induction Center to begin serving a draft-mandated term in the US Army.

He volunteered for regular duty, as opposed to a special entertainment unit, and spent a two-year stint at a military installation in West Germany, attaining the rank of Sergeant.

On these pages are views of Elvis' Army experience.

World's Most Famous GI

Above: Sergeant Elvis Presley very happily fields 'media flak' upon his discharge in March 1960.

Colonel Parker was close at hand upon Elvis' discharge, as is evidenced by the photo *at left*.

At right: Elvis waves 'goodbye to all that,' and hello to resuming his career. His stay in West Germany had one lasting effect on his life—he had Priscilla Beaulieu there.

Flaming Blues

This page: Elvis, reprising his military experience, as Tulsa MacLean in *GI Blues* (1960). *At right:* He evinced a much different persona as Pacer Burton in *Flaming Star* (1960).

Wild in Hawaii

This page: Elvis Presley, as Glenn Tyler, and Tuesday Weld, as 'Noreen,' in scenes from *Wild in the Country* (1961).

At right: Elvis and a bevy of female extras in a promotion still for *Blue Hawaii* (1961), which gave him a limited chance to don his old Army uniform *(above far right)*.

Elvis portrayed Chad Gates, who is seen *at above right* with one of his paramours in the film.

Many Elvises

Facing page: Elvis, co-stars and a special-effects double in *Kissin' Cousins* (1964). *Above, both:* Elvis and a young co-star in *It Happened at the World's Fair* (1962). *At left:* Elvis as Walter Gulick in *Kid Galahad* (1962).

Viva Las Vegas

These pages: Elvis and co-star Ann-Margret in their roles as 'Lucky' and 'Rusty,' respectively, in the April 1964 release of *Viva Las Vegas* (1964).

Elvis, as 'Lucky,' was an aspiring race car driver, and Ann-Margret's 'Rusty' was a swimming instructor. Songs include a duet, 'The Lady Loves Me,' featuring the two stars.

Three Light Films

Facing page: Elvis as Johnny Tyronne in *Harum Scarum* (1965).

Above: Elvis and supporting cast in *Paradise, Hawaiian Style* (1966).

At right: A publicity still for *Roustabout* (1964), in which Elvis played a carnival jack-of-all-trades named Charlie Rogers.

Double Trouble

Above and at left: Scenes from *Double Trouble* (1967), in which Elvis portrayed disco singer Guy Lambert, an otherwise happy-go-lucky fellow who is pursued through Belgium by a literal mob of people—some of whom love him and some of whom want to kill him. Also shown here is co-star Annette Day, as Jill Conway.

At right: In *Clambake* (1967), Elvis played Scott Heyward, a millionaire.

Charro!

These pages: Elvis in costume as reformed outlaw Jess Wade in *Charro!* (1969), with supporting cast and love interest, 'Tracie,' who was portrayed by Ina Balin.

This film is the only motion picture in which Elvis sported a beard. The fighting pose fits one of Elvis' personal interests—he had been a fan of martial arts since his days in the US Army, when he took his first lessons with an instructor in West Germany.

Sweet Memories

While motion pictures took up most of his time in the 1960s, Elvis longed to return to live performance in front of screaming, enthusiastic, fans.

Even as he worked on such films as *Clambake*, *Double Trouble* and *Charro!*, scenes of his earlier career—and the closeness to his adoring fans that he then enjoyed—washed through his mind.

These pages: A younger Elvis with his fans.

Three of Them

Elvis Presley had courted Priscilla Beaulieu since August 1959. They were married at 9:41 am on 1 May 1967 in Las Vegas. *Above right:* Elvis and Priscilla, just after exchanging marital vows. *At left:* The newlyweds prepare to cut their cake at the reception. *Above:* The rice rains down on Mr and Mrs Elvis Presley.

On 1 February 1968, Priscilla gave birth to Lisa Marie Presley at Memphis' Baptist Memorial Hospital. *At right:* Lisa Marie and her mom and dad emerge from the hospital.

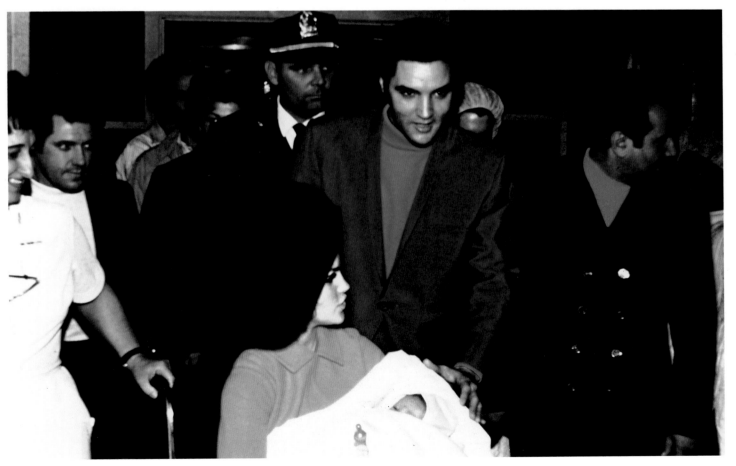

The Good Old Days

In the late-1960s, Elvis' fans prepared for the return of an Elvis they hadn't seen since the 1950s—a performer who shook the world with his dramatic pop renditions.

Above: Elvis at the microphone in the Sun Records studios, in one of his earliest recording sessions, circa 1954. His first hit was 'That's All Right, Mama.'

At left: Taking a breather during a session. *Facing page:* Charisma to burn, and a much-imitated pose.

Elvis Comes Back

His millions of fans also wanted to see Elvis live—and singing. He made his comeback on the concert stage via television.

The show was taped between 27 and 29 June 1968, and was aired on 3 December of that same year. It was a smash hit, and was proof of Elvis' blossoming forth as a musician once again. *These pages:* scenes from his comeback special.

The special featured the brand-new million seller 'If I Can Dream,' and a plethora of such Elvis classics as 'Heartbreak Hotel,' 'Don't Be Cruel,' 'Jailhouse Rock' and 'Are You Lonesome Tonight?'

Sincerely Yours
Elvis

On Stage Again

At left: A fan photo from his comeback special. *Above right:* Yet another flamboyant outfit.

He wanted to tour. Colonel Parker set up a contract with Las Vegas' International Hotel for 56 shows in 28 days in July 1969. Opening night was his first strictly live performance in nine years, featuring 'All Shook Up,' 'Blue Suede Shoes,' 'Tiger Man,' 'In the Ghetto' and other songs that were a cross-section of his musical career.

It was a triumph. *At right:* A marquee from one of Elvis' many subsequent Las Vegas stints.

Celebrity

Above: Elvis during a break from one of his late-1960s movies. *At far right:* Elvis in his car, surrounded by his fans, circa 1957.

He was a fan of policemen and criminology. On 21 December 1970, he scribbled a request to be made a federal narcotics officer, handed it to a White House security guard, and was immediately admitted to see US President Richard Nixon — who granted his request *(at right)*.

At left: Emblems of a lifetime of achievement, at Graceland. *Above right:* Elvis and Vernon, his dad.

The Way It Was

Facing page: Elvis, on tour, as represented in *Elvis: That's the Way It Is* (1970), one of two documentaries.

During its filming, Elvis recorded four songs: 'Snowbird,' 'Whole Lotta Shakin' Goin' On,' 'Rags to Riches' and 'Where Did They Go, Lord?'

His concert song selection eventually included 'Proud Mary,' 'Polk Salad Annie,' 'Bridge Over Troubled Water,' 'Let Me Be There' and the 'American Trilogy' medley of 'Dixie,' 'The Battle Hymn of the Republic' and 'All My Trials.'

This page: Two scenes from *Elvis on Tour*, the second of the 'on tour' documentaries, which won the Golden Globe Award for Best Documentary of 1972.

Aloha

Above and at left: Elvis in performance. In the 1970s, his live concerts were all sold out, and his television specials reached vast audiences. For instance, his *Aloha From Hawaii* show of 14 January 1973 was simulcast from Honolulu to 40 countries worldwide, with an estimated 500 million viewers.

With hits like 'Big Boss Man' and 'Burnin' Love,' Elvis' sound filled the airwaves again. Even so, it was painful for him at times. He and Priscilla—his true love and the mother of their only child—divorced on 9 October 1973. *Facing page:* On location for *Aloha From Hawaii.*

How Great Is Great

These pages: Elvis at work, with a fan and taking a break. Rock stars universally acknowledge his influence: 'Without Elvis,' said Buddy Holly, 'none of us could have made it.' 'That Elvis, man....wrote the book,' says Bruce Springsteen.

Elvis won the first of his four Grammy Awards in 1967 for the gospel album *How Great Thou Art*, which went on to win an unusual *second* Grammy in 1974. Another gospel album, *He Touched Me*, won him another Grammy in 1972.

Elvis also won The Bing Crosby Award of 1971—a special Grammy 'for creative contributions of outstanding artistic or scientific significance.'

Memphis Press-Scimitar

U.S. WEATHER FORECAST: A 60 per cent chance of rain with high in the upper 80s. Low tonight low 70s. High Thursday mid 80s.

SPECIAL EDITION

47TH YEAR   MEMPHIS, TENN., WEDNESDAY, AUGUST 17, 1977   TELEPHONES

Memphis Leads the World in Mourning the Monarch of Rock 'n Roll

A Lonely Life Ends on Elvis Presley Boulevard

A Tribute to Elvis

The unexpected death of rock 'n roll star Elvis Presley Aug. 16, 1977, was news of international impact. Almost every news agency in the world reported the tragedy under a Memphis dateline.

The public interest required that many members of The Press-Scimitar staff have a hand in compiling and presenting the story. Every conceivable angle was covered in a period of five publication days. Requests for copies of The Press-Scimitar containing coverage of the singer's death poured in from all over the world in great numbers. It was impossible to meet the demand.

Therefore, as a public service to its readers, The Press-Scimitar has reprinted in this special tribute edition all Elvis Presley stories and pictures published in the five-day period. With as few changes as possible, all stories and pictures that we published in the regular editions of The Press-Scimitar are reprinted herein. This edition plus a similar edition of The Commercial Appeal are offered to readers for 56 cents.

ELVIS PRESLEY, THE BEAT WENT ON — AND ON AND ON

Mourners In Waiting For Last Homecoming Of Revered Singer

Tribute Begins to Flow Freely For Pioneer of Rock 'n Roll

Death Sets Off Run at Record Stores

(Aug. 17, 1977)

Carter Pays Tribute to Elvis

(Aug. 16, 1977)

WASHINGTON (UPI) — President Carter said today Elvis Presley "permanently changed the face of American popular culture" and became a worldwide symbol of his country's "vitality, rebelliousness and good humor."

The President, in a statement issued by the White House on Presley's death, said the popular singer was "unique" and is "irreplaceable."

"Elvis Presley's death deprives our country of a part of itself," Carter said.

OVERCOME BY GRIEF FROM SEEING ELVIS
An unidentified woman receives assistance after she viewed body of singer

On the Inside

THE PROGRESSION of Elvis Presley's career is examined in a pictorial biography. Page 3.

SOME EDITORIAL COMMENT on the phenomenon of one of rock music's earliest and most enduring stars is offered on Page 4.

STAFF WRITER Perry Burch studies and much-discussed possibility that Presley suffered from a rare blood disease called lupus. See Page 9.

A FULL PAGE of color pictures of Presley's funeral day on Page 12.

He Gave It All

Elvis did extended stints in Las Vegas, his concert 'home,' and became somewhat of a fixture there, while also maintaining a grueling 'road' schedule—between 17 March 1975 and 1 January 1976, for instance, he toured 74 cities.

It all came to an end with his death on 16 August 1977—an event that filled front pages locally (*facing page*) and around the world. *Above and at right, both:* Visions of the Elvis that fans knew and loved.

Graceland

Located near US Highway 51 on the south side of Memphis, Graceland and its extensive grounds are a landmark for Elvis fans the world over. With a wealth of memorabilia from the great moments of an unforgettable life, Graceland has become a monument to Elvis Presley. *These pages:* Views of Graceland.

4E 77

ELVIS ARON PRESLEY

Elvis Presley was born in Tupelo, Mississippi on January 8, 1935, the son of Vernon and Gladys Presley. He moved to Memphis in 1948. Soon after signing a contract with Sun Records in 1954 he achieved tremendous popularity. His musical and acting career in records, movies, television, and concerts made him one of the most successful and outstanding entertainers in the world. He died on August 16, 1977 and is buried here at his Memphis home, Graceland.

In Memoriam

Facing page: Elvis' grave at Graceland, a site that is visited by thousands yearly—note that the spelling of his middle name here is actually a *misspelling*, for public relations purposes.

At right: Elvis' star shines bright on Hollywood Boulevard, in company with those of other great entertainers. He was *and is* so special to his fans that many refuse to believe that he is 'gone' in any literal sense of the word.

Above: A young fan poses by a plaque that only hints at the true story of Elvis Presley.

ELVIS PRESLEY

INDEX

Allen, Steve 6, 13, *13*
Aloha From Hawaii 6, 54, *55*
Ann-Margret 61, *60–61*
Balin, Ina *38*, 39
Baptist Memorial Hospital,
　Memphis 42, *43*
Beaulieu, Priscilla—see Presley,
　Priscilla Beaulieu
Blue Hawaii 6, 28, *29*
Cash, Johnny 9, *10*
Change of Habit 6
Charro! 6, *38–39*, 39, 40
Clambake 6, 36, *37*, 40
Coca, Imogene 13, *13*
Craig, Yvonne *30*
Crown Electric Company 6
Day, Annette 36, *36*
Dorsey, Jimmy *12*, 13
Dorsey, Tommy *12*, 13
Double Trouble 6, 36, *36*, 40
East Heights Assembly of God
　Church 6
Easy Come, Easy Go 6
Eden, Barbara *27*
Egan, Richard 6
Elvis on Tour 6, 53, *53*
Elvis: That's the Way It Is 6, *52*, 53
Elvis' 'comeback special' *2*, *46–47*,
　47, *48*, 49
Flaming Star 6, 26, *27*
Follow That Dream 6
Fun in Acapulco 6
GI Blues 6, 26, *26–27*
Girls! Girls! Girls! 6
Gleason, Jackie 6
Golden Globe Award 53
Graceland 14, 15, 50, *50*, *60–63*,
　61, *63*
Grammy Awards 56
Griffith, Andy 13, *13*
Hal Wallis Productions 6
Hart, Dolores 17, *17*, 20, *21*
Harum Scarum 34, 35
He Touched Me 56
Holly, Buddy 56
Hollywood Boulevard *63*
How Great Thou Art 56
International Hotel, Las Vegas 49,
　49
It Happened at the World's Fair 6, 30,
　30
Jailhouse Rock *4*, 6, *18–19*, 19
Jones, Carolyn 20, *20–21*
Kid Galahad 6, 30, *30*
King Creole 6, 20, *20–21*

Kissin' Cousins 6, 30, *31*
Las Vegas, Nevada 42, *42–43*, 49,
　59
Lewis, Jerry Lee 9, *10*
Live a Little, Love a Little 6
Louisiana Hay Ride 9, *10*
Love Me Tender 6, *16*, 17
Loving You 6, 17, *17*
Matthau, Walter 20, *21*
Memphis, Tennessee 6, 61
Metro-Goldwyn-Mayer 1, 6
Milton Berle Show 6
National General Productions, Inc 6
NBC-Universal Studios 6
Nixon, US President Richard 50,
　51
OC Hume High School 6
Paget, Deborah 6, *16*, 17
Paradise, Hawaiian Style 6, 35, *35*
Paramount Pictures 6
Parker, Col Tom 24, *24*, 49
Pepper, Cynthia *30*
Perkins, Carl 9, *10*
Phillips, Sam 6
Presley, Gladys Love 6, 9, *10*, 14
Presley, Jesse Garon 6
Presley, Lisa Marie 42, *43*
Presley, Priscilla Beaulieu 24, 42,
　42–43, 54
Presley, Vernon Elvis 6, 50, *51*
RCA Records 6
Roustabout 35, *35*
Scott, Lizabeth 17, *17*
Speedway 6
Spinout 6
Springsteen, Bruce 56
Stage Show 6, *12*, 13
Stay Away, Joe 6
Steve Allen Show 13, *13*
Sullivan, Ed 6
Sun Records 6
Sun Records studios 9, *10*, 44, *44*
Sun Records' Memphis Recording
　Services 6
The Bing Crosby Award 56
The Trouble With Girls 6
Tiu, Vicky *30*
Toast of the Town 13, *13*
Tupelo, Mississippi 6, 11, *11*
Twentieth Century-Fox 6
Tyler, Judy 19, *19*
United Artists 6
US Army 6, *22–25*, 23, 39
Viva Las Vegas 6, 61, *60–61*
Wallis, Hal 6

Weld, Tuesday 28, *28*
WELO Radio 6
West Germany 23–24, 39
Wild in the Country 6, 28, *28*

Songs

'All My Trials' 53
'All Shook Up' 6, 49
'American Trilogy' medley 53
'Are You Lonesome Tonight?' 47
'Big Boss Man' 54
'Blue Suede Shoes' 6, 49
'Bridge Over Troubled Water' 53
'Burnin' Love' 54
'Casual Love Affair' 6
'Dixie' 53
'Don't Be Cruel' 6, 47
'Heartbreak Hotel' 6, 47
'I Got a Woman' 6
'I'll Never Stand in Your Way' 6
'In the Ghetto' 49
'It's Now or Never' 6
'Jailhouse Rock' 6, 47
'Lawdy Miss Clawdy' 6
'Let Me Be There' 53
'Let Me Be Your Teddy Bear' 6
'Long Tall Sally' 6
'Love Me Tender' 6
'Money, Honey' 6
'My Happiness' 6
'Mystery Train' 6
'Old Shep' 6
'Polk Salad Annie' 53
'Proud Mary' 53
'Rags to Riches' 53
'Ready Teddy' 6
'Rip It Up' 6
'Shake, Rattle and Roll' 6
'Snowbird' 53
'That's All Right, Mama' 6, 44
'That's When Your Heartache
　Begins' 6
'The Battle Hymn of the
　Republic' 53
'The Lady Loves Me' 61
'Tiger Man' 49
'Too Much' 6
'Tutti Frutti' 6
'Where Did They Go, Lord?' 53
'Whole Lotta Shakin' Goin' On' 53
'You Ain't Nothin' But a Hound
　Dog' 6

STYLING FOR INSTAGRAM

Brimming with creative inspiration, how-to projects, and useful information to enrich your everyday life, Quarto Knows is a favourite destination for those pursuing their interests and passions. Visit our site and dig deeper with our books into your area of interest: Quarto Creates, Quarto Cooks, Quarto Homes, Quarto Lives, Quarto Drives, Quarto Explores, Quarto Gifts, or Quarto Kids.

© 2018 Quarto Publishing plc

First Published in 2018 by RotoVision,
an imprint of The Quarto Group.
The Old Brewery, 6 Blundell Street,
London N7 9BH, United Kingdom
T (0)20 7700 6700 F (02)20 7700 8066
www.QuartoKnows.com

10 9 8 7 6 5 4 3 2 1

ISBN 978-2-88893-350-2

Publisher: Mark Searle
Editorial Director: Isheeta Mustafi
Commissioning Editor: Emily Angus
Junior Editor: Abbie Sharman
Design: JC Lanaway
Cover design: Emily Portnoi and Jane Lanaway

Printed and bound in China

DEDICATION
*For Richard
brilliant photographer,
even better dad*

*'Stop trying to get it right.
Just take the picture.'*
SALLY MANN

STYLING FOR INSTAGRAM

Leela Cyd

ROTOVISION BOOKS

CONTENTS

Introduction   6
How to use this book   8

WHERE TO START   10
What it takes   12
Experiment   14
A way of seeing   16
Connect   18
Hashtags   20
Everyone's invited   22
Find your way   24
Edit, edit, edit   26

GET INSPIRED   28
Do some research   30
Compose as you go   32
Play with words   34
@cannellevanille   36

WHAT TO SHOOT   38
Look before you shoot   40
First impressions   42
The creative's home   44
Collections   46
Personal spaces   48
Assignment: the travel essay   50
@cestmaria   52

STYLE   54
Dark and moody   56
Light and airy   58
Modern   60
Speaking in colour   62
Vibe   64
Styling portraits   66
Chill   68
How to disappear   70
Charm   72
Play   74
Essence   75
Props   76
Give yourself a head start   78
@joyarose   80

LIGHT   82
Using natural light   84
Flattery   86
@zuckerandspice   88
Less is more   90
Assignment: the golden hour   92
Face the light   94
Shadow patterns   96
@anne_parker   98

COMPOSE 100

Off centre 102
Embrace the negative space 104
Styling food 106
Mix it up 108
Scale 110
Portraits 112
Angles 114
POV 116
Shake things up 118
Hands on 120
Blending the ingredients 121
Plain and simple 122
Learn your lines 124
Whacky and wonky 126
Create a story 128
  Beach picnic 130
  Feast of five pastas 131
  Desserts in the canyon 132
  Friends' weekend getaway 133
Start wide 134
Messy 136
Minimal 137
Create depth 138
Small moments 140
@littleupsidedowncake 142
Seeing the whole 144
Opposites pop 146
Floral 148
Playful 149
Resist uniformity 150
Capture emotion 152
@latonyayvette 154

PLACES AND SPACES 156

Moments in time 158
Colours of the market 160
Look behind the curtain 162
@jonnymagazine 164
Be an iconoclast 166
Shooting nature 168
Assignment: all change 170
A local perspective 172
@laurejoliet 174

HACKS AND TIPS 176

Always on 178
Don't stress the start 179
Easy adjustments 180
Bring the fun 182
Shooting in black and white 183
Equipment hacks 184
What next? 186

Glossary 188
Index 190
Author biography 192
Acknowledgements 192

INTRODUCTION

With a phone in your hand you can be a 'photographer'. There's no extra buy-in fee, you already have what you need, and 'auto' mode works just fine. With technology having evolved so quickly in the past decade, there's no reason not to try your hand at making beautiful images. A fancy camera is no longer necessary to make great pictures, but a creative mind still is.

I grew up with a photographer father and a writer mother. We always had visiting artists around our dinner table, and making pictures seemed to me as natural as breathing. From an early age, I understood that being a photographer/writer was a passport to an interesting life. It was also fascinating to meet the growers and creators of the subjects I photographed (thanks Mum). My job today as a photographer, author and stylist combines all the skills and awareness I developed from a young age – a love of documenting life and making it beautiful has set me on a never-ending quest. Following my passion has not always been a straight path but it's still the motivation for all my work.

This book is a collection of tips I've gathered from a decade as a professional photographer and a lifetime of being an artist. Each chapter will give you information in an easy-to-digest, practical way. I love sharing insights that can make a big difference to your approach to photography and fill your Instagram feed with gorgeous and compelling images – it took me years to figure out some of these things! My hope is that this book will encourage you to get your phone out and begin to make seriously beautiful photographs.

#AndHaveSomeFunAlongTheWay

Summer Drinks

brekky

HOW TO USE THIS BOOK

This book aims to help you make simple, yet extraordinary images with your phone and to build a strong and stylish Instagram feed. You may want to make images purely as an artistic endeavour, or perhaps you're building a brand and there's a need to create content everyday – or maybe your motivation is somewhere in between. This book will help give you a repertoire of practical skills and ideas on how to build up an engaging feed with different prompts and ways of seeing and photographing your world.

You can flip through and see what catches your eye, or jet straight to the chapter that will benefit you most. Are you a shopkeeper showcasing your curated wares? The Light chapter would be a great place to start. Got the travel bug, and want to share your explorations with your friends and followers? Jump to the Places and Spaces section. Perhaps you are an artist and need some help getting started with photography, in which case, head to the Get Inspired and What to Shoot chapters.

I'm endlessly curious and fascinated by other photographers and what their creative process looks like, so I've included nine case studies featuring interviews and photos from some of my Instagram heroines and heroes. These wonderful picture makers spill all the ins and outs of how and what they think of their photography practice. Get inside their heads as they explain how they chase specific lighting patterns around their house during the late afternoon sunshine; move intuitively from project to project (don't overthink!); and wrestle with what their followers want to see versus the fun images they just feel like pushing out into the world.

… from the people you meet, to the stories you encounter, to the pictures you'll create … I invite you to enjoy the ride of a lifetime…

I've benefitted from their responses and I know you will, too. Their images are amazing and they're creative geniuses!

You don't need an expensive studio or a fancy camera to make photos that sing, or a feed that stands out. You just need time, practice, determination and a steadfast commitment to daily posting. There is actually no real 'just' about that, but the journey is such a ridiculously gratifying one – from the people you meet, to the stories you encounter, to the pictures you'll create. I invite you to enjoy the ride of a lifetime, maybe as a new hobby or, for the lucky few, a whole new career.

① WHERE TO START

WHAT IT TAKES • EXPERIMENT
A WAY OF SEEING • CONNECT
HASHTAGS • EVERYONE'S INVITED
FIND YOUR WAY • EDIT, EDIT, EDIT

WHAT IT TAKES

Creating a post for Instagram with your phone is no different than working with a professional camera – beautiful, well-crafted imagery still shines. Phones are now so sophisticated that technology makes everyone a great photographer, making a successful image more about an idea rather than expertise. So where to start? Here are some helpful hints to keep in mind as you share your world.

1 DON'T SHOOT IN INSTAGRAM

The camera app that comes with your phone is much sharper, offers burst mode (great for action shots) and has a grid setting, which can be helpful when experimenting with composition.

2 TRAIN YOUR WAY OF SEEING

You need to exercise your eyes just like an athlete develops their muscles for a big event. The more you notice pattern, texture, light, shadow, foreground, background and shapes that interest you, the more practised you will be at finding and making moments that are unique to you.

3 POST EVERYDAY

Challenge yourself to find and create an image that excites you every single day. The practice will help you improve over time, which feels great. Your feed will become an amazing visual diary and your community will grow when you set this intention.

4 DEFINE 'SUCCESS' FOR YOU

Try not to worry about 'hearts' and comments. Instead, create work that challenges you and expands on the ideas or style of your previous post. Ask yourself: Am I excited about this? Does this photo make me feel something? Growth, variety and movement in your feed should be seen as a marker of success, not the external validation of followers.

5 TELL A STORY

Ultimately, a great image is all about composition and storytelling – are you creating dynamism and movement within the frame? Where is your eye drawn? Is it to the red nose or the tiara? And do you wonder just where these two are going on their bike? There are different moods for different perspectives. Experiment until you hit on the visual message that matches the story you want to tell.

EXPERIMENT

I prefer to learn by *doing* rather than researching or pondering. Skill in photography is built through practice, experimentation and hours logged rather than divine inspiration or natural talent. In this era where we all have a phone rather than (or maybe in addition to) a fancy manual camera, we can afford to be experimental and learn new things as we go along. Without the cost of film or software to hamper creativity, you've got nothing to lose.

1 START WITH A SUBJECT YOU LOVE
Already love cooking? Food and raw ingredients can be your
best muse. A fashionista? Begin with a few flat lays arranged
by colour or texture, or perhaps shoot details of garments
in different settings. Avid gardener? Make it a daily habit
to shoot the flowers that you're tending to. When you are
familiar with the subject of an image, you are able to see that
subject in new ways and create visually interesting pictures.

2 BEGIN AS A BEGINNER
Be easy on yourself. Know that it takes time to develop
abilities. It can be tough to be bad at something as an adult,
but give yourself room to just try, try and try again.

3 INSTAGRAM IS A VISUAL DIARY
As you scroll through your feed, your growth as an artist
becomes obvious. At first glance your images are a great record
of your life, but over time your feed will reveal where you've
been and where you're headed visually.

4 LEARN BY FAILING
If you're not failing at this, you're stagnating. Pushing yourself
to grow creatively may feel uncomfortable, and at times
frustrating, but that's okay. As you learn new ways of doing
and seeing your work, your creative outlook will expand.

5 DON'T WORRY ABOUT PERFECTION
Moving around – physically and mentally – to create new ways
of seeing and capturing images will produce an 'imperfect'
and non-cohesive feed (at least at the beginning of your
adventure), but you will find what you are drawn to in a more
authentic way than if you begin with a fully formed or fixed
idea of how you are going to approach a subject. Accidents
are your best friend right now.

A WAY OF SEEING

Photography is an illuminating way of seeing the world. It can be a daily meditative practice, a way to stoke your creative fire and a chance to connect with others. I think of making images as painting with light. Having motivation and a phone in your pocket can bring immediate gratification and the ability to quickly and easily share with others. You can hone your point of view by seeing the world in terms of light and shadow, lines and composition. Practising the way you perceive your surroundings will make you a stronger photographer. Here's how.

Where to Start

*I think of making images
as painting with light.*

1 NOTICE SHADOWS AND LIGHT

Tune in to different times of day. Try to shoot when your
environment looks prettiest: the breaking dawn coming
through your kitchen window and giving a glow to your cup
of tea; deep, crisp shadows thrown by a tree on the side of a
country road at midday; the last kiss of sunshine as it fades
behind the trees in your local park.

2 SUMMON YOUR SENSES

As you train your eyes to find the most beautiful lighting
and compositions, your other senses will sharpen. When I'm
photographing something I find stunning (a friend, a bouquet
or a delicious meal), the sounds around me get punchier, the
smells more vibrant, the flavours more delicious – all because
I'm paying attention while freezing this moment in time.

3 TAKE IT SLOW

Use photography to slow down. In this modern world where
we're darting from one thing to the next, photography can be
the best incentive to rest your attention on what pleases you.
It comes down to intention. If your objective is to create a
meaningful image, take some time and pause in the moment.

4 BREAK THE ROUTINE

Creating an image can be a liberating break from day-to-day
monotony. We all struggle with routine, work and attending
to responsibilities. For a few minutes each day, maybe more,
you can escape to a visual world – maybe an opulent lobby,
or perhaps a local park – and then share what you see with
the world.

CONNECT

When you have a phone with a built-in camera, you have the best job in the world – you are a photographer. You also have a responsibility to be bold, curious and adventurous. When crafting images, you have so much power – you can ask questions, discover new cultures and attitudes, explore places cut off to the casual passerby. Why? Because you have a camera and you can adopt the identity of 'photographer', the modern-day explorer. Here's how.

1 | BE A PHOTOJOURNALIST

If you have a blog or Instagram account, you are a content maker. You have full licence to explore topics that interest you, photograph them, and then publish what you've made. This means if you're into cooking, get to know the person behind the counter at your favourite delicatessen – then photograph and interview them. Love an outfit on a style maven? Ask if you can photograph her . . . she will probably be flattered. How about a craftsperson you've noticed making something beautiful while you're on holiday? Go and ask about their story and what they make – take photographs a few times during the conversation. You get the idea.

2 | CONVERSATION STARTER

The decision to 'be' a photographer, even for a couple of hours, can spark conversations that leads to unimagined directions and places. I'm normally a reserved person, but when I'm in photographer mode, I take on an exuberant, extrovert personality and boldly ask questions of people I find fascinating. Most of the time, when you are taking someone's photograph, they are happy to share a little about their world and perspective. As a photographer, you have an opportunity to dig deeper into the life of a stranger or a friend and learn something new.

3 | FIND YOUR TRIBE

When you're a photographer, you have an excuse to talk to fellow photographers. No one will relate to an experience of 'trying to get that shot' like another person in the field. My greatest friends are other female artists because it feels so good to be supported and understood by women with similar interests and struggles.

4 | SOCIALISE ON SOCIAL MEDIA

Through sharing your work, you find your digital tribe. Social media makes it possible to create connections with people from all over the world. People whose passions align with yours will find your work, comment and poof – a potential friend! I've met up with several online contacts made through my work and now I'm lucky enough to call them close friends.

HASHTAGS

Hashtags are the most popular means of categorisation on social media.
The pound sign (#) and a word can instantly organise your image into a group
labelled with the same identification and make the photo infinitely easier to find.
Hashtags also make it easier to connect with users with whom you share common interests.
Love them or cringe at the thought of them, hashtags are part of our vernacular
(the word was added to the *Oxford English Dictionary* in 2010 and the *Scrabble Dictionary*
in 2014). Here are some tips on how and when to best use hashtags with Instagram.

Love them or cringe at the thought of them, hashtags are part of our vernacular.

1 BE SPECIFIC

If you are working on connecting with your audience and other users, chose language that means something to the target audience. For example, if you are a florist, using #FloralDesign is fine, but be sure to include the type of flowers used in specific arrangements as well, such as #Geraniums #Dahlias #Roses #Delphiniums.

2 DON'T GET CARRIED AWAY

Don't use more hashtags than words in your caption. Using an endless list of hashtags is like screaming, 'find me' to your audience. Keep to ten hashtags or fewer per post.

3 SHORT AND SNAPPY

Keep hashtags to a single word or concise phrase. Keep obscure phrases to a minimum if you want your tags to be discoverable. When it's easier to type, it's easier to find. As an example, #PinkFrostedCake can just be #PinkCake.

4 CAPITALISE

Make sure your tags can be understood. If you string too many lowercase words together it makes them hard to read. The search function is not impacted by case. #toomanylowercaseletters #CapitalisationIsBetter

5 KNOW YOUR AUDIENCE

Hashtags are a great way to do some research and can show you the endless ways that other image-makers photograph the content you're drawn to. Exploring with hashtags can lead you to new feeds, as well as new phrases to use as hashtags so that you can attract like-minded people to your feed. #CopenhagenSunshine

E V E R Y O N E ' S   I N V I T E D !

For much of the twentieth century, photography was strictly for the trained craftsperson;
there was magic to being in the orange glow of a darkroom and conjuring up shapes on
a blank ghost of paper. It cost time and money to hone the ability to make images.
Now, most of us have phones with the capacity to create stunning, high-resolution
images. Becoming a photographer no longer requires an expensive 'buy in' of equipment,
and technology has democratised the practice, but the level of accessibility can be
overwhelming. Here are some questions to ask yourself before adding to the stream.

Where to Start

1 LOOKING VS SEEING

We *look* at a lot of imagery every day, but we *see* few pictures. How do you make an image stand out in a deluge of visual information? What does it take to make a viewer want to linger and *listen* to your take on a macaron?

2 WHAT DRIVES YOU?

Think about the adjectives you use when describing a powerful image – monumental, pristine, white, serene. Reference those words as the starting point to finding your muse.

3 KNOW YOUR GOALS

An Instagram account is free and easy to run, but you need to be clear about how you want to use this channel, and what it is you want to say. Are you looking for a casual audience of 'likes', or deeper engagement and commentary? Your images may be different for each goal.

4 CONSIDER YOUR FORMAT

Think of a phone as the default delivery medium when making your work. Shoot and adjust to ensure the image sings in this format.

Now, most of us have phones with the capacity to create stunning, high-resolution images.

FIND YOUR WAY

The wise words of Oscar Wilde, penned over a hundred years ago, still ring with meaning: 'Be yourself, everyone else is already taken.' Finding your own creative voice is a worthy pursuit. The Latin root of the word 'voice' is *vocare*, meaning 'to call, invoke'. Our voice is the thing that calls out in between the 'stuff' of life – the little spark in our head and heart that tells us to dig deeper and explore a topic. It is crucial to your creative development to listen and encourage this spark; it will lead you to your authentic vision and journey. Here are some ways to start.

1   JOURNAL

Each day for a month, explore your ideas and musings with a few pages scrawled in a journal. Even bullet points will do. You may find that by writing your thoughts and concepts down you become more aware of what moves you, and your ideas will rise to the top.

2   REMEMBER BEING A KID

When I was seven years old I was planning tea parties for my friends: twirling in a cute hand-me-down dress, picking flowers from the garden, making cupcakes with pink icing, and asking my dad to take our picture. I was basically art directing and styling my life, which has now become my job and creative vocation. Start with what you loved long ago. That will point you in the right direction.

3   IF MONEY AND TIME WERE ENDLESS

What would be the first thing you'd do? I'd buy amazing art, shop for a swanky dress and take all my friends for an extravagant meal. This list may be a dream, but it is possible to infuse some of the fantasy into my everyday creative life: I can go to a museum and take pictures, window-shop and document the process, and order an over-the-top dessert at a fancy hotel and photograph it. These are the anchors of my creative self: food, life and art. What are yours?

4   TRY EVERYTHING

Be bold, creatively and practically. Don't get bogged down by the details, or focus on heavy expectations and unrealistic goals. It's better to seek out the things that move you through active trial and error than to emulate someone else's vision or confine yourself to what 'should' look good.

5   OPPOSITES

When I am feeling uninspired by my creative work, I try to adopt a view that is the opposite of my usual outlook. This gets me out of my head, shifts the way I see a subject, and often leads to better work.

EDIT, EDIT, EDIT

It's hard to be ruthless when editing your own work, but to create a gorgeous feed
you've got to be unwavering. Editing images is something a lot of photographers
struggle with – we have a deep awareness of the context of each photo that makes
it difficult to discard images and keep only the cream of the crop. But a cohesive
flow of unified imagery creates a strong visual message. Here are a few tips
on cutting the fat and picking the right images for your Instagram feed.

1   CONSIDER YOUR AUDIENCE

Before you start making images, you should know whom those images are for. A loosely curated private account is great for keeping friends and family up to date, for example, but if you are broadcasting content for potential clients, customers or collaborators, it is best to stick to a specific point of view.

2   SUBJECT OR STYLE?

Stick to a single subject and don't deviate: Food, travel, portraiture and spaces are just four topics that can be explored from a million different angles. If you take a single-theme approach, even an occasional 'off-subject' image will dilute your feed. Alternatively, stick to a single style and diversify the subject. This can be a bit trickier, but is ultimately more interesting and rewarding. Decide what your overall vibe is: Bright and happy, feminine or colourful are all possible starting points. Only publish images that fall under the category you've selected.

3   KILL YOUR DARLINGS

Not publishing something you think is great is so tough! William Faulkner said, 'In writing, you must kill all your darlings'. Your affection for an image that doesn't serve your objectives should never save it from being discarded. That can be a real bummer, but let that frustrated feeling sharpen your focus on creating work that serves the purpose of your feed.

4   BUILD A STASH

Create a folder on your phone of your strongest work. This way, if you're feeling restless and want to post something, you'll have a pre-edited pool to select from. You can add to this stash in your downtime between photo shoots.

5   STEP BACK

If you're on the fence about whether to post or not, take a few hours to do something else, then return to the image with fresh eyes. The impulse to press 'publish' will have lessened and you will be able to assess if the image is worth publishing.

② GET INSPIRED

DO SOME RESEARCH • COMPOSE AS YOU GO
PLAY WITH WORDS • @CANNELLEVANILLE

DO SOME RESEARCH

For inspiration on ideas, technique and composition, I look to master artists of the past – painters, photographers and poets all have something to teach. The lesson can be as simple as a model's gesture or pose in an old painting, or as complex as the overall philosophy and environment in which an artist was operating. Digital access to artwork in museums around the world means there's no excuse not to explore history – from the convenience of a phone, of course, in between posts.

Digital access to artwork in museums around the world means there's no excuse not to explore history.

1 START WITH YOUR FAVOURITES

Do you love Caravaggio's dramatic use of chiaroscuro? Try replicating the contrast of heavy shadows and strong light in your photos. Start with your favourite artists but explore further and seek others in their canon. Use a hashtag to search for artists who fascinate you. Follow threads and leads – you never know what inspiration will be revealed.

2 SHOOT A POSE

Moved by the way a Greek sculpture of the human form is positioned and holding a gauzy fabric just so? Take a reference picture and when you're next photographing someone, direct them into a similar pose.

3 THINK CONCEPTUALLY

Explore the ways artists have addressed big concepts and look for a connection with what informs your work. Are you a modern-day feminist interested in goddess mythology? Look to the way goddesses have been portrayed in art throughout the world. Is the female form shown differently in European, Asian, American and African art? How can you embody your point of view on these themes through photography?

4 STORYTELLING

Literature and poetry can provide beautiful inspiration for visual storytelling. I love channelling a favourite story through a photograph or series. For example, after finishing *The Secret Garden*, I created a circular composition of trinkets and curios I imagined the main character may have carried in her pocket.

COMPOSE AS YOU GO

It's easy to move through a space blindly, following the path of a circle and finishing up where you started, without many ideas. Better to go slowly. Identify and capture themes as you consciously take your time. Any place, new or familiar, can become fascinating if you're looking for potential. Here are some tips to keep close at hand.

1 BE FLEXIBLE

The way you photograph one situation may not work for another. Set yourself up and frame your image according to what's in front of you. For example, when shooting a brightly lit building interior, standing in the centre of the space and facing the windows will create an airy composition. Moving very close into a sculpture in the same space, creating a single focal point (the sculpture) and letting the background fade into a blur, will give your image depth. One space, two very different approaches.

2 IT CAN BE SIMPLE

Not everything you see needs to stay in the frame. You can edit and simplify in two ways. The first is to crop out the extraneous items and focus on the subject of your picture. For example, if there is a beautiful kitchen set-up but a rubbish bin nearby, adjust the framing until the bin is almost but not quite included. The second way – which is not always an option – is to move something that is not working with your image out of the way altogether. Perhaps if it's a light rubbish bin, simply move it out of the frame, photograph the kitchen, then put the bin back.

3 ROTATE YOUR ANGLE

Sometimes I get stuck shooting everything in portrait mode. It's easy to mix up your perspective and the resulting image by rotating to a landscape composition. Even if you choose to crop the image into a square, the original horizontal or portrait compositions will affect the image slightly.

4 LOOK FOR SIGNS OF LIFE

Spaces can come alive through clues of who or what lives there. Be on the lookout for small scenes: for example, a solitary figure wheeling a bicycle along a tree-lined path can say a lot about that space and that person. If you are photographing an interesting person, look to situate them in an environment that hints at or embellishes their story.

PLAY WITH WORDS

I don't believe the artistic spirit comes down and hits you on the head every time you feel like making a picture; you need tips, tools and ways into an engaging idea. I love to play with words as a way of coming up with unique photos. I learned this skill working as a visual-display intern while at college. Each season we created a world for two characters – their clothes, mood, style of home, holiday destination and the music that they liked. When we had a sense of these imaginary women, we made artworks and displays that were aligned to their characters. You can do the same with photography.

I love to play with words as a way of coming up with unique photos.

1 CHARACTER DRIVEN

Pick a character from a book, a historical figure (Georgia O'Keeffe, for example) or a friend, and use them as your muse. Create images from what you imagine their point of view to be. Would they be messy and haphazard? Strong and bold? Where would they go and how would they dress? Start with these questions and see where your mind and phone take you.

2 TAGLINES AND TITLES

Use colourful phrases from fashion magazines as a starting point. Usually, an editor has come up with a witty phrase to describe the clothing and accessories featured in a spread. Phrases like 'Road Warrior', 'Dessert Vibes', 'Future Tech' or 'Modern Boho' all hint at fun concepts with which to frame a story and light up your imagination. Gather items you think fit into these story ideas (I love exploring second-hand shops), photograph the results *et voila* – something fabulous may occur.

3 MAKE A VISUAL PUN

Love crosswords or jumbles? Think of all the puns you know and create an image describing them. You may have a chuckle and be the only person who gets it, but that's okay.

4 MUSIC

Take a favourite song or lyric as the staring point for creating an image. From Beyoncé putting a ring on it, to the Beatles in a yellow submarine – the diversity of imagery and themes explored by musical artists is vast.

@cannellevanille

Aran Goyoaga
cannellevanille.com
arangoyoaga.com
vimeo.com/user56666335

Aran Goyoaga is a Seattle-based, Basque Country born-and-raised author, food stylist and photographer. She is the author of the book *Small Plates & Sweet Treats*, and the video series 'A Cook's Remedy'.

challenges

I am my biggest challenge most of the time! If what I am about to post doesn't feel true, or isn't how I want my work to represent me, I will stop myself.

tips

Cropping adds tension and helps viewers realise there is more beyond what they are seeing.

influences

Todd Hido, Ditte Isager, Juergen Teller, and Gentl and Hyers all have a very specific point of view when it comes to light.

composition

One constant across my work is very linear and symmetrical compositions; I use subtle breaks in the lines in order to add movement.

adjustments

I always metre and adjust white balance and make sure that my exposure is spot on. I always adjust contrast, too, and usually do a little sharpening.

3

WHAT TO SHOOT

LOOK BEFORE YOU SHOOT
FIRST IMPRESSIONS • THE CREATIVE'S HOME
COLLECTIONS • PERSONAL SPACES
ASSIGNMENT: THE TRAVEL ESSAY • @CESTMARIA

LOOK BEFORE YOU SHOOT

The most valuable time on a photo shoot is actually time spent *not* making pictures. There's so much to be said for taking in a space before you begin, chatting with people before pulling out your camera, or thinking about a recipe before taking a food shot. Take a few minutes to breathe and centre yourself. What are your goals for this image-making moment? If you begin in a relaxed state, your pictures will be better and the connection made will be more authentic than if you start shooting as soon as you walk through the door.

1   SURVEY THE SCENE

I do a walk-through of any space I'm photographing. This is either done on my own or in a twenty-minute conversation with a tour guide, or home or shop owner to understand more deeply the place I'm in. I ask which special areas they love to curl up in, or whether they have a favourite spot within their shop. Little nudges like these, and lots of follow-up questions, can open up interesting conversations and lead you to unique images. Doors will open for you.

2   CHAT WITH SUBJECTS

Most people find it difficult to be in front of a camera. A little lighthearted chat can help subjects feel comfortable. Prepare a few questions for the person ahead of time: 'How long have you lived here?', 'What's your favourite part of your job?', 'Do you have any pets?' are all things that I've asked when warming someone up to be in a picture. The questions can be silly (pets? Really, am I seven years old? But people *love* talking about their animals). If you are spontaneously photographing someone, compliment them and ask them a couple of questions: 'What brings you here?', 'Where'd you get that hat?' Almost anything you say will help to break the ice.

3   LOOK BEHIND YOU

Consider this scenario: you are caught up shooting a tray of pastries, trying to get every angle possible. It's crowded in the shop, a little confusing for you. You turn around to see a parade going past on the street outside – an event that's far more fascinating than a plate of croissants. Be sure to stay loose and look behind you; the best thing on earth may be passing you by.

4   IT'S OKAY TO GO BACK

Despite planning, there will be times when you get home and realise you missed the coolest room in the museum or forgot to go outside to photograph the gorgeous chickens. You want to slap your forehead for forgetting. Don't worry about it; just go back. It happens.

FIRST IMPRESSIONS

You only get to meet a person, a place or a beautiful object once before you become a little (or a lot) familiar. It's important to tune into the ideas and emotions that hit you immediately. Your responses to a first encounter can strike after the event, in the middle of the night, or while out and about shooting. Pay attention – these impressions can point you towards an intriguing story yet to unfold.

① LUCK

One way to make the most of first impressions is to take the shot and ask questions later. Be prepared to be lucky. When you see something of interest – someone pouring milk into their drink, for example – minimise the time between that spark of inspiration and actual capture. Don't waste time looking at the image on your screen or asking for permission.

② WRITE IT DOWN

Don't wait for inspiration to strike. Keep a pad of paper by your bed to jot things down. It's not only about having a great idea . . . but remembering the idea when you need to. Keep a running list of ideas to return to and explore.

③ FOLLOW THE SPARK

What catches your eye? Start there. Don't make it hard for yourself. Start by photographing the most captivating part of a space or the most striking feature of a person – their headscarf and bright red lipstick, for example. You can always return to the plan you thought you had.

④ PATIENCE

In contrast to the first tip, another approach is to take your time and relax in that first encounter. Compose something beautiful rather than taking the photo straight away – rearrange hats on a hat stand, place a vase of flowers on the table. Your work may exude a little more calm and a thoughtful attitude as a result.

It's important to tune into the ideas and emotions that hit you immediately.

THE CREATIVE'S HOME

Artists' and makers' environments have personality, humour and plenty of visual interest. The typical combination of a hodgepodge layering of artwork (traded, gifted or made by the home owner themselves), a myriad of furniture styles and a strong aesthetic sense coalesce into Instagram gold. The childhood home of your favourite artist or author could give you the perfect shot for an Instagram post.

An artist's home is usually imbued with history, memory and love.

1 TIME

Give yourself more time in a creative environment than you think you'll need. This is a mantra I'm still learning after a decade of shooting creatives' homes. There is much to take in, many conversations to be shared, maybe a glass of wine or tea, and loads of images to be created. Set aside an entire morning or afternoon to dive deeply into this world.

2 ECCENTRIC ELEMENTS

Interior designers look to artists and makers for inspiration. Don't worry about seeking out the 'coolest' homes featured in design magazines; they can all look the same after a while. An artist's home is usually imbued with history, memory and love through an eclectic blend of high and low style, and this combination always leads to interesting photographs. Seek out collections and the materials used to make them, then consult the tips in Collections (page 47) for ideas on how to document them.

3 BEYOND THE CANVAS

No access to an artist's home? No problem – expand your view of artists to include makers and art students. Historical artists' homes (now museums) are also fabulous to explore.

4 HONE YOUR VISION

Remember to keep the principles of composition, light and design in mind and not be overwhelmed by the layers of 'stuff' and the endless possibilities. Remember you are there to create dynamic photos. Even if the home is wild and over the top, you are the boss of the photo; you control what the viewer sees. Make sure there is still interplay between subject, foreground and background, light and shadow, and the overall mood of the image.

COLLECTIONS

Well-worn, loved curios and bits and bobs are one of my favourite subjects to photograph. They convey a sense of time and memory that is specific to their owner. A collection can sometimes tell the story of a person or a place more successfully than a portrait or a landscape shot of the location from which the little objects come. Ask to see what's in the treasure box . . . you may be surprised by what is revealed to you.

What to Shoot

1 TELL A STORY

The collections someone makes and treasures are intimate and unique to them. They tell a story of inclinations and methodology – after all, it takes time, judgement and focus to accumulate a collection. For example, a deeply personal, well-worn and beloved arrangement of pottery can produce incredible shots and reveal a fascinating narrative.

2 LEARN FROM THE PROS

Look to museums for ideas on arranging collections. These institutions are the home of exquisitely curated displays of historical artefacts, and natural and contemporary wonders. When you visit a museum, note the spatial arrangement of objects and try to replicate this in your next composition. Curators design displays with an eye on size, colour, material and theme to achieve harmonious compositions of seemingly disparate objects.

3 EXPLORE ARRANGEMENTS

Collections may be arranged very neatly or scattered randomly; either way, a composition made up of many little shapes makes for a fascinating image. If you feel comfortable (maybe it's your own collection of treasured shells), try varying the set-up – a grid of evenly spaced items looks very different to a lovely pile or diagonal swirl of things.

4 SEEK OUT UNIQUE SURFACES

The objects you are arranging are important, but take note of the way they relate to their background. Both an 'opposites attract' look (light objects on a dark surface) and a tonal approach (everything of a similar hue, including the surface) are great – just be aware of the look you want to achieve.

5 MAKE A DIGITAL SOUVENIR

Photographing a collection can be a great way to capture special objects or a themed collection without having to keep the pieces. I once created a tableau of bird-related treasures, photographed it, then simply parted ways with the objects. A print is now my visual reminder.

PERSONAL SPACES

The most visually interesting spaces are the most intimate. A precarious, imperfect or odd home or workshop tells a rich story of the inhabitant's life. To document these zones is to invite the viewer to step inside someone else's world. Interior design magazines are full of houses that look the same – trendy, austere and often unpopulated. A family or gaggle of housemates make a house a home; they make it real, and they can make for some very interesting photos. Here are some tips on how to capture personal spaces.

1 OVERVIEW IS IMPORTANT

An establishing shot may be taken from the point in a room that gives you the broadest view of the space, or shot outside to show a home's exterior. A shot of a workspace that includes a desk, computer and artwork helps tell the whole story of the space. Shoot horizontally or vertically, depending on the overall shape of the home – try portrait in a two-story space, landscape in a one-story home.

2 DOCUMENT REAL LIFE

The personal is inviting. Seek moments that showcase the everyday life of a home – a rumpled bed rather than a perfectly tidy bedroom, or a kitchen scene with flour and a sugary mess on the countertop – not an aseptic, clutter-free fiction. This is life and it's okay to show how it really looks.

3 LOOK FOR THE LIGHT

Turn on every light in the room and photograph the scene, then study the results. Sometimes, a fixture or feature comes alive and draws the eye when flooded with light. Other times, turning off all the lights and shooting with the windows as the only light source is far more elegant. Try both ways.

4 DETAIL. DETAIL. DETAIL

Think like a stylist when you walk into a space – pay close attention to the small things. Just because a TV remote control is hanging on the wall in the bedroom doesn't mean it needs to stay there for the photo. Move the prettiest cups and plates in a kitchen to the front of frame, place any dirty dishes in the sink and out of view, and if you can, take the extra seconds to wipe off a smudge. Just remember to return things to the way they were if the space isn't yours.

5 BRING FLOWERS

Flowers never fail to bring a pop of colour into a space, and can save a shot when nothing seems to be working. Bringing a posy of peonies and dahlias to your host's home is also a great icebreaker.

THE TRAVEL ESSAY

Looking to push your own creative buttons and shoot images like those in your favourite travel magazines? Compose a travel essay on your own city. Aim to create ten diverse images that fit with the style of your favourite travel magazine. This is a fun exercise to jump-start your creativity. Here's how to get started.

WRITE YOUR OWN BRIEF

Choose topics to give yourself a framework and make a list of the themes you want to explore. Subjects such as food, shopping, nature, art, grit, safety and people are all useful in describing the look and feel of a place. They'd all be on the shot list of any photo editor or art director.

FIND NATURE

Get outdoors and take a hike or bike ride, stopping every half-mile to make an interesting image of what you see. Find your fellow outdoor enthusiasts and ask about their favourite trails, go down a path as a curious kid would, go slowly and compose along the way.

BE BOLD

Ask people if they would mind being in a photograph and talk to them. See what they see. How does their neighbourhood influence them? Have they seen the city change much in the time they've been there? You never know where these impromptu conversations will lead. Carry a card in case they want to get in touch about the photograph. If they have really made an impression on you, get their address and send them a physical print of their image. It will cost you very little, and make their day.

TURN UPSIDE DOWN

Whenever you're feeling stuck with an image, change your position entirely. If you're shooting the same picture of the Duomo in Florence that every other person is shooting – looking up from around twenty metres away – turn your point of view around. Get on the ground and shoot from this unusual angle in order to make an image of an iconic building with an atypical and surprising quality.

@cestmaria

Marioly Vazquez
cestmaria.com

The creative mind behind Maria Marie, Marioly is a photographer and stylist living in Monterrey, Mexico. Her work is known for its unique use of colour and whimsical styling.

♡ style

I loved graphic design but chose the path of photography. That is why most of my photos have a graphic element to them. I like being able to illustrate with my photography.

PANTONE®
Confetti

♡ props

I love adding little props to my images as I feel it gives them personality. My favourite props are flowers – they give a pop of colour to any space or composition.

♡ colour

I have always had an inclination for a pastel palette. It helps me better express myself and portray subtleness, femininity and innocence.

♡ inspiration

My favourite season is spring. After a long winter, seeing spring's colours and light fills me with inspiration. Everything comes back to life, and that is what I like to capture.

♡ adjustments

My favourite adjustment is brightness. Although I usually shoot my images in well-lit places, I feel that this adjustment gives them a beautiful 'boost of life'.

composition

Shooting compositions can be tricky, which is why it is important to try new things. Always follow your gut and your aesthetic eye – if something doesn't feel right, try something different, but always stay true to your style.

④ STYLE

DARK AND MOODY • LIGHT AND AIRY

MODERN • SPEAKING IN COLOUR

VIBE • STYLING PORTRAITS • CHILL

HOW TO DISAPPEAR • CHARM • PLAY • ESSENCE

PROPS • GIVE YOURSELF A HEAD START • @JOYAROSE

DARK AND MOODY

Dark, moody images with just a hint of light and swathes of shadow have an emotional quality – melancholic, heartachey and wistful. There is poetry in the darkness (think Morrissey, fading bouquets and romantic gloom). Here's how to create this atmosphere.

1 INTENSIFY SHADOWS

I added darkness and increased shadows in this bedroom scene with a piece of black foam core. (You could also use a piece of poster board painted black.) Situate your subject near a window, preferably on a foggy day, or at least in indirect light. Place the foam core opposite the light coming in and fire away. Having this dark board just out of frame will enhance the shadows of whatever you're shooting by absorbing light and preventing it from bouncing back onto the subject.

2 USE A SINGLE LIGHT SOURCE

To create a richly shadowed photo indoors, it's best to use only one light source. The most readily available light is natural light coming through a window. Turn off all other lights, position your subject (colourful roses) near the light source and move increasingly further away from the light. Note the change in light quality – you still want to be able to see the subject, so experiment until you have just enough light to illuminate, and no more.

3 EDIT THE MOOD

Intensify or lessen elements of an image with an editing tool or app such as VSCO or Afterlight, or in Instagram. To amp up the moody, dark tones, add shadows before posting.

4 PLAY WITH EXTREMES

Experiment with different seasons, times of day and locations. All of these factors can add intense shadow and give a sense of a heavy atmosphere. Dawn and dusk are great times to start experimenting, as the overall light is not as intense as midday.

5 RESTRICT COLOURS

Restrict your colour palette. Having only a few colours – creams and greys, for example – can heighten the overall effect of the dark and moody style.

LIGHT AND AIRY

Want to create a sense of happiness and wistful beauty in your Instagram feed? Consider shooting with a light, airy style. All-over soft, natural light; very little – if any – shadow; sometimes a soft focus; and an uncluttered composition characterise this mood. Wedding photographers, magazine covers and many commercial outlets utilise this picture mode to embody a message of ease and joy.

1 TRICKS OF THE TRADE

Use a white foam core to decrease shadows and amp up the lightness of an image. Place your subject near a window or outdoors in indirect light and set up a piece of white foam core (or a piece of poster board) just out of frame. The white board will reduce the shadows that fall on the side of the subject facing away from the light source. It's a very useful, inexpensive tool for adding light without turning on a light bulb, which can add an unattractive yellow hue.

2 KEEP IT CLEAN

Simplify your composition. When in doubt, take it out! That's my mantra when working in this mode. The negative space surrounding the woman on a yellow stool lets the composition 'breathe', and creates an impact.

3 THE HUMAN TOUCH

When you're stuck with what you're shooting and confused as to how to change it, try adding a human hand or gesture. This can be as simple as a hand adding decoration to the food you're photographing, or having a friend walk through a table scene and bring a little movement into the image.

4 LET THE LIGHT GUIDE YOU

Utilise dawn and dusk outside, or midday when indoors. If you want soft shadows and don't have any white foam core, try shooting in the first and last few hours of the day, when shadows are lightest. Or, if you're indoors at midday, throw open one door or window and use the indirect light to create a soft image without intense shadows.

5 GIVE THE IMAGE DEPTH

Use macro (extreme close-up) or portrait mode to increase the airy feeling by creating a little depth between subject (shoes) and background (clothes). Both of these modes help to separate a subject's detail from the environment by introducing a lovely blur.

MODERN

The current profusion of images with harsh, contrasting shadows harkens back to the early days of photography, when a still life was set up to explore the capabilities of tone – showcasing every possibility of light and dark. In art as in fashion, music and food, everything old feels new again as the visual washing machine churns up modern versions of age-old themes. Catch onto this fun trend while it's still hot.

1 SHOOT IN DIRECT SUNLIGHT

To create the harsh shadows and light tones associated with this style, place your subject – a drink on a plain pink surface – in harsh sunlight during the brightest times of the day. The light is usually at its harshest at midday or in the early afternoon. Shadows will be long or short, depending on the exact time – explore both effects and see which you prefer.

2 ARTIFICIAL LIGHT

Replicate direct sunlight in a dark studio or room by employing a single direct light source. Place your subject in the middle of this light and explore the shadows and effects that the bright light creates.

3 ADD PUNCHY DETAILS

Think colourful and wild for props or surfaces – red dishes on a yellow background, for example. These little visual indicators add to the overall feeling of a modern look.

4 PLAY WITH THE FLASH

Try a flash; it can add to the 'weird' factor often used in modern-look styling. I like to use a flash on a very light environment, such as an already brightly lit room or an object on a white surface, and point it at the subject. The effect is an overall lightness to the image. Give it a go!

5 TRY IT ALL

Everything you think isn't going to work might work. This style gives you the opportunity to throw caution to the wind and really do the opposite of what you think will be beautiful. Shoot from a headstand position, pick your least favourite colour as your theme for the day, clear the table of all pretty food and shoot the empty glasses and plates – you get the idea. The results might astonish you.

SPEAKING IN COLOUR

Colours can say a thousand things words can't – they can invoke mood, elicit emotion
or stop you in your tracks. It's amazing to think of the simple power of colour.
The next time you're composing an image, choose a distinctive palette and let it
guide you. What do the colours say to you? What are you saying with the colours?

1 START WITH ONE

Choose a signature colour, a colour you are most drawn to. Start to note it in your everyday life – wear it, and try to locate it in other photographs. How does it make you feel when you see it? I get a rush of happiness when I see pinks – from magenta to the lightest blush, the colour makes me gleeful, and has since I was a kid. Starting with a single colour can show you how much can be done with one little corner of the rainbow, and is an easy avenue to a cohesive feed.

2 OPPOSITES ATTRACT

Experiment with contrasting colours and see how they emphasise or de-emphasise a subject – black and white, yellow and purple, blue and red. Note how the coloured ballet slippers here vibe off each other. If you investigate basic colour theory or can visualise the colour wheel, just think about using colours from opposing sides of the spectrum. They will 'talk' to each other in a vibrant way and provide a starting point.

3 TONAL PLAY

Another way to dive into colour is to create an image with subtle shifts in tone of one colour. Think of how elegant a woman looks in a monochromatic outfit. You can apply this sophistication to pictures using a palette with barely any variation.

4 RIOT OF COLOUR

Think of the joy you felt as a kid opening up a bag of sweets and seeing every colour of the rainbow. Or the happy thrill of looking up and seeing a multicoloured string of flags while on holiday. Pure delight will radiate from an image that includes all the colours you can find.

Colours can say a thousand
things words can't.

VIBE

Your vibe is everything when taking photographs – how you feel, communicate and conduct yourself instantly sets the mood for you and your subject(s). It's normal to have a few frazzled nerves or to feel a bit excited. Taking a few deep breaths; calming yourself down, centring your intention and plunging in with a good attitude will make the experience more fun. It will also sharpen your attention to detail, strengthen your connection to people if there's portraiture involved, and result in better images overall.

1   WEAR A POWER OUTFIT

This may seem silly but the right clothing can really put you in a good mood. When you don your 'photographer' outfit – whether a cool jacket and trainers, black trousers and a sweater, or a particular scarf – you must feel fabulous in it. Your confidence will set the tone for a great shoot.

2   SLOW DOWN

Before, during and after a shoot, slow down a little. I often have to remind myself of this, as I tend to move quickly through a space and a conversation. If you can go more slowly, you'll be doing the job more thoroughly, with more care and with less room for error.

3   ASK QUESTIONS

People love to talk about themselves! As you photograph a person or move through their home, ask questions: 'What's the story with the Bowie cushion?' They may respond with something that triggers a creative response in you and propels you to go deeper, connect more and create unique images.

4   BE YOURSELF

It might sound clichéd, but if you give the people you photograph an authentic impression of who you are, they will do the same for you. Don't get too caught up in how you think a photographer is supposed to act; if you are comfortable with yourself in the space, your vision is more likely to be realised in the images.

5   POSITIVITY

If you believe your shots will work well and expect to meet interesting people along the way to creating a few great photos, you're halfway to succeeding at creating a compelling Instagram feed. A light and positive mood can buoy your photography and sense of self. When directing people, give lots of positive feedback. Saying thank you is important as well, especially if you have made a genuine connection.

STYLING PORTRAITS

When creating a portrait, the background and environment are just as important as the figure. A simple background will help bring out the subject as the focal point; with little else in the frame, all eyes are on them. By contrast, setting your subject in a busy, natural environment can help tell their story, with objects or scenery expanding or explaining the narrative. There is a lot of room between these two extremes, so be conscious of the intent behind the creative decisions you make, and the story you want your feed to tell.

Style

1 **LOOK UP, LOOK DOWN**

When entering a space that will be the setting for a portrait, take in the entire scene. Take note of what is directly in front of you (furniture, windows, trees), but don't forget the world under your feet (an ornate rug or a carpet of little flowers in the grass). As well as looking down, remember to look up – you may find a dazzling chandelier that can become part of the composition and be used to illuminate the portrait.

2 **CONSIDER THE POSE**

What do you notice right away about the subject of your portrait? Maybe they have a beautiful smile or outrageous hair. Make whatever captivates you instantly the focus of your image by guiding them to a pose that showcases that feature.

3 **FIND THE RIGHT LIGHT**

Move the lighting around. In real life, people aren't always lit directly from the front. Think about how lovely it is to be at dinner with someone and have their face aglow with light from a nearby candle, or the beauty of the dappled light and shadows you see when hanging out under a tree on a summer's day. With any portrait, consider your lighting and how it complements or contrasts with your subject.

4 **CAPITALISE ON COMFORT**

Creating an environmental portrait puts the subject at ease. Right away, people are going to be more comfortable in their homes or gardens rather than in front of a backdrop or in a photography studio. Use this to your advantage. Ask your subject to perform a daily task for you to shoot; this enables them to loosen up and can make for lovely, engaging images.

5 **SIMPLE IS STUNNING**

Sometimes there's nothing better than a beautiful face with an intense expression. When in doubt, try sitting your subject on the floor near a window and in front of a minimal background and have a wide-ranging conversation with them in order to capture a pensive look.

CHILL

Getting a person to relax while you're taking their picture is an art unto itself. If they are in a relaxed state, they will radiate with authenticity on camera rather than sit flat with an air of fakeness.

1 AMBIENCE

Set the tone with music (and/or wine). Make a playlist to get everyone in the mood for what's about to transpire. On one occasion, a lovely designer opened a bottle of white wine at the beginning of our shoot together and I'll never forget how fun and kooky we got. The pictures turned out fabulous! It's all about being comfortable.

2 COLLABORATION

Make the model a co-conspirator. I say things like, 'I've been shooting a lot of people lately and there is a sameness about my portraits . . . What can *we* do that is unique? Help a sister out!' By asking the subject, they may give you a better pose than you could ever have imagined.

3 AVOID CHEESE

Don't tell people to 'say cheese.' If you want gorgeous photos, don't try and get people (especially kids) to smile directly at the camera. This will only get you strained 'picture faces'. It's better just to interact with your subjects and fire away as you play and chat.

4 ROLE REVERSAL

Share your camera with a friend and ask them to show you a location they would use to create an image. Take turns to photograph each other. Show the portraits to each other and discuss what you like and what you might change. You are now partners in this image-making endeavour.

5 COMFORT IN NUMBERS

Photograph your subject with someone they love – a baby (or babies), friend or a parent. You may not use this picture, but at least they will become more at ease in front of the camera. You can always ask the extra person to leave the scene (and help you to get the subject to crack up) after a few images.

HOW TO DISAPPEAR

If you are shooting an event, party or one-time-only scene, it's crucial to have a few things lined up: the proper gear (charged phones, enough space) and the right attitude to capture Instagram-worthy shots. I find the best way to do this type of thing is to go as stealth as possible, practically disappearing. This conscious style of working yields imagery that will have your feed radiating with emotions and authentic moments.

1   KNOW THE AGENDA

Do a little homework and find out when the event you'd like to capture is starting and get there early. Understand how the event will unfold and position yourself accordingly. Make sure you are at the right place, such as the front of the parade, at the right time.

2   GET CLOSE

. . . then back away. To highlight the expressive feelings of a party or even a wedding, get closer than you think is necessary. You're in photographer mode; it's okay to be a little bold. The physical closeness will be short lived and your pictures will feature a range of scale – from far away to very close. Closeness can show a gritty, raw beauty, while a more pulled-out shot can give the viewer a sense of the overall atmosphere.

3   DIRECT (SOFTLY)

Don't be afraid to help subjects get into a better position for a photo. They will appreciate looking beautiful later, and most people need a little guidance as to how to get there. It can be as simple as saying, 'Sit up straight'. It also tells people you know what you're doing, even if you don't. Encourage them with a 'You're doing a great job'. It never hurts.

4   CHASE THAT SHOT

Move your body to create the composition you want, instead of asking people to move for you. Keep moving through the space to find great images you haven't yet imagined. Don't get too comfy shooting from one spot – be fluid and rhythmic.

5   FOLLOW EMOTIONS

The most exciting elements to shoot at a heart-felt gathering are the emotions. If people are smiling, laughing or hugging, get in there quickly, photograph, and then get out of the way. I guarantee no one will even notice what you're doing, so be bold and then slyly disappear.

CHARM

How can you get people to warm up to you in only five minutes? How do you wrap someone around your finger and get them to reveal an element of their true self so that you can capture that spirit in a portrait? This is one of the skills of photography I am most interested in improving – it is a lifetime quest. Here's what I have learned about charming someone into a great photo.

1 BE A BIT SILLY

Come up with a goofy phrase. Mine are 'Work with me baby, work with me!' and 'You're a tiger, you're Tony the tiger, you're great!' These are both so stupid and inane, and that's the point. Hearing these silly lines from me always starts to crack up the subject. From there, we can start really getting to know each other, and the great images follow.

2 WARM UP

Know that your first twenty images are probably not going to be any good. The warm-up act is just that. Keep pushing the shutter button while you are saying goofy things (see above), and you'll both get more comfortable. Don't have high expectations of these first images – the good stuff is coming – just allow space to get there together.

3 NOT JUST A FACE IN A FRAME

When photographing people, and kids especially, they might not always want to look at the camera, but prefer to bend down to look at a rock, or even wear a mask. There are many different ways to tell a story, and you don't always need the person's face to be front and centre. Try capturing the person from different perspectives and angles. This might mean pictures of hands or feet. It makes for a very different type of portrait, but it's super interesting!

4 THE GOLDEN RULE

Never show a double chin if avoidable. This may mean shooting a bit from above or diagonally. Stand on a little step stool if you need some extra height.

5 PRINT A PICTURE

Always make sure your subject gets a copy of your image. In an age of digital photography and online feeds, having a physical print to frame or put on the fridge is a precious rarity.

PLAY

When photographing people, having fun is not only encouraged, it's a prerequisite for creating emotive, joyful photographs. So loosen up, get weird and don't be embarrassed to channel your inner child. Here are a few tips on how to play more while you're making pictures.

1 HAVE SOMETHING UP YOUR SLEEVE
Pulling out a clown nose, or dog treats are easy tricks – they seem so silly and irrelevant, but an inexpensive red rubber nose will make even the most serious of subjects double over in laughter, and the doggy treat will endear you to the dog owner forever.

2 USE HUMOUR
Saying things like 'Show me your strongest face, your sad face, your cross-eyed face, your Disney Princess face' will produce a couple of relaxed images that you can capture between and right after the subject's bursts of laughter.

3 FAKE IT
Fake laughs lead to real laughs. I always ask people to give me a fake laugh. It ends up being so awkward and unnatural that it inevitably turns into real laughter. It seems counter-intuitive but it works!

ESSENCE

Often the person with the phone or camera takes control, telling the subject to move their head this way or that. I say, sometimes you've got to give that control up to the subject. This invites them to put a whisper of their essence on display, and allows you to capture an unguarded aspect of their spirit.

1 GIVE THE SUBJECT CONTROL

Ask permission before entering a personal space or touching someone's possessions. I often sit at the same level or lower than a subject so they have a physical advantage and subtle sense of control over the encounter. Use this approach and your subject will find you less threatening. This is especially important with kids.

2 MOVE CLOSER

Once your subject is at ease, get closer than you think you need to be. Imagine someone with a camera trying to get a decent image of who you really are from fifteen metres across a room. It is difficult at best.

3 BE NICE

In general, people want each other to succeed. An earnest attempt at a meaningful encounter prior to and while taking photographs rubs off on the subject; they will become more themselves if they sense you are a real person with good intentions.

Ask permission before
entering a personal space.

PROPS

It can really help to have a few things stashed in a bag to help bring out humour or add a pop of colour and interest to a shot. If you don't use the stuff in the bag, that's great. But if you do need a little something, you'll be glad you came prepared.

If you do need a little something,
you'll be glad you came prepared.

1 TEA TOWELS

I like to have a stash of tea towels when shooting a food scene. These cheap and cheerful props give me options; I can use one or two as a background if the table I'm working with is just not doing it for me, for example. It's worth having the option of something different. Lifesaver and costs just a few pounds!

2 A SCARF

A colourful scarf can add vibrancy to someone's face and act as a pop of colour in a picture's plane. It can also double as a pretty layering piece on a boring bed. If the scarf is semi-sheer, you can use it to filter direct sunlight and produce a soft shadow on your subject.

3 FLOWERS

Even a neighbourhood bouquet picked on a walk can be handy – you can add the flowers and foliage into a quiet, monochromatic scene (white shoes on cream tiles); tuck a flower behind your subject's ear; or decorate a tablescape with a few petals.

4 A LIL' SOMETHING

A gesture of goodwill, such as a nice chocolate bar, is always appreciated. If you are taking shots in a shop, someone's home or even a public setting, a small gift and saying 'thanks' will go a long way to let someone know you value their time. It can also look cute in a vignette scene or help someone warm up – who doesn't like an unexpected nibble of chocolate?

GIVE YOURSELF A HEAD START

Setting yourself up for success is ninety per cent of the work in creating a great image. You do this by considering as many factors as possible: environment, time of day, style of photo. Once you've identified what you need to bring, wear and prepare for, you have the building blocks of a beautiful image.

1 LOCATION, LOCATION, LOCATION

Choose the right spot to show off your subject. This can be a local park that has a pretty garden, a colourful wall, a tidy room in your house. Anywhere can work – the point is to keep an ongoing list of pretty places to use for creating gorgeous images that pop.

2 TAKE NOTES AND MAKE LISTS

Think about what you want to get out of your shots and the story you want your Instagram feed to tell. Do some sketching or list a few goals. You might also have a list of different shots you want to get before you call it a wrap. Bring your notebook with you, because mid-shoot you will forget everything!

3 ARRIVE EARLY

It never hurts to have time to take in a scene before a location opens and fills with people. Take some shots of an empty venue to get a sense of the light, and identify the best zone for a photograph.

4 FLIRT A BIT

I mean this in a totally non-sexual way, but the act of chatting up your subject, paying them a few compliments – regardless of gender – will loosen them up and make them laugh. Now you're ready to take their picture.

Once you've identified what you need to bring, wear and prepare for, you have the building blocks of a beautiful image.

@joyarose

Joya Rose Groves
joyarose.com

© Cara Robbins

Joya Rose Groves is a lettering artist and illustrator, painting and living with her husband and daughter in their seaside home in California. After college Joya spent two years abroad, journalling and illustrating her travels, which eventually lead to embracing ink play as a career.

inspiration

For the past couple of years I have focused on finding beauty in imperfection – scuffs on my boots become a patina, the mess on my workspace a pile of possibilities.

props

Sometimes I just throw props in and see what happens! A perfect minimalist scene with perfectly placed details can be beautiful, but it might not always be fun. HAVE FUN!

styling

I used to feel like a phoney arranging things just so they looked good on Instagram. Then I started working on some tabletop styling and loved it: I got over my fear of being a phoney!

challenge

My biggest challenge is prioritising experiencing a beautiful place with friends and family over getting a good shot of the experience. A gorgeous online presence does not equal a rich and beautiful life!

adjustments

Right now, I love to warm and brighten photos. I use a warming filter (M5 on VSCO) and brighten if needed. The trick is never to have filters on full saturation – a little goes a long way.

 **favourite location**

I like to take photos outdoors – any time of year, any time of day. I love natural textures – trees, grass, sea, wood. Also, I have ghastly carpet in my house; maybe my preference for the outdoors comes from trying to avoid getting that blasted stuff in the photo.

⑤

LIGHT

USING NATURAL LIGHT • FLATTERY
@ZUCKERANDSPICE • LESS IS MORE
ASSIGNMENT: THE GOLDEN HOUR • FACE THE LIGHT
SHADOW PATTERNS • @ANNE_PARKER

USING NATURAL LIGHT

To be a photographer/stylist is to be keenly aware of light, the critical ingredient in making a subject and image come to life. Natural light, sometimes called 'available light', is the easiest to work with, and readily available for many hours of each day. It also gives us 'the golden hour', which allows photographers to get soft, glowing shots that radiate warmth. There is such beauty in keeping things simple and relying on available light. Here are some tips on how best to use natural lighting and instantly improve your photos.

1   DAWN AND DUSK

The early morning and late afternoon hours offer the softest natural light. The calm of dawn and pretty pinks of twilight are subtle and gorgeous. The absence of harsh shadows, as in the India shot, make it easier to capture a flattering image of a person, place or object.

2   AVOID ARTIFICIAL

When shooting indoors, turn off all the lights – they cast a yellow shade as opposed to neutral-coloured natural light that can be seen falling across the furniture and plants in this interior shot. Place the entire set-up – person, object or both – near the window to take advantage of the natural light source. If the sun is blazing through the window, put up a small white sheet or scrim to diffuse the light.

3   LEARN TO LOVE CLOUDS

Gloomy weather creates ideal lighting conditions for almost every subject. The clouds filter light in a clear, soft way and produce a beautifully subtle white light, perfect for creating evenly lit flat lays and inviting interiors.

4   UNDEREXPOSURE

Focus on the brightest point of an image – a mirror or the sky, perhaps; your camera's exposure will automatically balance to the point of focus. Bring the exposure down a little from the automatic setting (this is generally done by tapping inside the frame and adjusting the brightness toggle). You can always brighten and boost the colour and light within a digital image, but it's nearly impossible to recover something that's overexposed or 'blown out'.

5   LOOK FOR SHADE

It may seem counter-intuitive to seek out some shade with all this talk of natural light, but placing your subject – ducks, people, anything – in shade and increasing the brightness after you shoot gives more control of overall exposure and avoids strong, distracting shadows.

FLATTERY

Ever notice that there are a few super-photogenic people in your circle of friends –
those unicorns who know how to face the light and pose just so? Most of us are
shy in front of a camera, and are used to looking at photos and feeling 'blah'
about what we see. But with a little practice and some good lighting, you
can coach your subject into a gorgeous image that you will both be happy with.

Light

1 LET THE LIGHT SHINE

Direct the subject to face the light – it's a natural Photoshop tweak that helps eliminate furrows and creases and can reduce bags under the eyes. Use what nature provided, but don't be afraid to gently suggest that your subject powder their nose or throw on some lipstick.

2 MANIPULATE THE LIGHT

A white bounce card can help round out shadows. Use a big piece of white foam core or even a white T-shirt stretched over a piece of cardboard to bounce light into dark areas on the opposite side of the light source.

3 CONSIDER THE SUN

If you're shooting a portrait outside, keep your subject out of direct sunlight – it will cast shadows and emphasise every wrinkle and imperfection. Schedule the shoot during the 'golden hour', when the soft lighting will make everyone look gorgeous and create dreamy highlights.

4 USE WHAT'S AROUND YOU

If you're shooting indoors, use a lamp or a window to direct flattering light onto the subject (just watch out for a yellow cast if using a lamp). Position it just outside the frame so that it illuminates the side of your subject's face. For a more direct light, position the light source in front of the subject. The light source can also be positioned so it is seen in the shot and fills the frame with light, giving the subject a radiant glow. Whatever you do, try not to have the light coming from below, which will give a spooky, Halloween look – one that is generally unflattering (except to young trick-or-treaters!)

5 BE PLAYFUL

Help your subject play, dance, smell the roses and move around. Try to find emotion within this person – it will help him or her relax and feel a bit more confident in front of the camera, which is ultimately the most flattering look of all.

@zuckerandspice

Sam Zucker
zuckerandspicetravel.com

Sam is a freelance photographer, videographer, and food and travel writer, based in Barcelona, Spain. Originally from Boston, Massachusetts, he is also a trained chef and gastronomic–historical tour guide.

♥ **tip**

Shooting into the light directly or indirectly almost always gives me a more interesting and dynamic image than one that is shot with the light source at my back.

♥ **composition**

I have the rule of thirds in mind often, if not always. I also frame my compositions using leading lines whenever possible. I tend not to shoot with the subject in the centre of the image unless I can be sure I will have a balanced composition.

♥ **colour**

Vivid colours are attention-grabbing – important for driving engagement on social media. I much prefer contrast-rich, colourful shots to 'washed-out' pastel or monochromatic photos.

♥ **planning**

Waking up early to photograph a location during the golden hour puts me in a different mood to having my camera around my neck throughout an entire day of travelling.

♥ **passions**

Initially I took photos as a hobby whenever I travelled. As I started working as a professional photographer I started treating each trip as a way to showcase what I love to do. I now get paid jobs that include travel.

♥ seasons

I love shooting architecture and street scenes in impressive cities like Barcelona and Madrid, just after sunrise when the light is soft and the streets are empty, although late afternoon and sunset are also lovely. The season doesn't matter too much – each has its unique beauty.

LESS IS MORE

When shooting digitally, once you blow out something (overexpose an area within an image), it's gone forever. It's better to underexpose, leaving some areas a little too dark, and then lighten the image in post. This gives you more flexibility during the editing process, which is always a good thing. You can reduce the highlights in an overexposed image using the 'highlight' button on the Instagram editor – just move the slider to the left until the brightness is reduced a touch.

Light

> Once you blow something out,
> it's gone forever. It's better
> to underexpose.

1 EXPOSED SKIN

If you're in direct or 'hard light' – during the middle of a bright day at the beach, for example – find the right exposure for the subject's skin, zoom out and then recover highlights later.

2 HATS OFF

Hats are problematic in hard light. If your subject is wearing a hat in bright sunlight, it will create an irreversible shadow across their face, impossible to balance in post with under- or overexposure. Ask them to tip the hat back a little, wear it backwards or even play with it as a prop so that you can expose for an even pattern of light.

3 SNEAK A PEEK

Use the live view on your phone to your advantage; you can really see what you'll get this way. Try moving your focus and exposure point around by touching different areas of the picture plane on your camera screen. Note the difference when you touch the darkest, lightest and mid-points.

4 REVERSE ENGINEER

Use the shadows tool in Instagram to recover the darkest parts of the photo (shadows cast by leaves) and make more detail (flowers and sunlight on leaves) visible. By lightening the shadows, rather than using the brightness tool (which brightens indiscriminately), you'll improve the dark areas but the light parts of the image won't be altered.

ASSIGNMENT
THE GOLDEN HOUR

During the first two hours of sunlight (dawn) and the last two hours before the sun sets (dusk), shadows are slight and the glow of indirect light showcases highlights, mid-tones and shadows in a round, soft way. The magic of the golden hour gives everything you shoot a special radiance. So set your alarm for a dawn stroll and get out before dinner to make some heart-breakingly gorgeous images.

PLAN YOUR SHOOT

You've got to do a bit of homework when working with the golden hour. Go scout locations you think might work later in the day or early the next morning. Plan your composition and note any details that might be relevant later in the day. Take reference pictures, jot down notes and return later.

NOT JUST FOR OUTSIDE

The golden hour affects the indoors, too. The light that bathes your subjects in a warm glow outside will creep through the

DIRECT WITH EASE

It's much easier to direct people during the first and last hours of sunlight. There is no harsh light to cause them to squint, meaning you can put them directly in front of a barely there fading or rising sun without any issue.

windows of a space. Try opening a door behind you to let in as much of the golden hour as possible, and relish in the long shadows and flattering luminosity.

KEEP AN EYE ON THE SKY

What if it's foggy or overcast? Unfortunately the golden hour is affected by clouds. Cloud cover during these times will obscure the subtle shimmer and shadows and make the overall lighting even. This is another look entirely and isn't a bad one. Just be aware of it – you may want to reschedule.

GET TO KNOW THE GOLD

The golden hour is great for lens flare, backlight and front light. If you practise, you can really manipulate the way the soft light affects your images. Have your subject directly facing the golden light for an even, golden glow. Do the opposite and have the golden light behind your subjects, creating a subtle light all around their perimeter and a lovely golden atmosphere. If you shoot during the first or last glimmers of the golden hour, you may get a few lovely lens flares, which will add some groovy imperfection to your images.

FACE THE LIGHT

The quickest, easiest way to flatter a person with lighting is to have them face the light
– either straight on, where the light is positioned right near the camera, or from the side,
to direct light across half the face, with the other half in soft shadow. As photographers,
we are painters of light; it's the most important element of an image, so it's critical
to understand how it interacts with a person, location or object.

Light
94

① KNOW YOUR LIGHT

Lighting – natural, or from an artificial set-up – is the best tool for bringing out all the good in someone's face and neutralising the less attractive parts. Your photos will benefit enormously when you learn the language of light. 'Photo' means 'light' in Greek, and it's the core of this practice.

② GIVE DIRECTION

With your subject facing the light, you're only halfway there. Most people look better if they stick their face out a smidge from their neck and body; this creates a visual separation between face and body. It's subtle but helpful. As ever, take regular breaks and compliment your subject.

③ FIND THE BEST ANGLES

When you first meet someone whom you'd like to photograph, take note of what it is about them that immediately strikes you as distinctive and interesting. It doesn't have to be a traditionally beautiful feature – it could be a gesture, a way they hold their head or a quirky smile. Think about ways to accentuate their unique look in a flattering, beautiful fashion.

④ SUNGLASSES

Sometimes you just can't get rid of squinting eyes, or you find that your subject looks mega-tired from the previous night's partying. When all else fails, try sunglasses. They make a lot of sense outdoors and offer an insight into the personality of the person you're photographing. Indoors they may look a little silly, but that's okay – the shot might end up being fabulous.

⑤ BUTTER UP

If skin is showing, use oils. For beautiful, subtle highlights, I like to ask my subject to rub some oil on any skin that's visible – apart from the face, which looks better matt, so is usually best with a light application of powder.

SHADOW PATTERNS

Vivid stripes from Venetian blinds, dappled sunlight from an overhead tree, lace patterns formed by grandmother's curtain in the kitchen window can add a thrilling element to an image. They can also be problematic, distracting the viewer from the subject. Using contrasting shadows is a purely aesthetic decision – I love the effect of strong shadow play and the dramatic feeling that it elicits. Shadows can provide visual interest, direct a viewer's attention along the picture plane, and add contrast and depth.

1. KEEP TIME IN MIND

Shadows are longest around early morning and late afternoon, although this is impacted by season and latitude. Observe shadow patterns in your location if you plan on shooting a dramatic, shadow-laden look.

2. ADD SOME DRAMA

Shadows can bring an exciting element to an otherwise dull composition. Switch your focus to the shadow itself – with the subject just a sliver in the frame – and tell the story of the gesture, object or person in an unconventional way.

3. PLAY WITH PROPORTIONS

The closer you are to the light source, the bigger your shadow will be. Experiment with shadow length, shifting both yourself and your subject's position in relation to the light source.

4. PLAY WITH PERSPECTIVE

Get above a scene to see how shadows can play a key role in a composition. I love to go to the top of a shopping centre or tall building and see how the trees or people interact with the street surface. Sometimes the beautiful shadow patterns are more interesting than the subject.

5. TAKE CONTROL

Make your own 'gobo'. A gobo is a dark plate with some type of perforated stencil that lets in a controlled point of light. It's an industry tool used to create specific light patterns. I often use a homemade gobo to replicate shadows found in the real world. This can be as simple as a branch of a tree held up to the light source – usually a window – to filter the light and create a dappled pattern on a basket of peaches.

@anne_parker

Anne Parker
madebyanneparker.com

Anne is a food and prop stylist based in Portland, Oregon. When not constructing beautiful tabletops, she can be found snuggled in bed watching documentaries about the 70s, adventuring with friends, and taking her time to appreciate all of life's tiny details.

© Chantal Anderson

 favourite

Almost every evening when I'm home, I find myself snapping photos as the sun is going down and there is a beautiful orange glow streaming through the windows. It's such a fleeting moment, but it never ceases to draw me in.

 style

Oftentimes, when I look at my images I feel like they're so busy that there's too much going on. I love bold simplicity, and always have to remind myself that less is more.

inspiration

My photography is really just capturing what I'm drawn to, and how I live in the world. In life, I always prefer dim natural lighting to artificial light, and I think that's reflected in my photos because that's the environment I'm in.

Insty-love

I'm happy to know that the content I've produced has resonated with some people. Through Instagram, people started to contact me, asking me to style photo shoots.

challenge

At first I was very specific about what I posted, and wanted every photo to be perfect. Now I sometimes post photos that I know won't get many likes. If I like what I'm doing, I'm happy.

 theme

My photos revolve around interiors, food and the outdoors. I'm definitely not as good at shooting people, and that's something I'd like to improve. When I do freelance jobs, I see how so much of the success of portrait photography relies on the photographer's rapport with their subject, and the direction they give, which is intimidating to me!

6

COMPOSE

OFF CENTRE • EMBRACE THE NEGATIVE SPACE
STYLING FOOD • MIX IT UP • SCALE • PORTRAITS
ANGLES • POV • SHAKE THINGS UP • HANDS ON
BLENDING THE INGREDIENTS • PLAIN AND SIMPLE
LEARN YOUR LINES • WHACKY AND WONKY
CREATE A STORY • START WIDE • MESSY • MINIMAL
CREATE DEPTH • SMALL MOMENTS
@LITTLEUPSIDEDOWNCAKE • SEEING THE WHOLE
OPPOSITES POP • FLORAL • PLAYFUL
RESIST UNIFORMITY • CAPTURE EMOTION
@LATONYAYVETTE

OFF CENTRE

The easiest way to create a dynamic composition, no matter which aspect ratio you're working in (square, rectangle, etc.), is to keep the subject out of the centre of the frame. This approach works to make the viewer's eye dance around the image. Focusing on a subject centred in the frame will instantly pull and hold the viewer's attention to a single point.

1   BISECT THE HORIZON

A horizon defines a midline; by bisecting the frame in the bottom third or top third, you can make a livelier image. Bisecting the horizon line with, say, a church spire, gives the image openness and allows the viewer to focus on the subject. It can also provide space for the placement of text .

2   CREATE MOVEMENT

Keeping things out of the centre creates movement. By placing a subject or part of a subject in the foreground or middle ground off centre, you're asking the viewer to move their eye around the page, and so take the time to digest the picture.

3   SUBJECT AND SURROUNDINGS

When the subject is off centre, other parts of the composition then become more relevant. For example, if you're shooting outdoors, placing a big arching tree off to the side pulls the viewer's attention to other areas of the picture plane – a gorgeous sky in the background, perhaps, or a group of people hanging out at the base of the tree.

4   RULES ARE FOR BREAKING: CENTRE IT!

Sometimes you've got to upend what you know and put the subject in the centre of the frame. Emphasising a particular quality of a subject (perhaps its circular shape) by placing it dead middle of the picture plane can be an effective way to amplify a message. There's an awkwardness to this style of image that can be appealing and fun.

When the subject is off centre, other parts of the composition become more relevant.

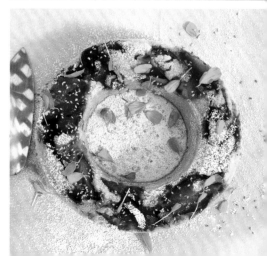

EMBRACE THE NEGATIVE SPACE

Negative space is simply the area around and between the main subjects in an image. People have been using the power of negative space since they began painting in caves. The technique is critical in all art forms: sculpture, painting, drawing and photography. Using negative space is all about balance and creating a relationship between context and subject. Here are a few tips to keep in mind when composing an image with negative space.

1 MOOD AND EMOTION

Negative space provides the mood, emotion and context of an image. The setting and the space that the subject inhabits are huge factors in the story an image tells. Think of a figure positioned at the bottom of a frame, surrounded by a grey background. Now think of that same figure surrounded by a bright sky – each scene tells a very different story.

2 EMPHASISE THE SUBJECT

The space itself can also become the subject, providing the viewer with information and context. Use negative space as an intentional feature of your composition to emphasise what's important – for example, the grandeur of a castle. Explore the emptiness and look at all of a subject's surroundings – the spaces you originally dismiss as uninspiring may become the shapes that frame or define your image.

3 ADD MYSTERY

Negative space brings a little mystery to a composition. Think of the lilt of a piano at the beginning of a piece; it tantalises then playfully carries you into a full sonata. Negative space is the lilt of the keys – it doesn't reveal all at once, but asks the viewer to investigate the subject and setting more carefully.

4 CROP IT LIKE IT'S HOT

You can always crop in, but can't do the reverse. I like to shoot with a lot of air and negative space in my photos. I can always decide to trim the edges and reduce the amount of negative space to make it less extreme, but it is difficult to add negative space without resorting to time-consuming post adjustments.

5 PAUSE BUTTON

The barrage of imagery we are exposed to on a daily basis is overwhelming; negative space provides a visual pause. With so many figures, shapes and pieces of information to take in, negative space above a colourful arrangement of vegetables, for example, can provide room for a mid-scroll pause.

STYLING FOOD

If you can view food as a series of compositional elements –
colours and shapes – rather than a delicious meal, your pictures will be
stronger and more dynamic. Think like a painter rather than an eater and
view foods based on size, colour and their relationship to each other.

1 PLAY WITH YOUR FOOD

Rearrange. Rearrange again. Edit, remove and then add plates or pans. Play until you see something unexpected and striking emerge. Take some time to be silly; try scattering colourful petals across a cake. Most importantly, be flexible and let go of what you think your food image should look like; something far more interesting can appear when you're experimenting.

2 NATURAL INGREDIENTS

The best food pictures start with the best-looking natural ingredients. If you have the desire to make the food you're styling, start with beautiful produce from a farmers' market; it makes all the difference. Real food looks natural, romantic and alive – so much better than the supermarket stuff.

3 TRY PATTERNS

A fun way to get out of a rut is to try lining up a series of little plates of food, a tea set or raw produce in a square, circle or more complex mandala shape. You can try arranging objects from small to large, in a grid, or group by shape or type of item. Just try it; you'll get something fun.

4 MULTIPLE ANGLES

It's easiest to shoot food from above, in an aerial view – this aspect flattens food and plates into a 2D plane and emphasises patterns and shapes. Move the set-up around to see if you can find a better angle, such as super close up or straight on. Let the food you are shooting guide you, and use the shape of the food as a starting point. If a wine glass is tall and thin, you might start with a vertically aligned photo to echo the shape of the glass.

5 STYLE THE PLATE

You have control over the entirety of the picture plane. You've styled the food and plates in an overall composition – but you can also control the life happening on the plate. Watch food programmes on TV to see how chefs are plating and use this as inspiration to make a statement with food.

MIX IT UP

When styling a flat lay of found objects, a product story or a food scene, an aerial perspective is the easiest to manipulate. You can include large, medium and small shapes in an infinite number of arrangements. From complex patterns to a sparse scattering of objects, the way you compose will help you tell the story. Use a compositional approach to create your own worlds and photograph them.

From complex patterns to a
sparse scattering of objects,
the way you compose will
help you tell the story.

1 START WITH SURFACE

The place where your objects sit is critical. A lively, green
chequered textile creates one mood, while a whitewashed
table will give you an entirely different look. Whatever you
choose as a surface, pay attention to the way it interacts with
what you place on it, and the use this interplay to build a
visual story.

2 THREE DIFFERENT-SIZED SHAPES

When setting a table or arrangement of any kind, including
at least three different shapes of varying sizes – a teapot, a
sprig of berries and a large platter; a shoe, a hair pin and a
single flower – instantly creates an interesting composition
and infuses the picture with flow and dynamism.

3 SPARKLE WITH DETAILS

I love to include small flowers, stones or candles to light up
pieces in an arrangement. These small compositional gestures
can make the scene pop and dance like little sparkles in
viewers' eyes.

4 WOW ELEMENT

Everyone loves something unexpected that makes them gasp
with glee. A pop of colour or an unexpected shape – a sparkly
necklace, a trace of lipstick on the rim of a glass, a slice of
cake, a handwritten note, a vintage coffee tin – adds an
element of interest and can take an image from fun to
fabulous. Whatever the surprising component, place it
in the shot at the last moment; this trick can often work
to bring a composition together in a new way.

SCALE

Varying the scale of your photos – from extremely close up to very far away –
is key to keeping your shooting style fluid and your images varied. You don't want
to miss a detail because you're busy only shooting skies, or vice versa. Stay nimble
and physical as you move through a shoot. Sometimes photography feels like a sport,
so be ready to move your body as you vary the space between you and your subject.

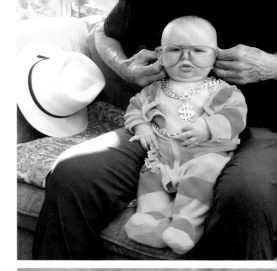

1 SHOT LIST

Having a mental running list of differently scaled shots – from extremely tight to very far and everything in between – will fill your Instagram feed with a diverse body of work. Something always looks better from a certain point of view (unknown before you begin), and covering all these bases will help you arrive at the best shot.

2 OUT OF SCALE

Placing subjects out of scale can be thought provoking and sometimes funny. The disparity of a baby wearing an adult's glasses is hilarious, memorable. Getting very close up can produce a minimalist image, where line, shape and form become elemental and elegant.

3 MINIATURES

Small is charming – seek it out when you can. I grew up with a love for dollhouses and the tiny worlds I could create within them. When you see a small object, pick it up – maybe it's a blossom or shells found on a beach walk. Learn to be a miniature-treasure collector and document your finds as if they were twenty times their size – sometimes an object can take on new interpretations, depending on how close in you photograph it.

4 BIG, MEDIUM, LITTLE

In landscape images, scale becomes critical. I love to have small things in the foreground, such as wildflowers or a moving tree branch; this way the viewer 'goes through' a porthole of sorts and meanders to the back of the image, where the hills and horizons meet again. The play of shape and scale adds movement, story and interest to the image.

PORTRAITS

Anyone can make a picture of a person that looks like it came out of a school or college yearbook. But how do you create a portrait that hints at a subject's inner world? Placing someone in their natural setting (known as an environmental portrait), or shooting in close up with little background, are both stylistic decisions that can be used to highlight aspects of a person's character.

1 FOCUS ON THE EYES
Everything in a portrait can be soft except the eyes. If the eyes are out of focus, the whole picture looks off. Tap your phone's screen at the eye area, or focus on the eyes with your camera every time you take a shot, just to be sure that the eyes are clearly captured.

2 BURST MODE
There will always be times when you find the perfect angle, with sunlight falling in a spectacular way, and your subject's eyes are closed. To avoid missing the moment, shoot a burst of three or five shots. Review the shots and keep only the good ones. Be ruthless – your storage settings will thank you.

3 TAKE CHARGE
'Focus on the ceiling, look towards the window, try your hands in your pockets, how about gesturing towards me, now taste a spoonful of the marmalade, what's your plan this summer?' These are all questions and directions I have used to bring something new out of a subject. Grabbing a subject's attention and showing them you have the situation under control lets them know you are in charge and puts them at ease. Directing and asking questions will help build a relationship between you and your subject and help produce a portfolio of varied images for your feed.

4 TRY BOSSINESS
If you don't have great chemistry (it happens every now and again) then try authority. Be assertive; tell your subject where to go, show them how to stand, and make them move: 'Turn this way, turn that way'. You have little to lose, and you want to get the perfect shot.

5 BE IN A PICTURE
Every now and again, I like to have my picture taken. It reminds me of how awkward it can be and how it takes time to get comfortable with a photographer. It's humbling to be in front of the camera and feel uneasy – do it every now and again to be able to connect with your subjects more readily.

ANGLES

Like a sharp lawyer, I love the knowing the angles. Angles are intersections of line or
shape – they're where things come together. These compositional moments are not
exclusively austere, man-made or architectural. They also occur in nature: an angle
can be found in the curve of a winding stream or a sweeping branch.
Look at the intersections of things and see where they lead.

An angle can be found in the
curve of a winding stream
or a sweeping branch.

1 PERSPECTIVE

The horizon has two-point perspective – objects appear
smaller on each side of a single viewpoint. The convergence
of a staircase at a distance is one-point perspective. The best
way to learn how to use perspective is make a small lesson for
yourself: 'Play the angles'. Try shooting a series of one- and
two-point perspective images, and note how they affect the
feel of your final image.

2 NO SHARP ANGLES

The flip side of looking for straight angles is to seek situations
or objects where they are altogether absent. Everybody loves
the soft, pure, puffy roundness of a baby's feet.

3 MANY ELEMENTS, SINGLE FRAME

There are a multitude of in-between angles – from the
softness of puppy paws to the harsh separation between
skyscraper and sky. Try combining the two opposites. It
gets exciting when you find severe angles within a soft
environment – for example, the chubby legs of a baby, so
close they are unrecognisable, or the severity of soft birds
on a single power line. Angles when mixed with different
textures, tones and colours become shapes. Shapes become
paintings, and then you are on your way to becoming an artist.

4 INTERSECTION

Picture a room where two walls meet bathed in natural light
– one wall will be brighter than the other. This already creates
an interesting lighting pattern, but position a person in that
intersection and you've got a thing going on, where one half
of their face will be in shadow, the other brightly lit.

115

POV

Point of view is literally the position you put the camera in when viewing a scene, and more abstractly, your personal taste and style expressed through photography. It can be malleable, but over time consistent threads will start to emerge in your work. Just when you think you've got your POV down, push yourself to shift it to keep your your Instagram feed engaging, and your creativity on its toes.

1 HORIZONTAL VS VERTICAL

When the world of image making was filtered through the lens of an SLR camera, everyone thought in horizontal alignment. Cameras in mobile phones have shifted this mindset to the vertical. If you are used to making horizontal images, change to vertical, or vice versa. Your eye level often defines point of view. It is the most expected vantage point. When you shoot from somewhere other than eye level – down low, for example – you are rearranging everything. So do not simply put the camera up to eye level; be a cowgirl or cowboy and shoot from the hip.

2 AERIAL

Understanding the range of POVs available to you is useful for furthering the point of your image. Aerial shots (a bird's eye view) can be taken from an airplane to shoot a valley below, or from a balcony for a new perspective of a street scene. Taking the subject's POV by shooting from eye level gives the viewer the sense that they are part of the subject's environment, not looking down on it. Making pictures from the ground is a sort of 'worm's eye view' and can make everything appear larger.

3 LITERAL POINT OF VIEW

It can be interesting to shoot from right above a subject's shoulder, and include a trace of the side of their face, a lock of hair, or their hands in the frame. The viewer will 'become' that subject when the image is created from this angle. We want to embody that person, we see what is shown – it's a slim amount of information, but it can say so much.

4 SEEK YOUR POV

I love bright colour – I'm drawn to colourful scenes over and over again, so my point of view involves a happy, jolly palette. Because I know that's a strong part of my point of view, I'm constantly trying to refine my understanding and mastery of colour – studying the way certain shades vibe with one another, and how subtle shifts in colour can create a very different feeling to that produced by strong clashes of, say, bright pink and yellow against pastel green.

SHAKE THINGS UP

Often the limitations you have are self-imposed. Get rid of them.
Don't be afraid to *take* a picture or *make* a picture. Give yourself the
power to try something different. Be unpredictable. Success can be a terrible
mistress, lulling you into believing that you have the answers, and making you fear
stepping away from what has worked before. When you think something doesn't
work, try to correct it by doing what you know works, then try exactly the opposite.

1 WHAT IS UNEXPECTED?

Disregard any 'rules' you know: the rule of thirds, the 'don't put things in the centre' rule, the 'start with natural light' idea. Throw out your notions of what you do and how you do it, and you'll start surprising yourself.

2 CHANGE YOUR PERSPECTIVE

The same subject shot from three different angles can become three entirely different images. A bamboo forest shot straight-on looks like a series of vertical lines meeting a blue sky. Shot from ground level looking up, the view is mostly of the canes with light patches of sky. If you were to shoot directly above the bamboo, the picture plane would be filled with green colour and texture. Try varying the perspective on any subject to shake things up.

3 CHANGE THE STYLE

When you find yourself relying on a single way of seeing to compose your photographs, it's time to change things up. If your default setting is a 'bright and airy' style with a single point of focus and very little shadow, make your next picture all about heavy contrast with piercing highlights and near-black shadows. The same subject will take on an entirely different feeling when you change the lighting and style.

4 START WITH ONE THING

When I get stuck and in a creative rut, or the options for creating an image become over- or underwhelming, I just start with one thing. I take a seasonal fruit, a collection of vintage silverwear and kitchen utensils, or a small bouquet of flowers I picked on the way to the studio, and I try to make the best photograph of that one thing that I can. From there, the light or the way the little items move or interact with the background colours . . . all of it leads me to the next thing. So instead of stressing and not getting started, just simplify, then carry on.

HANDS ON

A simple gesture – a flick of the wrist, or a gentle grasp – can do so much to convey feeling and mood. When you're stuck on how to proceed with a portrait, zoom in on what the hands are doing. If they're doing nothing, ask your subject to casually put their hand on their face, run a hand through their hair or touch the brim of their hat.

1 ADD MOVEMENT

Hands are not often still. Even if your subject is seated in the middle of a stark room their hands may be moving through a range of subtly different positions. This motion and expression of body language can permeate the entire picture. Try asking them to put their hands in their pockets, or encourage them to use their hands while telling you about their day.

2 ADD LIFE

When shooting a still life, or a travel or food story, I like to shoot a version as is, and a version with hands in it. When we see only a model's hands and not the rest of their body, we imagine the hands as our own, which leads us to be more connected to the image.

3 CONNECTION

Clasped hands instantly convey a sense of connection. If the hands are those of two people intertwined, we know they're close – maybe they're family, lovers or friends. No matter what the relationship, it is always an intimate act that resonates on camera.

BLENDING THE INGREDIENTS

The figure-to-ground relationship – the relationship between subject and background – is the most important compositional concept you can master. Paying attention to the entire picture plane, not just the subject, produces visually harmonious and integrated images.

① ATMOSPHERIC CONDITIONS

The easiest way to find a subject and a ground with very different colours is to make pictures outside the brightest points of the day. Wake up early and make your shooting time between five and eight in the morning, then go out again after five in the evening.

② LIGHTS AND DARKS

Having a broad range of colour and tone will help define a subject against a background. The subject or an area near it is usually illuminated, and the rest of the picture plane is typically in medium tones or shadow. The light falling on or near the subject – on towers of brightly coloured macarons, for example – tells the eye where to look.

③ ANYTHING CAN BE THE SUBJECT

A road, an object, a room or a single light beam can be the 'figure' in your composition. While our first inclination is to start with people, push yourself to look beyond this first impulse to find the natural subject line of a room – it could be a chair, a crack in the wall, the angle at which two walls come together, or a shaft of light falling through a window.

PLAIN AND SIMPLE

To create anything that is simple and stunning requires skill and practice. Think of tasting the best bread and butter of your life; it's not a complicated dish, nor is it expensive, but when it's right, it is sublime. The elements that combine to produce the perfect baguette – bread, water, salt and yeast – have to be flawless. The rise and the baking require a refined skill that takes years to master. In photography, your ingredients are light and rudimentary shapes, and the skill is in manipulating the composition to create feeling within an image. Simple is not easy, but it's worth trying. Here are some strategies to consider.

In photography, your ingredients are light and rudimentary shapes.

1 INSPIRING PHOTOGRAPHERS

Ralph Gibson is one of my favourites. His books *Days at Sea* and *The Somnambulist* are great. The black-and-white photographs show simple relationships between subjects like a hand, a shadow, sand and the sky. Rarely are there more than three physical objects or elements in an image.

2 VISUAL HAIKU

Seek the special within the mundane. Note how light comes through a door or casts a shadow on the wall, or how a friend's hair is illuminated by an overhead light as she exits the car. See what you discover when you seek out the simplest of subjects and compositions.

3 SYMMETRY VS ASYMMETRY

The simpler the symmetry, the greater its impact in a photograph. Try your composition in different ways. For example, if you're shooting a flower, get tight in and show the strong, repeating lines of the overlapping petals. Then zoom out a tad and reveal the whole bloom centred in the frame with almost no negative space. Which is better? Both can work, they're just different.

4 SIMPLICITY IS STUNNING

When photographing people, start with a simple, stunning image. A single figure against a dark wall, without context, can be super-striking. It may take more effort on your part to relax and engage your subject when working in such an intimate setting, but it's worth a shot.

LEARN YOUR LINES

When shooting architecture or interiors, be aware of the horizontal lines
(the base of a building or room, and the tables or windows within it) and vertical
lines (where two walls come together, furniture, a building's height). When these two
things are out of whack and off axis, because they are tilted or warped, an image
tends to look unprofessional. There are a few helpful tips that can jump-start your
understanding of this concept and give your images polish.

1 GRID IT UP

The grid function on your phone or camera will make it easier to keep compositions straight. Vertical lines converge when you are looking up or down. The eye naturally corrects for this effect, removing the warp of perspective, but the camera does not. When shooting interiors this can result in tall items converging to create a visually uncomfortable effect. Using the grid function will help you isolate and align the area you want to shoot straight.

2 PERSPECTIVE

An architectural drawing is a beautiful example of a 3D object (a building) flattened into a 2D object (a drawing). Studying these drawings can help you to identify where on the horizontal and vertical axes straight lines occur – awnings, floor tiles, worktops. Being able to identify the straight lines will help you stand in the best position to capture them.

3 FIX IT AFTER THE FACT

If an image is a little skewed, you can edit to straighten the lines using a lens correction filter or the rotate tool, rotating the image slightly. Making this adjustment will crop off some of the image, so be aware of this.

4 THROW AWAY THE RULES

Don't worry about keeping lines plumb and true – get weird, forget the 'right way' and see how a marina scene or any space looks from a diagonal, intentionally warped angle. What do you get? Do you like it? Two of my favourite photographers, Todd Selby and Garance Doré, embrace this off-kilter look to brilliant effect.

Being able to identify the straight lines will help you stand in the best position to capture them.

WHACKY AND WONKY

It's fabulous to be off-balance and strange, rather than straight and formulaic. Learn the rules, abide by the rules, then throw them out the window and try for the opposite effect. Aim to visually unhinge your viewer. Get low, get high up – shoot from under the table and obscure most of the image with a dark blur (the underside of said table). Shoot at high noon with everything in the centre of the frame and see what happens. You get the idea. Even if you don't keep at it, get whacky and wonky every now and then to rattle your brain into seeing new possibilities and give your feed a visual jolt.

1 GET UP HIGH

Find some safe footing at the top of a building. Use your camera or phone as a periscope to capture a breathtaking perspective. If you look at an image and you get vertigo or the hair on the back of your neck stands up, you have probably created something impactful.

2 MAKE IT MEMORABLE

An image of four fingers grasping the edge of a ledge would lead a viewer to assume there is a body dangling below that ledge. But the reality could well be someone crouched on a stoop below the 'ledge' to create the illusion of risk and drama. The image implies a narrative. Make it funny, risky, exciting and thrilling.

3 COPY UNTIL IT BECOMES ORIGINAL

Look to other photographers making weird, fun work. Investigate their images with a critical eye – do they shoot super close up with a bright flash? Try it. Do they cast models from Gumtree rather than a modelling agency for real-life grit? Try that, too. Do they shoot dead flowers rather than freshly picked blooms? Copy, copy, copy until others' approaches transform into a new way of thinking for you.

4 SHAPE PLAY

When I'm just about being playful and feel like a creative workout, I try to relate shapes to each other. Can a mango look the same as a little vintage dish which also looks just like a bar of fancy soap? They're all ovals so they all go in the shot. It doesn't matter that they don't relate to one another – because they're all in the same image, viewers will string a story together.

CREATE A STORY

A camera or phone can allow us all to be visual storytellers. An image is quickly digested, and a photo can do so many things – delight, haunt, surprise – so a succesful Instagram feed is one that is filled with memorable shots. You can work up many 'sketches' or 'drafts' before getting to something masterful; the more you do it, the more articulate your story will become. Pretty soon, the idea in your mind matches what you create. Whatever story you're telling, a mastery of light, a strength or subtlety of colour, and bold, graphic composition are always the criteria for creating thought-provoking images

1 MAP OUT A PLAN
Create a shot list or series of sketches exploring different ideas or approaches that you can then use as a map when you're in the moment and it feels overly complicated, or if you run out of ideas. This handy reference will give you creative inspiration and might include a close-up, a profile, an environmental image, a vertical and horizontal alignment, and one crazy idea: bring on the hair rollers and playing cards.

2 RELATIONSHIPS
To create a great story you need to see the subtleties in relationships between people. Relationships can be romantic, or about growth and time. An image of a grandparent and a child is a story loaded with emotion and speaks about the passing of time, and the bonds of family.

3 CONTEXT IS EVERYTHING
To create a nuanced image full of description and meaning, think of where you're situating your subject as much as the subject itself. The space between things can add emotion, visual pause, and give the viewer graphic clues.

4 DIPTYCH OR SERIES
Use a diptych or a series of images to build a narrative. A photo essay in a magazine typically uses ten to fifteen images. There is usually a wide, establishing image; then medium shots; and a few detail shots. Your Instagram feed is a storytelling device with many images comprising a whole. Think of scale, colour, theme and how well the photos relate to each other as you post.

5 LAYER
Layer the subjects to create a deeper story of a place, person or feeling. A story is stronger and more memorable when an image uses multiple visual indicators. Think of this image in your mind: two friends laughing with each other, sitting in dappled light on the step in front of a green door. Here you have information about the two people (jovial, lighthearted) and their location (outside a home).

CREATE A STORY

BEACH PICNIC

Setting up a picnic on the beach is a cute way to bring together a range of elements, from food and portraiture to travel and textural details. Enlist a couple of friends to be your models – payment can be in the form of a spread of delicious food – and ask a stylish pal to be in charge of props. If you have access to a farmers' market, gather a selection of the best-looking fresh fruit. Add a chopping board, your favourite cheeses and a bottle of wine and you're set.

GET ORGANISED

If you can, go to a familiar beach and scope out the best spots and the best time of day to shoot. If it's summer time, plan to shoot when the sun is lower in the sky. Look for an area that isn't too crowded so that you don't have to work too hard to avoid random people in the background.

SET THE SCENE

Lay out your largest elements first – picnic blanket, basket, models – then add your smaller items, such as a chopping board, plates and fruit. By working this way you can easily see big compositional shapes and use the smaller elements to create a diagonal flow within the composition. Keep major components out of the centre of the frame, and remember to leave some negative space.

MOVE AROUND

If you've put a lot of energy into creating a scene, it can be hard to remember to move around when shooting. Work through a mental shot list of various angles and scales. Get in very close on some details – focus on one person with their plate of food, perhaps – and be sure to capture the overall scene with a wide shot.

FEAST OF FIVE PASTAS

I love doing a deep dive into a favourite food – for me this is pasta!
I find so much beauty and inspiration in the different shapes, varied
methods of preparation and styling options. Working with a subject I
love offers limitless potential to create stunning pictures and gorgeous styling.

CHANGE UP STYLES

To showcase a collection of similar items – in this case, pasta – try varying the backgrounds and styles you shoot them in: try cooked and uncooked, use different backgrounds, bowls and light sources. Let your imagination run wild for an hour or two.

ENLIST A FRIEND

It's too much to try and cook five different pasta dishes in one day and do a good job photographing them. If you can get a friend (even a parent!) who's a great cook to do this part, you'll be miles ahead. Split the leftovers and you will both have a week's worth of readymade dinners.

PROCESS SHOTS

Remember that ingredients can be just as interesting, if not more so, than the finished dish. As you go along from dish to dish, consider the beginning, middle and end of the meal – the ingredients, a hero shot of the pasta and maybe an empty plate with a few crumbs nearby.

DESSERTS IN THE CANYON

I have a passion for sweets, and they make some of the very best photography subjects. Typically they are cute (smallish in size), carefully prepared, luscious to behold and, most importantly, they make everyone lick their lips and want to eat them. I'd say that's a great starting point for a shoot.

FORM PARTNERSHIPS

Build relationships with your local bakers or pâtissieres. When someone brings an outstanding cake to a party, I compliment the creator and follow up with them to get the recipe. It's very helpful to know people in fields that complement your own – reach out and ask if you can photograph their creations.

BE A LOCATION SCOUT

Use your everyday life as a scouting mission; remember the interesting and special spaces you have come across when you're planning a shoot. Friends of mine have taken over a cool old motel with a rough-and-tumble cabin vibe that works well for a rustic desserts shoot.

THINK LIKE AN ART DIRECTOR

Prepare a shot list of diverse images – whole desserts, slices of pie, a single small pastry and the person who baked everything. By being aware of the range of images you may want to make, you'll come away with a body of work that's interesting, not just one great picture.

FRIENDS' WEEKEND GETAWAY

Is there anything better than being with a group of friends in a stunning location, wearing fun outfits and eating fabulous food? I'd be hard pressed to come up with a more perfect, or photogenic, weekend. The next time you're organising an adventure, throw a few extra dresses into your bag and invite your girlfriends for a few days on the road and a chance to play dress up.

GET CRAFTY

Bring the ingredients for activities – this always makes for a good time and helps everyone relax for a few photos. I like decorating biscuits and painting. Both help tell a story of a fun girls' weekend and provide cute props.

NO 'MODELS,' NO PROBLEM

Regular people are gorgeous. The more I go along in photography, the less interested I am in 'perfection'; I'm looking for quirks, scars, goofy grins. Confidence in front of the camera is sexy – working with friends creates a relaxed atmosphere and will help you make images that reveal their natural beauty.

WHAT'S IN FRONT OF YOU

The best location or scene may be right in front of you. Don't get caught up in trying to make it to the next activity. Take in the moment and see what's right there. Maybe your hotel room has a fabulous bathtub or fabulous retro blanket; you may find you can create an entire visual story in a single room.

START WIDE

Films usually start with a predictable pattern of images: overview, medium shot, tight shot and then detail. The wide shot establishes the scene. When shooting any series of photographs for Instagram – travel, lifestyle, food or even a portrait – the same pattern can be used. Start with an overview to establish the scene, then move closer in as you continue to shoot. Once you're *in* the scene, turn around or take a breath and ask yourself, 'What am I missing?'

Start with an overview to establish the scene, then move closer in.

1 FILM SCHOOL

Study wide shots from films and think about them when creating your own composition. From contemporary to classic, note how the first thing you see sets the mood of the entire film. Some greats are the 1963 version of *Cleopatra*, which begins with a carefully constructed set of ancient Egypt and a throng of extras in red tunics; the first scene in *Indiana Jones*, which is all about a boulder coming towards our lead character; and *Lord of the Rings*, which sets the scene with a series of epic landscapes. None of these are by accident.

2 COMPOSITIONAL RULES

When setting the scene for your visual narrative, keep the compositional rules in mind. Think of the foreground (paved square), middle ground (terraced buildings) and background (blue sky) – do you have something in all three planes? Can you walk through the scene visually?

3 CAMERA LEVEL

Hold the camera or phone at waist level rather than at eye level. By shooting from mid-body height, you will capture sky, horizon and ground in equal proportion. Shooting from a lower position makes it easier to represent horizontal and vertical lines as straight, too, and will give your shots a more purposeful composition, avoiding the amateur look of eye-level shots.

4 WATCH YOUR EXPOSURE

Aim to show the scene in its best light. Position yourself high above the scene and wait for sunset, twilight or dawn. Shoot at a slightly underexposed level to capture vivid colours; you can always brighten the darks by adjusting the 'shadows' setting in Instagram editor.

MESSY

Working in an all-over-the-place, messy style is the most fun compositional approach. The more irreverent and free from expectations you feel and act, the better. Keep a light rein on all this wild abandon; there's a fine line between dishevelled, lived in and funky, and total, senseless chaos, so be mindful and ride the edge of the two looks.

① REMEMBER NEGATIVE SPACE

A messy composition still needs negative space to work. Begin by loading up the composition – lots of ingredients for a food scene, a collection of beachcombing treasures, or an array of bits and bobs for a still life – and remove piece by piece to create a little negative space.

② GIVE PHOTOS A LIFE FORCE

Even a touch of messiness brings a life force to an image by signifying human interaction with the setting. Resist the temptation to clean everything away after a party and try shooting the scene with evidence of a good time in place – a few crumbs, lipstick stains on the china, wine spilled on a white cloth. You may find a far more interesting image than you did at the start of the party.

③ DROP IT

When garnishing food or creating a messy scene, scattering from above is a beautiful way to replicate the random patterns found in nature. Instead of systematically placing individual leaves with tweezers, sprinkle them from above – where they fall is where they should be.

MINIMAL

Creating a subdued, sparse composition is tough – but when you nail it, the balance of light, line and shape sings. A pared-back composition can say more than a frantic or busy arrangement. The next time you're creating a still life, a portrait or even photographing a room, consider removing elements to bring the essence of your subject to the fore.

1 MASTERS OF COOL MINIMALISM
Tina Modotti's still lifes and Robert Mapplethorpe's intense studies of flowers are the epitome of a cool perfection without artifice or fluff. Images of a single item ask more questions than they answer, and that's what makes them so haunting.

2 SIMPLE IS NOT BORING
Once you've chosen your subject, try simplifying the scene. This could mean shifting your shooting position to omit trees from the perimeter of an image of the sky, or filling the foreground with a jumble of shells and pebbles breaking across the horizon.

3 INCLUDE NEGATIVE SPACE
Minimalist photography is as much about atmosphere as subject. If you want to incorporate an object, try including a small figure and a lot of sky. Negative space is your main tool for directing the eye to the subject, or lack thereof.

4 CROP
Centring your subject, then cropping most of it out of the frame creates intrigue and an element of surprise, making an image that viewers will linger over. This is particularly effective when photographing people.

CREATE DEPTH

Including layers – something close to camera, in the midline of sight and far
behind the subject – creates depth in a photo. A sense of three-dimensionality
in an image creates dynamism and interest in the picture plane. A layered
image is not sterile or flat; it more closely resembles real life and the way we move
through spaces. It's an instant boon to your work to think in 3D rather than 2D.

1 CREATE OBSTRUCTIONS

Look for objects you can use to protrude into the edge of the frame and obscure the composition of a simple shot. A cluster of leaves held close to the lens can create the effect of shooting through a tree; a piece of glass can add a subtle blur in a corner. Breaking into the edge of the frame will add a sense of space. Placing leaves very close to the lens makes them appear soft and blurry, and introduces a soft field of colour that works to direct the eye towards an architectural detail, such as this spiral staircase.

2 SELECTIVE FOCUS

Focusing on one point and slightly blurring the rest of an image will create depth of field. Use depth of field to help isolate what you're looking at, and add a subtly emotive feeling to an image. On a phone use 'macro' mode; for a camera stop all the way down to your lowest aperture. An isolated focal point – a person with gorgeous hair pulled from the background, or a fun cocktail in someone's hand – forces a viewer to pay attention to what occupies that point.

3 FAMILY PORTRAIT

Here's little exercise . . . Construct a family portrait with a teenage girl in sharp focus, sitting looking at the camera. To the side, slightly behind the girl and softly out of focus, have a woman looking at the girl. In the background have a man out of focus but implying a masculine figure. You have just created a story about a family by using different depths of field.

4 PORTRAIT MODE

Using portrait mode on your phone will isolate your subject and slightly blur the background. This is a quick way to add intensity and the feeling of space to an image. Remember, your subject doesn't necessarily have to be a person – you may choose to focus on swaying branches, heavy with elongated leaves.

SMALL MOMENTS

You can create intimacy with a small, specific detail – light catching on a cluster of wildflowers, the way a feather intermingles with a leaf, a pool of chocolate oozing from a perfectly baked chocolate chip biscuit. These minutiae prompt the viewer to build a story in their mind. So get in tight, closer than you think you should be – the more zoomed in and less specific you are, the more space you give the viewer's imagination.

Compose

1 | DETAILS MAKE THE STORY

Accessories or details on an outfit can help embellish a scene. A hand-stitched seam, a bright red bow, layered costume jewellery or a worn-in, sun-bleached hat will help the viewer construct a narrative around your subject.

2 | LOOK FOR HANDS AND GESTURES

We speak volumes with body language. A great photographer can capture nuanced expressions to reveal a person's quirks or the bond that exists between two people. Pursed lips and a concentrated gaze give the viewer a window into who the subject is. When you have faces in an image, they belong to specific people and not the viewer. When you have interlocked body parts or nervous feet, your images convey the singularity of the subject(s) you're portraying.

3 | SLIVER OF LIGHT

Just a whisper of light within a mostly dark picture plane can become a striking story; a poem rather than a billboard.

4 | MACRO SETTING

The macro button allows you to get close up and retain detail. The focal point (a cup of tea) will be sharp, while the image's perimeter or background (pastries and cherries) may fall out of focus. The effect of this focal play is to create a sense of depth in your image.

5 | GO SLOW

Finding details and small moments is about taking your time. I try to arrive early when I have an appointment and spend time observing my surroundings. This 'spare time' allows me to capture the small moments of beauty – perhaps a delivery of flowers sitting on the pavement outside the florist's – that I would have missed if I was rushing to arrive on time.

@littleupsidedowncake

Sanda Vuckovic Pagaimo
littleupsidedowncake.com

After a year working in IT, Sanda realised that it was not a road she wanted to continue on; something else was commanding her attention – organic food and food photography. She now works from home and fully enjoys what she does. Every day.

♡ time
Every season, every time of day has its own beauty. It can be a challenge to transmit that beauty in an image if the light is too strong, the grass too green or the background too busy.

♡ light
I use direct light when I want to create a very strong message, and diffused light when I want a more romantic, subtle mood.

♡ composition
I usually think in advance about colours and props, but composition and mood are mainly decided on the fly. I think when composing I put a bit of myself, my mood, my life, memories and personal story into it.

adjustment
I usually use the VSCO app on my phone images and adjust for brightness. I also use Afterlight for framing images.

satisfaction
Instagram is my favourite social network platform. I have met so many great people through my work on the app – some in person.

If I shoot food, I may not only shoot a plate
of food, but also a portrait of someone
eating it, or perhaps the cook who made
it, a glimpse of the space around it, or even
the mess on the table after the meal is over.
This way the atmosphere around a dish is
captured and passed to the observer – a
story is told.

SEEING THE WHOLE

Everyone starts with the subject. Try a different technique and start with the environment. Shoot the negative space: the spaces between things. The figure-to-ground relationship is critical in this approach. Practise shooting this way and you'll never see the 'thing' you're shooting without also seeing the world it lives in. The setting can be a complicated, junk-filled bedroom, or a simple wall of solid colour. Whatever it is, make sure you're aware of how the colours, textures and shapes are interacting with the subject.

1 HUMBLE PIE

A good portrait does not always scream, 'Look at my face'. It can be subtle and nuanced, with the subject positioned in a corner of the frame and peering out from a dark interior. This set-up can convey a sense that the subject has secrets they are not revealing. You can amplify this atmosphere by creating a lot of space around the subject and including only part of the figure in the frame.

2 BACKGROUND

When shooting food, pay attention to the table or cloth on which the plates are set. If the food is complicated and full of garnishes, balance the whole by using a simple linen tablecloth, or have fun and play with pattern by using a wild, colourful cloth as a contrast to a single bowl of white rice.

3 IN THEIR ELEMENT

Compose an inclusive setting by placing a subject in their world and asking them to do their thing. A chef? Photograph them in their kitchen preparing a dish. A craftsperson? Shoot them in their shop making something they are proud of. By placing the subject in their world you see the way in which they interact with it and capture context.

4 CLUES AND CONTEXT

When shooting a building, landscape or landmark, the sky and ground areas are as important as the subject. Can you exploit clouds, rain or rays of sunshine to add a certain mood to the overall scene? Perhaps flowers are growing at the base of a building where concrete meets metal? Or are the feet of busy commuters swarming all around the subject? Being sensitive to the details surrounding a subject may lead to a more intriguing image.

OPPOSITES POP

Experimenting with opposites is an effective approach when you want
to get out of a creative rut. This method is like wearing pyjamas to school
or eating breakfast for dinner. Doing or thinking exactly the reverse of what
you're 'supposed' to do is inspiring, energising and downright delightful.

1 GET UNCOMFORTABLE

Do the reverse of whatever you're comfortable with. Your 'look' may be minimalist, reserved compositions of very few items; if so, go Rococo with a riot of objects in the frame. If you are always shooting food or still lifes, grab some friends and do a portrait session. Your models will all appreciate a new headshot and you will have flexed new creative muscles.

2 MAKE MISTAKES

Moving away from what comes easily to you is not always fun. It's hard to grow creatively, but pushing into unknown territory is how you do it. When you create an image, look at it to figure out how to make it better, but also try to exaggerate the 'mistake' or weakness. I know it sounds crazy, but push in both directions. You may surprise yourself!

3 ASK QUESTIONS

Never look at your work and say to yourself, 'What do I have?' Always ask, 'What have I not tried?' and dive in again. By training yourself to go deeper and be more thorough with your process of investigation, you'll learn and advance towards creating a beautiful and inspiring Instagram feed.

4 START IN A DIFFERENT WAY

If your habit is to set a still life using only your favourite fruits, try working with all of the 'ugly' fruits you find at the market, or 'deconstruct' the fruits you typically use by peeling and cutting them and see how this impacts your approach and the image you create. Starting out by throwing your creative eye off balance will almost always lead you to somewhere different, and perhaps, to produce something extraordinary.

> Doing or thinking exactly
> the reverse of what you're
> 'supposed' to do is inspiring.

FLORAL

The rich and evocative language of flowers has been used to incite passions and describe feelings for centuries. In some cultures the yellow rose signifies friendship and joy. A red rose expresses love. Fill your Instagram feed with images that tap into the aesthetic qualities, colour and symbolism of flowers.

1 COLOUR

First and foremost, flowers can add a bright pop of colour to a composition. White in a floral landscape brings a mellow mood for the eye to rest upon; a bouquet of white lilies in a plain room adds a subtle spirit and beauty; and a loose arrangement of blooms will light up the corner of a kitchen scene.

2 LIFE CYCLE

Fresh, dried, in the process of dying – there is beauty in every stage of the life cycle of flowers. Old Masters included decaying flowers in their still life paintings. Follow their lead and bring emotion to your image by including objects that are past their 'prime'.

3 SCATTER

I love flowers in their glorious entirety of form, but I sometimes prefer the compositional element created by breaking them down into petals and leaves. Scattering these smaller shapes across a picture will add movement, texture and small points of interest that carry the eye around the image – not to mention a hint of romance!

PLAYFUL

In order to make subjects respond and engage in the process and to create images with a relaxed sensibility, it's imperative that you radiate lightness. Having a playful, curious attitude while you're working will make the process of creating playful, energetic images more intuitive.

① PLAY WITH COLOUR
Pile all the yellow objects you have onto a white surface; shoot and then reverse the set-up and shoot white on yellow. Arrange a collection of clashing colours on a pedestal that almost matches the backdrop to generate an uncomfortable, silly, vibrant feeling. Colour can make you laugh if you get the vibe right, so keep playing until something tickles your funny bone!

② ARRANGEMENT
Set a timer, and using the same ten objects, come up with as many arrangements as you can in ten minutes. This exercise is like freehand writing or sketching before you paint; it opens you up to possibilities and warms up the creative muscles.

③ DISCOVER
Take five minutes everyday to collect a handful of objects that represent the place you are in. Situate them on any available surface – I have used baking trays – and make a little portrait of the collection. This creative game will heighten awareness of your surroundings and acts as a great lesson in how to create visual interest using whatever is around.

RESIST UNIFORMITY

Experimenting with chaos and rejecting order is a fun compositional device.
When styling a scene, I'm always thinking about the message I'm trying to convey,
and the arrangement that will best communicate that message. Natural, unfussy
and perhaps somewhat loose styling says something very different to a neatly
arranged grid with minimal props. Decide what you want to 'say' and get busy!

Abundance gives
you room to play.

1 QUANTITY MEANS QUALITY
Start with more than you think you need: more vases, more
jugs, more pots, more candles, more people. It's easier to take
away a surplus than to hustle up more of whatever you need
at the last minute. Abundance gives you room to play and
experiment as you build a scene up and then edit out
elements to get the composition that works.

2 ONE GOOD, MANY BETTER
One kitsch plastic clock on a wall can look fun, but an array
of six clocks each showing a different time is a party. This
strength-in-numbers approach works in many situations;
look for retail displays with the regularity of items arranged
according to a particular set of criteria – lots of narrow vertical
shapes, for example – or at a farmers' market, where fruit is
lined up in lovely little baskets. More is better.

3 SEEK MASTERS OF ORGANISATION
Once you start looking at the way information and items are
displayed, you'll see tidy grids of cute objects everywhere.
You can find great work on this theme with the hashtag
#ThingsOrganizedNeatly.

4 SEEK MASTERS OF CHAOS
There is a fine line between a photo of a pile of junk and
an artfully crafted disarray of beautiful materials. Pile a
collection of lush fruit with strongly contrasting colours on
serving dishes, and let the shapes flow and spill over the
edges. Think of nature when composing in this way – leaves
fallen from a tree and scattered on the ground in a beautiful
random pattern – and try to emulate that perfect sense of
chaos by leaving elements in your composition where they fall.

CAPTURE EMOTION

Photographing emotional scenes may be the hardest thing to do. It can make you and your subject uncomfortable. In situations of great emotion you want to put down the instrument and be a human being. You have to *be there* for these moments, establish who you are, and have trust built rather than walk in the door and press the 'capture' or shutter button. It is critical in these settings to show those present that you respect them – and possibly love them – and that taking photographs does not diminish your feelings. After this is clear, go in and photograph as close as you can. The tears of joy and the tears of sorrow, that's where the good stuff is.

1 RITUAL AND CEREMONY

Social, religious and political ceremonies are where passions collide. These events can be hectic and fast moving, so wear a comfortable outfit and be ready to move around the scene. Exercise your skills in getting close to people and shooting by starting with a little rapport building. Ask them nicely about their reason for being there, then fire away.

2 PRACTISE ON YOUR FRIENDS

Become the 'photographer' at every wedding, birth or big event in the lives of friends. It may be that they have hired someone else 'officially', but the people you know and love so intimately make great guinea pigs and these, typically, relaxed situations are an opportunity to try out new things that can later be applied in images you create for your feed. Ask friends to hug, ask them to laugh – invariably it turns into real laughing and then it's just a hoot.

3 TOUCH

There's nothing more awkward than friends or loved ones posing for a camera and not interacting with each other. You can direct them a bit, never touching them, but motioning for them to put a hand on a shoulder, whisper a secret, gesture at each other. This will help warm them up and reveal the love shared between intimates.

4 THINK ABOUT EQUIPMENT

A high-end camera makes you more formidable; a phone makes you more like an average person. Don't think file size or pixel count; think of what will work best for the situation. If you are at a formal organised event it may be that the authority of a camera is the better choice, while an intimate scene in an ocean setting at dusk is best captured through the familiarity and casualness of a camera phone. Use what most helps you capture the idea you're going for.

@LaTonyaYvette

LaTonya Yvette Staubs
latonyayvette.com
blog.latonyayvette.com

LaTonya Yvette Staubs is well known on the internet as simply LaTonya Yvette. She is a stylist, activist, writer and mother of two. Her blog, LaTonya Yvette, has captured, with candor and grace, notes on motherhood, style and all of life's ebbs and flows.

 style

I live and work in the same context. I use 'intersection' a lot when describing my work, and everything I do in passion and work is truly a representation of a woman standing at an intersection.

 adjustments

I recently started to skip the filters, and it's been the biggest eye opener in how I view imagery. I take down highlights in the photos section on my phone while it's raw and play around with what that does for the colours.

 tips

Clean your lens before snapping. Get down to their level. Let the camera be a prop, but not the lens in which you view the scene.

 colour

I see the world through colour. I am drawn to it in my clothes, in writing descriptions of scenes, in noticing things about my children, and my social media feeds. It is who I am.

satisfaction

Having people be moved. Truly. I love the way Instagram has become this thread with which we are all connected. That feels like good work to me. When I'm eighty-something and asked 'Instagram – what? What did you do?' Well, I moved people.

♡ challenge

My biggest challenge lies in translation.
What did an image mean to me when
I shot it, and what does it mean to me now,
sharing it on this platform? Is the story told
without me using words? Or can my words
evoke the true nature of what I am feeling
and what this scene made me feel? Or is it
getting lost in translation?

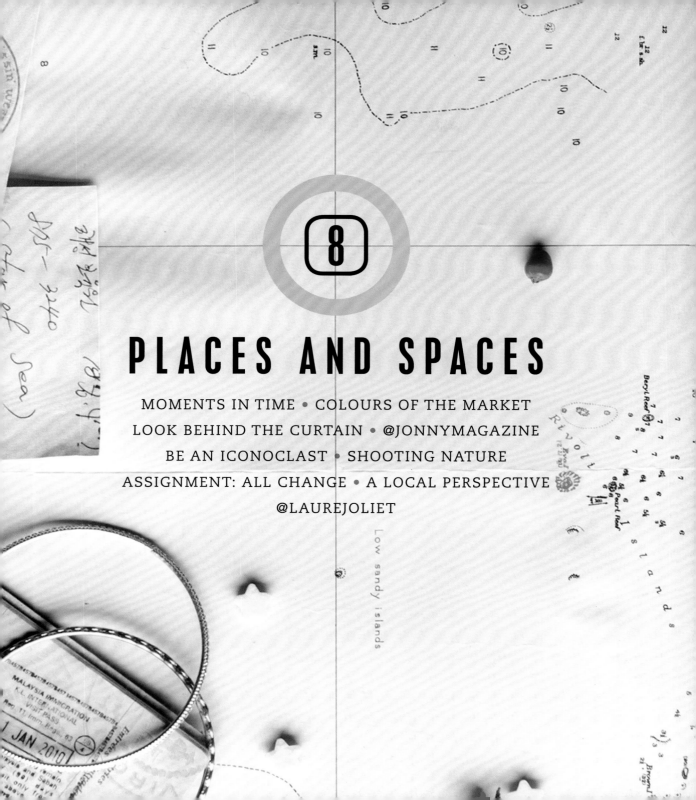

8

PLACES AND SPACES

MOMENTS IN TIME • COLOURS OF THE MARKET
LOOK BEHIND THE CURTAIN • @JONNYMAGAZINE
BE AN ICONOCLAST • SHOOTING NATURE
ASSIGNMENT: ALL CHANGE • A LOCAL PERSPECTIVE
@LAUREJOLIET

MOMENTS IN TIME

Before I book a trip, I research major festivals at my destination. Capturing the exuberance of a unique local experience adds authenticity and energy to my images and dazzle to my life. There's nothing like getting caught up in a throng of revellers – the dancing, food, colours and music are all so grand – I'm dancing in my chair at the thought.

1 THINK LOCAL PRESS

Local print media – *Time Out* magazine, a local newspaper or even flyers posted around an area – are all excellent resources for discovering street fairs, festivals and markets. So even if you can't plan your trip around some annual event, there is probably something shaking while you're there – you just have to find it. I once happened to be in Florence, Italy, for Easter and witnessed the most surreal Renaissance-costumed procession: an ox with head-to-toe floral decorations, colourful smoke, a bejewelled carriage and the release of a dove to signal spring. It was incredible!

2 STAKE OUT A SPOT

Go out early, get a coffee, mill around, watch the light and imagine what may transpire. Wear comfortable shoes, bring some playing cards and settle in for a front-row view of your unfamiliar surrounds – the attitude of a patient, curious observer will get you much better photos than if you try to shoot your way through the back of a million heads.

3 PLAN AND BE PATIENT

Public events can be three-, four-hour or sometimes all-day affairs. After taking the time to assess the place, the space and the people, let events unfold. Don't be in a rush to 'get' your shots; there is an energy and momentum to these situations. Commit to being there and being ready to capture the magic you discover. I couldn't have planned to get a shot of rally car drivers enjoying an ice cream.

4 STAY LATE

The aftermath may offer just as many opportunities for great shots as the main event. When people are clearing out, confetti is strewn all over the street, costumes and decorations are piled in a corner, and the performers are stopping for a cappuccino in their sparkling outfits; you see the juxtaposition of glitz and grime and have the opportunity to capture some really interesting images.

COLOURS OF THE MARKET

A lively market in a foreign country (or the farmers' market down the street) can be one of the most productive locations for creating dynamic imagery. The colours, layers of texture and charismatic vendors fascinate photographers and viewers alike. Carve out a couple of hours to celebrate the intersection of commerce and humanity, an age-old combination!

1. GET BRAVE

It's no good being a disinterested observer when photographing vendors and market goers – it is critical in this situation that you adopt a very confident, extroverted persona and ask people questions. Fake it if you have to. Vendors will warm to you as you ask about their products: then you can casually ask if you might photograph them. Compliment their smile, stand or earrings – whatever it takes. People usually say yes.

2. SEEK PATTERN AND REPETITION

A market stand is often a vendor's main source of income, so they take great care to display their goods in an enticing and organised manner – rows of strawberries, mounds of blood oranges and baskets of flowers all create visually arresting and graphic images.

3. WHITE TENTS

Ever wonder why all your pictures from a farmers' market look so pretty? The white shades under which the sweetcorn is sitting create a diffused light, perfect for enticing produce shots – take advantage of this ready-made filter and shoot an array of pretty fruits, vegetables and flowers.

4. SHOPPING WHILE SHOOTING

Shooting while carrying a lot of stuff in your hands is very difficult, so go with a plan. Better yet, shop and shoot simultaneously, but get a friend to carry everything so you are free to observe, capture a moment and share a laugh.

5. VARY IT UP

Shoot detail, medium and wide shots. The story you are chasing may be better captured in a portrait of someone surrounded by produce than a busy wide shot of market goers. Often you can't tell where the story is strongest until you review your images. So cover the market with the zest of a seasoned photojournalist and give yourself options.

LOOK BEHIND THE CURTAIN

Go behind the scenes – into the workshops, kitchens and laboratories of the world. There are always people dedicated to a craft, working their butts off, who would love to chat with a curious photographer. It's easier than you think. It's a matter of mustering up a little courage and asking to speak with the creator. This question can give you access to a whole new world. The payoff is vast, and allows you to form connections and capture backstage images of a place and its people.

There are always people dedicated to a craft, working their butts off, who would love to chat with a curious photographer.

① INVESTIGATE SCHOOLS AND ATELIERS

I love to go to cities with Carnival or Mardi Gras, not only New Orleans, but Rio and Trinidad and Tobago. I came across some float workshops in India and met some incredibly talented papier-mâché artists. Many craftspeople and artisans work in isolation. All you have to do is express an interest, begin a conversation and let the images come to you.

② MEET THE CHEF

If you have an amazing meal in a restaurant, ask to say 'Hi' to the chef. You already have a great conversation starter: the food you've just eaten. Michelin-star restaurant or roadside diner, you never know what you'll find behind the scenes. Even if you only get to spend five minutes in this hidden world, photographing food, culture and the spaces where these topics intersect is always wonderful.

③ SEEK HIGH AND LOW

Maintaining a single behind-the-scenes perspective while travelling can be exhausting. Keep your creative and physical energy up by mixing fancy and gritty scenes. Look for workers' canteens with plastic tablecloths and opulent dining rooms with velvet seats. The experiences you have, and images you make, will be completely different, but you may also be surprised to discover similarities.

@JonnyMagazine

Jonny Kennedy
jonnymagazine.com

© Daryl Phelps

Jonny Kennedy is a Londoner working in book publishing. Since picking up a camera just two years ago, he has explored his creativity and photography skills to the full, and is always on the hunt for something new, exciting and – most importantly – fun.

♡ **challenge**

London is a busy city, so the biggest challenge I face has to be the number of people. They can get in the way of a great shot, but it's OK, I'm fairly patient.

♡ **colour**

I'm from London, which can be a pretty grey city, so I guess subconsciously I'm looking for colour – something that stands out and is just plain fun.

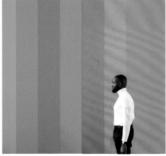

♡ **inspiration**

I'm definitely drawn to faces and people within their own environment – not so much a sit-down portrait, but everyday things: taking the bus to work, a market place, a cyclist on his way home.

♡ **adjustments**

If I do use filters it's subtly. I may brighten a little – it goes with my colourful themes. I want the black to be a real black, not faded, to give an image more depth and impact.

♡ **favourite**

I like the soft light of autumn and the dramatic shift from the bright sun and green parks of summer to the misty mornings and leaves on the ground.

composition

Always go with the flow, and don't try too hard – it doesn't have to be perfect. Imperfections are also interesting. Take the same image from many different angles; you'll be surprised by how different the results can be.

BE AN ICONOCLAST

We know what the Eiffel Tower looks like – so, too, the Tower of Pisa and the Taj Mahal. These landmarks are etched into our minds, but it is the job of a photographer to see and document ubiquitous subjects in a fresh and arresting way and displace the norm. It can be tricky to shoot iconic locations, but armed with a few tips and a new attitude you'll be getting weird in no time.

1 EMBRACE OR AVOID CROWDS

When visiting a monument, go very early before anyone gets there – as I did when visiting the sculptures at Pietrasanta – or celebrate the fact that there are throngs of people with you. Both situations hold beauty. A setting devoid of people can amplify the stoicism of a monument, while a chaotic sea of humanity can reinforce the significance of a place.

2 ASK AND YOU SHALL RECEIVE

If you strike up a conversation with a curator, official or docent at a museum or monument, it just may open doors. Sometimes getting access to a new angle is simply a matter of making a connection with the person who has inside knowledge, and a key.

3 SOUVENIR SPECIAL

Don't ignore the gift shop or souvenir vendors. A tray of miniature Eiffel Towers or a row of gondolier's hats may have more charm than the real deal.

4 FORGET ZOOM

Never shoot a site with a long lens or extreme zoom. Your image will be flat and boring. Look for something intriguing in front of the monument – a couple embracing, oblivious to the importance of the site behind them, or a kid eating an ice lolly and looking bored even though he's at a 'wonder of the world'.

5 GET ON THE WATER

When all else fails, take a river cruise or ocean ferry. Stack the cards in your favour and take a twilight cruise. Look for reflections in the water, or in the glass of the boat. Can you capture the monument and people viewing it in the same frame? An image of the Eiffel Tower and a couple reflected in the window of a boat travelling on the Seine may hold more romance than the iron monument alone.

SHOOTING NATURE

Showing the natural aspects of a place defines a location. Picture Los Angeles with
no images of the sea, Kyoto without cherry blossom, the Sydney Opera House
without the harbour – impossible, right? If you love being outside, you've probably
seen a landscape photo that has made you gasp. Photographing nature is a chance to
disconnect from the day-to-day grind, meditate, seek a stunning composition and
breathe fresh air. You may have to be patient and wait for the light to be perfect or a
bird to fly through your scene, but the anticipation is half the fun. Relax and enjoy.

1 — LEAD THE EYE

When dealing with a vast expanse of outdoor space, you have to be ruthless in your composition and edit down the overall view. Variations in shape and line will draw the viewer's eye over the picture plane. A long road with a tree in the distance could be framed with a green crop in the foreground (small shapes), the stretch of road (line) and fluffy clouds in the background (large shapes) to direct the viewer's gaze. Together these elements make for an intriguing photograph.

2 — ADD PEOPLE TO SHOW SCALE

To show how big and wonderful a place is, add a human to the scene. This effect is amplified if the person is a child.

3 — WILDFLOWERS

Know when the wildflowers are in bloom, and if you can, plan your travels to coincide with this explosion of earthly colour.

4 — CREATE AN ALTERNATIVE PORTRAIT

Use collections from nature to create a 'portrait' of a place. Gather small elements – rocks, shells, seaweed, stones, sticks – and assemble them in a grid of uniform rows. This subtle narrative about a place is a great creative exercise, and it is always fun to forage around for little treasures.

5 — FOG, RAIN, SNOW

The great outdoors are not always sunny, and nature is not always inviting, but don't hesitate to shoot in the rain or snow. You have less competition and often the light is much softer. The morning sun filtered through fog creates a beautiful glow across a landscape. Just remember to dress appropriately.

Anticipation is half the fun.
Relax and enjoy.

ASSIGNMENT
ALL CHANGE

The journey is the destination is an old maxim, but it's the absolute truth. Shooting the 'getting there' – the bus stations, train rides, motorbikes, taxis, tuk tuks, ferries, rice boats, tiny airports and bicycles – can showcase an integral element of the day-to-day functioning of a culture. The trick to creating interesting images is in the way you perceive this often-mundane event and transform it into an intriguing photo assignment.

GO LOCAL

Using local transport is a sure way to engage with the world you have entered. You have to figure out how to buy a ticket, plan your route and spend time (perhaps hours) with a large number of people you don't know – sometimes all in a language you don't speak. As a guest you can be curious and ask questions of your travelling neighbours. You can photograph them, too – just politely smile, perhaps laugh a little and you may be on your way to having a life-altering conversation with a new friend.

PRACTISE
It takes persistence and repeated failure to succeed in photographing someone right next to you. True, it is not easy . . . but you want that intimacy. It makes a photo great.

RIDE THE TRAIN
A train journey can feel like being in a bustling mobile city filled with people, noise, games and food. Don't miss a moment of this fleeting, transitory community. Take pictures, bring food to share, have people take pictures of you, then reciprocate. Show them the results on your screen; it's a great way to start a conversation.

TRANSPORTATION OF GOODS
Step out of the passenger car and try shooting carts, trucks or motorbikes loaded with the stuff of everyday life – livestock, produce, flowers, building materials. The sky is the limit. You just never know when someone on a scooter will zoom by with a baby on their knee and full-size fridge strapped to the seat.

A LOCAL PERSPECTIVE

Travel isn't just about where you go; it's also about how you see the world. Photography offers a golden ticket to deep exploration, to peel back layers and develop a real sense of a culture. If you have a camera or phone and are curious, it is possible to learn something new anywhere you go. Be bold and go forth with the assumption that your thoughts and questions are relevant and your images meaningful. This attitude may feel unnatural at first, but with practice and the successful images that result from this tactic, you'll find it easier and more fun. Don't only take this approach when travelling – it can also be used in your hometown to create images filled with authenticity.

If you have a camera or phone and are curious, it is possible to learn something new anywhere you go.

1 ASSIMILATE

Get a haircut; buy a coffee from a locals' café; take the commuter bus crammed with people (and sometimes chickens); go to a communal bath or spa for an alarmingly vigorous massage with oils you can't identify. Photographs of these scenes will be quirky and distinctive.

2 LEARN A GAME

In Asia, dominos and chequers rule; in New York City, people play chess on permanent boards in Washington Square Park; cards are universal. If you know a game or two, playing with locals can be a great icebreaker and lead to some memorable shots of your opponents, their friends and the scene.

3 TAKE DRIVING LESSONS

This may seem like offbeat advice, but since taking tuk tuk driving lessons in Southern India at age 16, I've asked for them in nearly every country I've visited – the teachers are always baffled, but accommodating. The hilarity that follows will make your sides split and guarantees wonderful, funny pictures.

4 GO ON A FOOD TOUR

Having a guide show you the local specialties (at home or abroad) gives you a break from research, and provides a fresh perspective and new knowledge. You can create your own tour by using a favourite food to map your route through a city; shops with great pastry is an itinerary I love to follow. Get to know a neighbourhood by visiting every eatery in the area and photographing your progress.

@LaureJoliet

Laure Joliet
laurejoliet.com

© Jeffrey Brodsky

Laure Joliet is a Los Angeles–based photographer with an eye for living things and lived-in spaces. Her images are intimate, inviting and unpretentious – they immediately convey the fundamental magic of spaces lit mostly by the sun.

♡ inspiration

I'm always curious to see new places, meet new people, and capture the quirks of how they live – this spirit is what drives how I photograph. My passions inform my subject matter!

♡ tip

When shooting a beautiful room with your phone, make sure to tap the shadows so that your exposure adjusts – it will normally brighten up the whole image and make the room feel dreamier and truer to what you are seeing with your eye.

♡ approach

I show up with a curious attitude. I don't overplan – I have a loose framework for parts of town, restaurants, stores and sights I want to see. I try to leave enough time for the unexpected.

♡ challenge

I mainly use phone shots for Instagram, so the biggest challenge can be the phone shortfalls. Shooting in low light can be frustrating, as can loving a shot and wishing I had it as a larger file. But overall I am so grateful for my phone.

♡ adjustments

I like to bump brightness a touch, add contrast, sharpen a little. It makes the image feel crisp but still real, and just helps to define it on the screen.

theme

I am always looking for the light! I think about negative space a lot, so I look for ways to include some emptiness in a photo. The emptiness helps your brain to dream and fill in the blanks, so the less you show, the more evocative a photo is.

HACKS AND TIPS

ALWAYS ON • DON'T STRESS THE START
EASY ADJUSTMENTS • BRING THE FUN
SHOOTING IN BLACK AND WHITE
EQUIPMENT HACKS • WHAT NEXT?

ALWAYS ON

You always have the most important pieces of equipment with you –
your brain and determination. If you don't have your camera, use your
phone; if you don't have your phone, borrow one from someone
standing next to you and email the images to yourself.

1 ## THE TOOL IS IRRELEVANT
The cameras in our phones are capable of capturing
complex images full of luminosity and detail. Entire
magazines are being shot with iPhones (*Bon Appetit*,
among a host of others), so there are no excuses not
to try if you have an interest.

2 ## DOWNSIZE THE CAMERA, UPGRADE
THE PHONE
An older phone can produce great shots, but
technology upgrades and slow performance can
interfere with its function. When the time comes to
upgrade your equipment, buying a new camera is not
necessary. Upgrading your phone is a less expensive
way to improve the quality of your pictures and access
the latest technology.

3 ## CAPTURE THE UNUSUAL
Stay as alert and present as possible, all day, every
day. Once you train your eye you'll notice so many
more out-of-the-ordinary moments. It won't take
long for you to start finding extraordinary ways to
capture the mundane, either. Train the eye and the
rest will follow!

DON'T STRESS THE START

It will take time to get the shot you want. Regardless of the subject,
the magic shot is always caught somewhere in the middle of a session –
at the sweet spot where everyone is relaxed, and there is a sense of
partnership between photographer and subject.

1 SET EVERYONE UP FOR SUCCESS

Make sure everyone you are photographing is well fed,
physically comfortable, groomed, rested and happy
with the music playing. If you are photographing
fashion, make sure that clothing is free of logos and
comfortable to move in. Having these basics down
before you begin will help bring everyone into the
moment and make them ready to create a timeless
image. These preparations can also provide an
opportunity for some great spontaneous shots.

2 SLOW DOWN

Pace yourself; take some deep breaths before, during
and after a shoot. Encourage everyone around you to
do the same. Stretch a little, take a toilet break, look in
a mirror and say to yourself, 'You got this' (it's cheesy
but it works). Direct, breathe, review, readjust, tweak,
laugh, then repeat the cycle all over again.

3 ENCOURAGEMENT

I start with a host of compliments for all of my
subjects. It's a genuine approach and makes people
relax and feel good. I'll say something like, 'I love your
outfit! It's going to look great with this background I
picked for us'. Or, 'You're going to make my job easy,
you look gorgeous'. This approach lessens a subject's
expectation of feeling awkward in front of the camera
and sets a positive tone for photographer and subject.

EASY ADJUSTMENTS

One person can look at an image and think, there's too much contrast; another may feel the same image is snappy. What is most important as a photographer is to understand your own style and preferences; try everything until you arrive at what you like best.

I bump up the brightness
very slightly to add luminosity
and joy to an image.

1 CONTRAST

What the camera sees is often a smidge flat to my eye. I like
to counter the uniform, slightly dull look by increasing the
contrast. The trick here is not to go overboard; a little tweak to
contrast went a long way to making this rustic kitchen interior
pop. Start by dialing the contrast all the way up, and then
bring it back until you get it where you want – just a little
better than in camera.

2 BRIGHTNESS

Unless I am shooting a 'dark and moody' look, I bump up the
brightness very slightly to add luminosity and joy to an image.
Take care not to overdo this adjustment, though; it can blow
out the lighter parts of your images.

3 SHADOWS

Adding light to shadows will reveal more information in the
picture plane (details of the trees surrounding the building);
adding darkness will make the image more dramatic. Pick
what works for you. I go both ways, depending on the image.

4 ROTATE

Use the rotate tool on architectural or interior images to get
vertical and horizontal lines straight. An adjustment of just
two to five degrees can make all the difference.

5 HIGHLIGHTS

The highlight tool is useful when you've shot in bright sun,
such as a scene of boats in a marina, or had to expose for a
medium part of the picture plane. When areas of an image are
too bright and lack detail, you can add visual information in
those zones by bringing the highlights down.

BRING THE FUN

You cannot underestimate the power of a silly attitude,
an outgoing vibe and a few simple tools to get a photo shoot
going smoothly. Atmosphere is everything – the tone you
set is key to creating succesful images.

1 MUSIC

Music is always a good means of loosening people up.
I love to create a playlist that goes with the mood of
the shoot – if I'm shooting a French floral tea party,
I'll find 60s French female singers and make a playlist
that lasts for a couple of hours. For a portrait shoot,
I love Motown; it makes everyone feel awake. Kids
love show tunes (I do too), which makes it easy for
everyone to sing!

2 BE THE CIRCUS CONDUCTOR

How many photographers does it take to move
a light bulb? Answer: It's irrelevant. The point is,
the light bulb needs to be wherever you think it
looks good on the subject. Maybe it's switched
off altogether. You're the conductor. You have to
direct. Don't be passive.

3 CHAT THEM UP

Banter like 'You've modelled before, haven't you?'
makes everyone giggle. The stupider the chit chat,
the better. 'Work with me baby, work with me!' is
my all-time favourite (I got it from my photographer
father). Keep talking. Keep shooting. Have your subject
look away from the camera and then again towards
you. People love being treated like a glamorous
celebrity. Help them live in this illusion.

SHOOTING IN BLACK AND WHITE

Black and white abstracts, imbues nostalgia and flattens a scene.
It simplifies, but it is far from boring. There's a romance to it that
can't be topped. Colour is *Amelie*, black and white is *Casablanca*.
It makes subjects appear timeless.

1 LOOK FOR CONTRAST
When composing for black and white, think in
extremes: strong blacks and bright whites. This will
help capture tones between each end of the tonal
spectrum and keep the picture plane interesting.
A woman in a white shirt wearing sunglasses and
standing in front of a dark background has the
ingredients for making a beautiful black-and-white
image. When composing in black and white, shoot
for the shadows to avoid losing them. This can blow
out the highlights, but they can be recovered in post.

2 TONE AND TEXTURE
Instead of looking for contrast, focus on subtle shifts
in tone. Removing colour removes distractions and
increases the visibility of slight shifts in shades of
grey. This also has the effect of increasing a viewer's
awareness of texture.

3 THINK TIMELESSNESS
Timeless subjects are strong choices when
shooting in black and white – still lifes, family
portraits, historic sites. A dramatic lighting
pattern will emphasise graphic shapes in the
shadows and produce pretty highlights.

EQUIPMENT HACKS

There is not much needed to start making amazing images other than a phone or camera. I wouldn't run out and buy a thing. Chances are, all the tools you could want can be found around your house. With a little preparation and ingenuity, you can set up a mobile photography studio in no time.

1 BODY TRIPOD

If you have a wall, you have a tripod. Brace your back against a wall, squat slightly and push into the surface with your back, making a chair shape with your legs. Now you have a steady position to shoot from. Your forehead is pretty flat. It may look funny, but put your phone against your forehead. Take a deep breath and shoot (this will steady the shot, keeping things in focus). Your shoe can also be a great tripod; a camera or phone nestled in a shoe is secure and shake-free.

2 REFLECTOR CARD

Anything white or light coloured can become a decent reflective card. Even a white shopping bag can bounce light onto a display of flowers – ask a friend to hold it up. You can throw a white T-shirt over a piece of cardboard, or even ask someone wearing a white T-shirt to stand next to your subject, opposite the light source.

3 MACGYVER ANYTHING

With an attitude that there is no problem that can't be solved and a refusal to say, 'I can't do that', there is always a solution to be found. Duct or gaffer tape are incredible inventions; tape your phone to a wall or mirror, set the timer and – boom – jump into the shot. The headphone volume button on your headset is a remote shutter when you are in your phone's camera app. Just turn up the volume to 'snap' a picture. Add a tiny drop of water to your lens for a hazy effect, then clean up right away to prevent damage. Chat to other photographers; learn from everyone about hacks and fixes you can incorporate into your photographic process.

4 SUNGLASSES AS POLARISING FILTER

On a very bright day in a location that has lots of lights and darks, it can be helpful to tone things down with a filter. I use my sunglasses by putting a lens right in front of the phone's lens. This tones down the brights while maintaining the saturation. You can then boost the overall brightness in post, taking care to keep the highlights in check.

WHAT NEXT?

I'm not sure where photography and Instagram are headed. What I am sure of is that every wave of technology is exceeded by something new and different, almost as soon as it arrives. The only constant is change and evolution. What doesn't change is that the cream still rises to the top; those who have interesting, curious ways of tackling creative problems and coming up with unexpected solutions are the ones who push the medium forwards. This evolution doesn't always come from the people designing the tools. Rather, it's a conversation between artists, makers, technologists and the audience that moves imagery, and the way we view it, forward.

Staying nimble and on your toes creatively will help you evolve along with the technology.

① STAY NIMBLE

The most important thing to keep in mind when making images and pushing them out to the world via Instagram is to not get complacent. You cannot be successful doing the same thing day in and day out. Be flexible and make choices that are uncomfortable. Staying nimble and on your toes creatively will help you evolve along with the technology – your portfolio will thank you, and this attitude will lead to a more interesting life.

② KEEP ENGAGING

The easiest way to get out of a rut and burst through to a reinvigorated style, point of view or creative beat is to keep engaging with others in your field. If you are a photographer, reach out to an interesting stylist for the jolt of new ways of seeing. Talk to art directors about where they see your work headed. Pair up with a farmer to shoot their land, the food they grow, the home they live in – the pictures will be a lovely thank you to the farmer for their help in leading you to a renewed sense of creative purpose.

③ EARLY ADOPTERS

Don't get bogged down by technology, but stay engaged and relevant. It's not the medium that defines amazing artists; it's their creative approach to working in and being curious about the new tools available to them. David Hockney's artistic career has seen him work in classical drawing and painting, photo collages, video and digital paintings done on an iPad. Don't begrudge changing technology – figure out how to make it work (and make it fun) for you in your artistic practice.

GLOSSARY

AFTERLIGHT

An image-editing app for iOS, Android and Windows. Using inbuilt tools, filters, customisable textures, borders and frames, it allows you to create unique mobile photo edits quickly and easily.

ARTIFICIAL LIGHT

Light supplied by lamps or lighting rigs to produce various effects. Can be used to replicate natural light or to introduce a specific aesthetic effect.

ASPECT RATIO

The proportional relationship between the width and height of an image. Instagram's original square format was a 1:1 ratio.

AVAILABLE LIGHT

Also known as "ambient light" or "natural light." The light available in a setting without the addition of artificial sources.

BLOWN OUT

Overexposed highlights that are all white and lack detail.

BOUNCE CARD

A reflective piece of card used to help direct and soften the light from the sun or an artificial light source.

CHIAROSCURO

An oil painting technique developed during the Renaissance, in which strong contrasts are used to create drama and to give objects 3D form.

COLOUR CAST

A tint of a particular colour across part or all of an image. Artificial light set-ups can create an orange or yellow cast. Applying a blue filter can reduce an orange or yellow cast. An amber filter will balance a blue cast.

COMPOSITION

The placement and arrangements of elements within a photograph.

CROPPING

The removal of areas of an image to improve the framing and highlight the subject.

DEPTH OF FIELD

The distance between the closest and furthest points at which an object is in focus. Can be used to direct a viewer's eye to certain elements in an image.

ESTABLISHING SHOT

An image used to set up or explain the context of a series of images.

EXPOSURE

The amount of light received by the sensor of a camera via the lens.

FIGURE-TO-GROUND RELATIONSHIP

A clear distinction between the subject (figure) and the background (ground); a light subject on a dark background, or a dark subject on a light background.

FRAME(ING)

The placement of the subject(s) in relation to other elements in an image.

GOLDEN HOUR

Also known as the 'magic hour', the golden hour takes place during the first hour of sunlight in the day, and the last hour before the sun sets. It is known to be one of the most favourable times to shoot because the light from the sun is softer and creates a warm glow.

HARD LIGHT

A light source that creates hard, crisp-edged shadows.

LANDSCAPE MODE

An aspect ratio where width is greater than height.

Natural light

Negative Space

LIVE VIEW
A digital camera or phone's ability to display an onscreen preview of the image in front of the lens.

MACRO
A mode on some cameras (or a lens) used to capture extremely close-up details of an object.

MUSE
Traditionally, an inspirational goddess of Greek mythology. Used generally to describe a person who provides creative inspiration to an artist.

NATURAL LIGHT
See available light.

NEGATIVE SPACE
Also called 'white space', the space around and between the subject(s) of an image. Negative space gives the eye a place to rest and can highlight the subject(s).

PERSPECTIVE
The relationship between the size of objects within an image and their distance from the eye or the lens. Distant objects appear smaller, while parallel lines appear to converge.

PHOTOSHOP
An image-editing program for Macs and PCs. The industry standard since 1988, the name has come to be synonymous with digital editing.

PICTURE PLANE
The surface in the foreground of an image that corresponds exactly with the material surface of the image – the point of visual contact between the viewer and the picture.

POINT OF FOCUS
The object in a photo that is most in focus, and to which the eye is naturally drawn.

PORTRAIT MODE
An aspect ratio where height is greater than width.

POST
Adjustments made to an image after it is taken.

SCRIM
Fabric used to diffuse light.

SHOT LIST
A checklist of images. Used to ensure a range of subjects, poses, locations, framing and scale.

SOFT LIGHT
Light that produces soft, diffused shadows that appear to wrap around objects – created by cloud cover, or with the use of a scrim to filter the light.

SUBJECT
What is shown in a photo.

TONAL RANGE
The difference between the lightest and darkest areas of an image.

VIGNETTE
An image where the edges have been softened, feathered or blurred.

VSCO
An image-editing app for Android and iOS, with superior filters (called presets) and granular editing tools (to adjust tone, saturation, etc.), which connects to its own publishing platform, Grids. VSCO allows you to take, edit and share photos, all from within the app (#vsocam).

INDEX

A

adjectives 23
aerial views 107, 108–109, 117, 127
angles 114–115
anne_parker 98–99
architectural drawings 125
arriving early 79, 141
artificial light
    avoiding 85
    flash 61
artists, inspirational 31, 36
asking questions 18–19, 41, 43, 65,
    147, 170
asymmetry 123
audiences, considering 21, 23, 27

B

background 13, 33, 45, 47, 59, 61,
    66–67, 77, 103, 105, 112, 119, 121,
    130–131, 135, 139, 141–142, 145,
    169, 179, 183, 188
beach picnic 130
black and white 63, 123, 183
black foam core 57
bossiness 113
brightness tool 91, 181
buildings
    original viewpoints 51
    rotate tool 181
    showing context 145
burst mode 13, 113

C

camera levels 135
cameras 153, 178
cannellevanille 36–37
centred compositions 103
cestmaria 52–53
chaos 136, 150–151
clothing 65, 179
clouds 85, 93, 145, 169, 189
clown noses 13, 74
collections, photographing 45, 46–47,
    119, 149, 151, 169
colour 15, 47, 49, 52, 61–63, 106, 117,
    121, 128–129, 144, 148–149, 151,
    154, 160, 164
    restricted palette 57
compliments 41, 79, 95, 132, 161, 179
concepts, developing 31
contrast tool 181
craftspeople 19, 145, 162–163

creative voice, finding 24–25
creatives' homes 44–45
cropping 137

D

dark and moody style 56–57
dawn 59, 85, 92–93
depth, creating 59, 138–139
desserts in the canyon 132
details 140–141
digital souvenirs 47
direct sunlight 61, 87
directing people 65, 71, 95, 113
disappearing 70–71
Doré, Garance 125
double chins 73
duct tape 185
dusk 59, 85, 92–93

E

editing 26–27
emotion, capturing 152–153
establishing shots 49, 129, 134–135
experimenting 14–15, 118–119
exposure 85, 90–91
eyes
    focusing on 113
    training 13, 16–17, 178

F

failures 15, 147
Faulkner, William 27
feast of five pastas 131
festivals 158–159
fictional characters 34–35
figure-to-ground relationships 121,
    144–145
first impressions 42–43
flash 61
flattering shots 86–87
flexibility 33
flowers
    as a gift 49
    photographing 77, 148
    wildflowers 169
foam core 57, 59, 87
fog 37, 57, 169
food
    behind the scenes 163
    food tours 173
    styling 77, 106–107, 143, 145
friends, practising on 153
friends' weekend getaway 133

G

gaffer tape 185
games 173
Gentl and Hyers 36
gestures 141
getting closer 71, 75
Gibson, Ralph 123
gifts 77
goals 23
gobo 97
golden hour 92–93 *see also* dawn;
    dusk
Goyoaga, Aran 36–37
grid function 125
Groves, Joya Rose 80–81

H

hands 59, 120, 141
hashtags 20–21
hats 91
hazy effects 185
Hido, Todd 36
highlight tool 181
Hockney, David 187
horizon, bisecting 103
horizontal images 33, 117
horizontal lines 124–125, 181
humour 74

I

inner child 25, 74
Instagram, shooting in 13
Isager, Ditte 36

J

Joliet, Laure 174–175
jonnymagazine 164–165
joyarose 80–81
journals 25

K

Kennedy, Jonny 164–165
kill your darlings 27

L

landmarks, original viewpoints for
    51, 166–167
landscape composition 33, 117
landscapes 111, 145
latonyayvette 154–155
laughs, fake and genuine 74
laurejoliet 174–175
layering subjects 129

Pancake perspective

Moody moments

lens flare 93
light and airy style 58–59
light/lighting
    avoiding artificial 85
    experimenting 49
    flash 61
    natural 84–85
    portraits 67, 87, 94–95
    single source 57
    sunlight 61, 87
lines 124–125, 181
lists 79
literary inspirations 31, 35
littleupsidedowncake 142–143
locations 79

M
macro mode 59, 139, 141
Mapplethorpe, Robert 137
markets 160–161
messy style 136
minimal style 137
mistakes 15, 147
modern style 60–61
Modotti, Tina 137
moody style 56–57
movement, creating 103
moving objects 33, 49
museums 45, 47
music 35, 69, 182

N
nature 51, 168–169
negative space 59, 104–105, 136–137

O
off-centre composition 102–103
one-point perspective 115
opposites 25, 61, 146–147

P
Parker, Anne 98–99
patience 43
people
    directing 65, 71, 95, 113
    enlivening spaces with 33
    giving control to 75
    relaxing 41, 68–69, 72–73, 79, 179, 182
    see also portraits
personal spaces 48–49
perspective 115, 119

phones, upgrading 178
'photographer' outfit 65
photographers
    copying 127
    talking to 19
planning 78–79
playful images 149
point of view 116–117
portrait mode 59, 139
portraits 66–67, 86–87, 94–95, 112–113, 123
printed images 51, 73
props 52, 74, 76–77, 80
puns, visual 35

R
rain 37, 169
reflector card 185
remote shots 185
research 30–31
rotate tool 125, 181
rule breaking 119, 126–127

S
'saying cheese' 69
scale, varying the 110–111
scarves 77
Selby, Todd 125
shade 85
shadows
    adding light to 181
    in direct sunlight 61
    patterns 96–97
shadows tool 91
shaking things up 118–119
shapes, playing with 127
simplicity 33, 67, 122–123, 137
skin
    exposure 91
slowing down 17, 65, 179
snow 169
social media 19
souvenirs, digital 47
stash building 27
Staubs, LaTonya Yvette 154–155
stepping back 27
storytelling 13, 31, 128–129
    beach picnic 130
    desserts in the canyon 132
    feast of five pastas 131
    friends' weekend getaway 133
subjects, choice of 15, 27

success, defining 13
sunglasses
    as polarising filters 185
    in portraits 95
sunlight, direct 61, 87
surveying the scene 40–41
symmetry 123

T
taglines as inspiration 35
tea towels 77
Teller, Juergen 36
titles as inspiration 35
train journeys 171
training the eyes 13, 16–17, 178
transport 170–171
travel 50–51, 172–173
tribe, finding your 19
tripods 185
two-point perspective 115

U
underexposure 85, 90–91
uniformity, resisting 150–151
unwanted objects 33, 49

V
Vazquez, Marioly 52–53
vertical images 117
vertical lines 124–125, 181
vibe, finding your 64–65
viewpoints, unusual 51, 166–167
visual diaries 13, 15
Vuckovic Pagaimo, Sanda 142–143

W
water
    effect on lens 185
    shooting from 167
white bounce cards 87
white foam core 59
wide shots 134–135
Wilde, Oscar 24
wine 69
words
    adjectives 23
    hashtags 20–21
    playing with 34–35
worm's eye view 117

Z
zoom 167
Zucker, Sam 88–89

Leela Cyd

© David Kilpatrick

@leelacyd
leelacyd.com

Leela Cyd is a photographer and author living in Santa Barbara, California. She lives a block from the ocean with her husband David, and son Izador. Leela's work centres around the intersection of imperfect beauty, beloved travels to far-off places, colourful styling, food stories and joyful moments at the table with friends. She shoots and writes wherever she goes, often for publications such as the *New York Times*, *Kinfolk* and *Sweet Paul*. Leela has also photographed and authored three cookbooks: *Food with Friends*, *Tasting Hygge* and *Cooking Up Trouble*.

 thank you

I would be nowhere without the lively bunch I hold close around me – the people who make my days worth noting.

 thank you

I am grateful to my parents, Richard and Cissy, for encouraging me to work on this book and share my story – and for all their babysitting to allow me time to write. You embolden me to reach higher than I think I can go.

 thank you

Gratitude to my big brother Nick, who with his humour and upbeat take on life teaches me to enjoy the ride.

 thank you

To my husband David for more than a decade of helping me to unfurl my creative wings, and his unfailing patience while I'm getting a shot on my tippy toes in some far-off place.

 thank you

Biggest thanks of all to Izador Cosmo, my son – you came into my world, charmed me silly and I found my favourite subject for ever and ever.

 picture credits

The publisher would like to thank Shutterstock.com for permission to reproduce their images:

iPhone by Zeynep Demir, 4–5, 7, 9, 51, 93, 130–133, 171, 176–177
Flat lay by Arkhipenko Olga, 28–29
Flat lay by Volodymyr Hlukhovskyi, 176–177

contributors

Unless otherwise noted, image ©:

Aran Goyoaga, 36–37
Marioly Vazques, 52–53
Joya Rose Groves, 80–81
Sam Zucker, 88–89
Anne Parker, 98–99
Sanda Vuckovic Pagaimo, 142–143
LaTonya Yvette Staubs, 154–155
Jonny Kennedy, 164–165
Laure Joliet, 174–175